The Man Who Wrote Mozart

The Man Who Wrote Mozart

THE
EXTRAORDINARY LIFE OF
LORENZO DA PONTE

ANTHONY HOLDEN

Weidenfeld & Nicolson
LONDON

First published in Great Britain in 2006
by Weidenfeld & Nicolson, a division of
the Orion Publishing Group Ltd
Orion House
5 Upper Saint Martin's Lane
London
WC2H 9EA

1 3 5 7 9 10 8 6 4 2

A CIP catalogue record for this book is available
from the British Library

ISBN–13 9 780 29785 080 9
ISBN–10 0 297 85080 6

Designed in Monotype Bell by
Geoff Green Book Design, Cambridge

Typeset, printed and bound in Great Britain by
Butler and Tanner Ltd, Frome and London

The Orion publishing group's policy is to use papers that are natural,
renewable and recyclable products and made from wood grown in
sustainable forests. The logging and manufacturing processes are expected
to conform to the environmental regulations of the country of origin.

www.orionbooks.co.uk

FOR ALAN SAMSON
the onlie begetter

Contents

'I can never remember without satisfaction and joy that Europe and the whole world owe the exquisite vocal music of this remarkable genius largely thanks to my own perseverance and determination.'

Lorenzo Da Ponte, of Mozart

List of Illustrations

King's Theatre, Haymarket, London (Mander and Mitchenson Theatre Collection)

Interior of King's Theatre (Mander and Mitchenson Theatre Collection)

Nancy Grahl, Da Ponte's wife (Private Collection)

Nancy Storace (Weidenfeld Archieve)

Michael Kelly (Lebrecht Music and Arts Photo Library)

Columbia College, now Columbia University (courtesy Author)

Lorenzo Da Ponte, the professor (courtesy Columbia University)

Manuel Garcia (Lebrecht Music and Arts Photo Library)

Maria Malibran (Giuditta Pasta House, Elevio/Art Archive)

The first opera house in the United States (Museum of the City of New York)

The National Theatre burning down in 1839 (Private Collection)

Lorenzo Da Ponte in old age (Private Collection)

Da Ponte's tombstone (Dan Swift)

Prologue

I T IS typical of him to wind up where you would least expect: a Jewish-born Catholic priest, poet and womanizer, grocer and bookseller, professor and librettist, born in the mid-eighteenth century in an ancient hill town near Venice, but buried here in this rackety, depressed suburb of New York, with the jets into JFK roaring overhead.

His remains were lost in 1903 during the mass move of coffins from Manhattan's old Catholic burial ground in the Bowery to the Calvary Cemetery in the bleak Woodside district of Queens. Twenty minutes across the East River, sandwiched between the two main expressways into Manhattan, this is the world's largest cemetery. His is but one of three million graves in its vast, 365-acre wasteland.

This model immigrant, credited with introducing Italian opera and literature to the United States, the first Professor of Italian at New York's Columbia University, now lies among vaudeville and silent-movie stars, boxers and baseball players, senators and mobsters. Countless Irish and Poles as well as his fellow Italians reflect the remarkable range of New York's Catholic immigrant community. The names on the gravestones beside his are Orestes Basile and Umberto Nangeroni, Enrico Viani and Julia Byrne, Mamie C. Harahan and Jane Annie Devlin, the families Valvo, Gulizia and Falco, Cahill, O'Downell and Downey.

Not far away lies Steve Brodie, a late-nineteenth-century Bowery bookie famous for jumping off the Brooklyn Bridge into the East River for a $200 bet – and surviving. Here lies Vito Bonaventure, a 1920s Mafia boss shot to death in the driveway of his Brooklyn home; the mid-twentieth-century mobster Anthony Carfano, known as 'Little Augie Pisano', killed after refusing to meet Vito Genovese, *capo di capi* of the

xii   *The Man Who Wrote Mozart*

Genovese family; the short-lived gangster Francis 'Two Gun' Crowley (1911–32), whose life inspired the James Cagney movie *White Heat*; Joseph 'Socks' Lanza, born 1901, one of those few mobsters lucky enough to die of natural causes, at the age of sixty-seven.

Built in 1846 by the trustees of St Patrick's Cathdral, when their original Manhattan cemetery ran out of space, Calvary was originally intended for Catholic soldiers who had fought on the Union side in the American Civil War. Among those buried here are fifteen winners of the Congressional Medal of Honor, all killed in that conflict.

Across the street, fifty yards away through the side gate at the junction of Review Avenue and Laurel Hill Boulevard, in what is now a largely Hispanic, Ecuadorian and Romanian neighbourhood, sit the lumpen head-quarters of Wheaton World Wide Moving and American Compressed Gases Inc. Beside them is a scrap-metal dump, over which seagulls circle in search of food. In section 4B of the cemetery's south-west corner, beneath the Brooklyn–Queens underpass, sanitation trucks thunder by and another deafening jet makes its final turn into John F. Kennedy Airport as the visitor stands beside the stone marker designating his final resting place – which can't even spell his name right:

LORENZO DAPONTE (1749–1838)

Lorenzo Daponte, Italian-born poet and librettist to Wolfgang Amadeus Mozart for the operas *Le Nozze di Figaro*, *Don Giovanni* and *Così Fan Tutte*, emigrated to the United States in 1805 and tutored American youth on Italian culture, becoming the first Professor of Italian Literature in America. Founded the first opera house in this country in New York City in 1833, re-interred 1903, in Calvary Cemetery, Queens, New York.

This monument placed by the Italian Heritage and Culture Com-mittee of New York, the Native New Yorkers Historical Association, Councilman Morton Pouman of Queens, New York, Calvary Cemetery and the Woodlawn Cemetery in the 177th anniversary year of Daponte becoming an American Citizen.

Dedicated during Italian heritage and culture month Oct. 1987.

Da Ponte's nine-decade life embraced the birth and death of Beethoven and Schubert, Keats and Byron, Walter Scott and Napoleon Bonaparte as well as Mozart.

It was fifty-five years before his death in New York, at a party in another world – the Habsburg Vienna home of Baron Raimund Wetzlar von Plankenstern – that Da Ponte first met the man without whom his name would now be forgotten, without whom we would not trouble to delve into the astonishing detail of the many lives he lived over his near-ninety years.

Baron Wetzlar was an enlightened man. The son of a wealthy Offenbach banker, ennobled after converting from Judaism to Catholicism, the guitar-playing Baron and his Viennese wife Maria Theresa would later host piano contests at their summer villa between Beethoven and the Austrian composer-pianist Joseph Wölfl.

That was not until 1798, when the Baron was in his mid-forties, and post-revolutionary Enlightenment thinking had caught hold of Europe. Fifteen years earlier, in the Vienna of Emperor Joseph II, Wetzlar had made a rather more significant contribution to musical history by taking under his wing an impecunious, unemployed, little-known and newly married composer-pianist from Salzburg.

As their landlord, Wetzlar let Wolfgang Mozart and his bride Constanze live rent-free at his 'Little Herberstein House'. When he needed their rooms for other guests, the Baron would pay not merely the Mozarts' rent but also their removal expenses to temporary lodgings on the Kohlmarkt – No. 7, now an elegant forecourt boasting an antiques arcade at the heart of a smart shopping street.

Small wonder Mozart speaks of Baron Wetzlar as 'a good and true friend' in letters to his father, Leopold, in Salzburg, dated 21 May and 18 June 1783. In the second, the young composer congratulates his 'très cher Père' on becoming a grandfather for the first time, while apologizing with some embarrassment that his newborn son bears Wetzlar's name before his:

> I immediately sent a message to Baron Wetzlar, who ... came to see us at once and offered to stand godfather. I could not refuse him and thought to myself: 'After all, my boy can still be called Leopold.' But while I was turning this round in my mind, the Baron said very cheerfully: 'Ah, now you have a little Raimund' – and kissed the child. What was I to do? Well, I have had him christened Raimund Leopold ...

In another of his many letters to his father, dating from eighteen months earlier, 13 October 1781, Mozart had spelt out his view of the relationship between words and music in opera. Then writing *Die Entführung aus dem Serail* (*The Abduction from the Seraglio*), his first stage piece for Vienna, the twenty-five-year-old composer insisted that 'the poetry must be altogether the obedient daughter of the music'. But a collaboration between musician and poet should still, he went on, be very much a meeting of two minds, functioning as equals.

It was at Baron Wetzlar's party, in mid-1783, that Mozart met such a man. Two years after his arrival in Vienna, the musical capital of Europe, where his ambition to compose Italian opera had met with little success, the struggling twenty-seven-year-old composer was thrilled to make the acquaintance of Austria's celebrated theatre-poet, Abbé Lorenzo Da Ponte.

Six years Mozart's senior, the dashing Da Ponte was a favourite of the music-loving Emperor and the toast of Vienna as the author of libretti for the court composer, Antonio Salieri, and others. 'We have a new poet here, Abbé Da Ponte, who has a huge amount to do in revising pieces for the theatre,' an excited Mozart wrote to his father. Soon he would persuade Da Ponte to work with him on a daring new opera, based on a subversive French play banned by the Emperor.

Mozart had originally been summoned to Vienna in March 1781 by his (and his father's) employer, the Prince-Archbishop of Salzburg, to join his travelling court at the celebrations of Joseph's accession as sole ruler on the death of his mother, Maria Theresa. Fresh from the success in Munich of his opera *Idomeneo*, in Vienna Mozart was outraged to find himself seated between the valets and the cooks at the Imperial dinner table; he ate in silence, he told his father, as crude jokes made their way round the table. His resentment towards his employer was increased by the Prince-Archbishop's refusal to let him perform at events attended by the new Emperor. Within six months, famously kicked in the pants, Mozart had quit his job in disgust.

He stayed on in Vienna, frustrated in his ambitions to land a post at the Emperor's court, but content to do freelance work – composing and performing, in private and in public – in a city with a boundless appetite for music. Mozart made a modest living by teaching, playing at patrons' houses, publishing his music and composing to commission. It was also in Vienna, on 4 August 1782, that he married Constanze Weber, to a distinctly muted response from his formidable father.

1782 had also seen the staging of *Die Entführung*. A *Singspiel* to a German text by Gottlieb Stephanie the Younger, the work defied convention with its long, elaborate arias. But no less a figure than Joseph Haydn told Mozart's father that his son was 'the greatest composer known to me in person or by name; he has taste and, what is more, the greatest knowledge of composition'. Yet the Emperor's sole comment on the *Seraglio* was: 'Too many notes, my dear Mozart, too many notes!' Joseph preferred the music of Salieri and the Spanish composer Martín y Soler.

Mozart yearned to make his name by abandoning the German tradition for Italian opera. 'The best thing', he wrote to his father, 'is when a good composer, who understands the stage and is talented enough to make sound suggestions, meets an intelligent poet, that true phoenix.'

Within two years of writing that letter, Mozart found his 'true phoenix' in the unlikely, maverick figure of Lorenzo Da Ponte – the truth of whose chequered past, let alone his equally eventful future, neither he nor the rest of Vienna could know.

Lorenzo Da Ponte in late middle age, after an engraving by N. Rogers.

PART ONE

Veneto

1

The 'Clever Dunce'

THE EIGHTEENTH-CENTURY Jewish ghetto in the ancient Italian hill town of Ceneda, fifty miles north of Venice in the foothills of the Dolomites, has long since disappeared. All that remains is a Hebrew inscription over a doorway in what is now the historic 'old town' of the wine-rich city of Vittorio Veneto – named for the defeat here of Austrian invaders in October–November 1918, the climax of centuries as a strategic fortress crucial to the defence of the Venetian republic.

Today there is a war museum in the piazza at the heart of Ceneda, named after Pope John Paul I, its Bishop before his short-lived papacy in 1978. Vittorio Veneto's 'old town' also boasts a Via Lorenzo Da Ponte, and even a bronze statue of Mozart's librettist beside its market square, erected by the community in 1999, the 250th anniversary of his birth. The Da Ponte family had loomed large in the vivid history of Venice, boasting senators and ambassadors, prelates and painters, even the Giovanni Antonio Da Ponte (1512–97) who, appropriately enough, designed and constructed the Rialto Bridge.

The name would have meant nothing to Emanuele Conegliano, the high-spirited, rough-hewn Jewish boy who played in these streets, in this piazza, in the 1750s. Born in Ceneda on 10 March 1749, Emanuele was the first child of a Jewish couple named Geremia and Rachele (or 'Ghella', née Pincherle) Conegliano. After bearing him two younger brothers, Baruch and Anania, Emanuele's mother died when he was only five. A tanner by trade, despite loftier ancestry, his father Geremia was ill-equipped to care for, let alone educate, his three sons. At the age of eleven, Emanuele remained illiterate, running wild through the streets of Ceneda and the foothills of the mountains where Titian was born. A bright boy with a taste for poetry, but largely ignored by his father, Emanuele was nicknamed 'the clever dunce' by his better-educated but wary contemporaries.

Not until he was eleven did Emanuele's indigent father make a gesture towards his education by hiring him a rudimentary-sounding tutor, the son of a peasant who (according to his pupil in later life) may have 'abandoned the plough and the ox for the schoolmaster's rod, but still kept in the schoolroom the harshness and boorishness of his forebears'. After several months, Emanuele had learned nothing.

An inquisitive and apparently able boy, who already spoke elegant Italian, he had a prodigious memory and a gift for repartee. Surprised that Emanuele seemed to be profiting so little from his lessons, his father one day decided to investigate. He found his son in tears as his tutor beat him about the head – his 'daily' method of 'stimulating' the boy's brain. Geremia Conegliano seized the tutor by the hair, dragged him out of the room and flung him down the stairs, followed by his inkwell, pens and Latin textbook. Thus ended his brief attempt to broaden his son's horizons.

An affectionate father, then, if somewhat feckless, but ambitious for his children. As one of the American friends of the boy's old age put it, 'There must have been some fine hereditary instincts, or some rare aspirations, or he would not so readily have grown out of and beyond the inauspicious circumstances of his lot.'

Three years later, at the age of fourteen, Emanuele's life changed radically for the least likely of reasons. A widower for ten years, his forty-year-old father had fallen in love with a sixteen-year-old Christian girl, Orsola Pasqua Paietta. Before he could marry her, Geremia and his three sons all had to be received into the Catholic faith. So it was that on 29 August 1763, in the Baroque duomo which still stands in Ceneda's central piazza, Emanuele and his family were baptized by the Catholic Bishop, Monsignor Lorenzo Da Ponte.

It being the custom for converts to take the name of their sponsor, Geremia became Gaspare Da Ponte, while Baruch and Anania became Girolamo and Luigi. As the eldest son, Emanuele assumed the Bishop's own name. Barely a year after his bar mitzvah, Emanuele Conegliano was suddenly a Christian named Lorenzo Da Ponte.

His father married Orsola less than two weeks later, on 10 September.

Emanuele-turned-Lorenzo's new stepmother, only two years his senior, would in time present him with no fewer than ten more siblings: three more brothers and seven sisters.

The Jewish origins of Lorenzo Da Ponte, as he would now be known for the rest of his life, swiftly became an almost guilty secret. He himself never referred to them, even in the memoirs he wrote late in life. 'As I am not writing the memoirs of a man illustrious by birth, talents or rank,' he begins, somewhat disingenuously, 'I shall say little about my family, my birthplace and early years, for they are matters entirely unimportant in themselves and of very little moment to my readers.' As Da Ponte's eventful life unfolded, the faith into which he was born would occasionally be used against him by the few privy to his past. So he preferred, in an intolerant age, to shroud his origins in mysterious obscurity.

As a Jewish boy in mid-eighteenth-century Italy, he was in truth lucky that his forebears had come to Ceneda a hundred and fifty years earlier from the nearby town of Conegliano, which remained the family name until its wholesale conversion to Catholicism. While part of the Venetian Republic, Ceneda was much less harsh in its treatment of Jews than Venice itself, where 'Hebrews' were tolerated because of their usefulness as moneylenders – a trade forbidden to Christians – but forced to live in squalid conditions on the island of Sinalunga, later known as the Giudecca. It was late in the sixteenth century, when Ceneda's economic fortunes flagged, that its Bishop invited Israel Ebreo da Conegliano to move the few miles north to open a bank there. While confined to a ghetto, and forced to wear red berets or headscarves, the Jewish community of Ceneda lived a more comfortable life than those in other North Italian cities of the period. The Conegliano family prospered, providing seventeenth-century Venice with some of its most celebrated physicians – who no doubt treated the wealthy Da Pontes.

Conversion to Catholicism, simply in search of a better life, was not uncommon in eighteenth-century Italy. But it was rare to have so specific a reason as Geremia Conegliano and his four sons that August afternoon as they joined the Bishop's procession down the winding path to the duomo from his official residence, the Castello di San Martino, which stands guard over the picturesque hill town to this day.

Also in the procession were the many members of the Bishop's household, both lay and clerical, led by his liveried company of halberdiers, beating their drums as the church bells chimed. This was the fifth successive day of such services, an occasion for much pomp and circumstance. Also the feast of the beheading of St John the Baptist, it began and ended with a salvo of cannon from the slopes of the Monte di San Paolo, which rises high above Ceneda. After the service the Conegliano family, now the Da Pontes, processed with the Bishop and his retinue back to his castle to continue their celebrations as fireworks lit up the piazza.

With the Bishop of Ceneda as his sponsor, young Lorenzo's fortunes now took a timely turn for the better. Renowned for his generous acts of charity, not least the renovation of the cathedral at his personal expense, this kindly man could tell that his young namesake was an intelligent boy, for all his lack of formal education. At fourteen, although ignorant of all other subjects, the child was at least literate; already he was a voracious reader of the volumes of poetry he had found abandoned in his father's attic. Among them were the works of Pietro Metastasio, Caesarean Poet to the Holy Roman Empire, whose verses aroused in his young mind 'the sensation of music'.

So the Bishop enrolled Lorenzo (and one of his brothers, Girolamo) in his episcopal seminary, where he was taught by caring masters and enjoyed access to a superb library. In two years he had mastered Latin, usually the route to the priesthood – his father's and the Bishop's aspiration for him, though Lorenzo himself knew it would be 'directly contrary to my vocation and character'. Modern languages, even Italian itself, were not on the syllabus. By the age of seventeen, young Da Ponte was fluent in Latin, verse included – he could compose a long oration and some fifty verses, he boasted, in half a day – while still barely able to write a literate sentence in his own tongue. A letter of even a few lines would contain a dozen errors.

The day was saved, and Da Ponte's future fundamentally altered, by the arrival on the seminary staff of a learned young Abbé named Cagliari, a recent graduate of the renowned University of Padua, where Dante and Petrarch were read and taught as assiduously as Virgil and Horace. With two young schoolfellows who would remain his friends for life, Michele Colombo and Girolamo Perucchini, Da Ponte began to enjoy a genial rivalry in the composition of Italian verses.

Hoping to touch his father for some money, Lorenzo thought he might stand a better chance of success if he appealed to him in verse. So he wrote his first sonnet, which began:

Mandatemi, vi prego, o padre mio,
Quindici soldi o vento, se potete,
E la cetera in man pigliar vogl'io,
Per le lodi cantar delle monete . . .

(Send me, I pray you, O father mine,
Fifteen shillings, or twenty, if you can,
And I will take my lyre in hand
To sing the praise of money!)

No sooner had he finished this quatrain than he heard a loud guffaw behind his back, and turned to find his friend Colombo reading over his shoulder. Colombo proceeded to mock Da Ponte's doggerel by chanting it in the drone of a blind Italian street beggar, strumming an imaginary lute as he sang. Tormented this way for several days, Da Ponte determined to set aside idle pleasures and make an intensive study of the Italian poets.

In less than six months he had learned by heart almost all of Dante's *Inferno*, as well as many Petrarch sonnets and *canzoni*, plus the 'finest' passages of Ariosto and Tasso. At the same time he secretly wrote – and promptly burned – more than two thousand lines of his own verse, determined to reach a standard at which it would transcend mockery. He had his reward in the shape of a sonnet he wrote to mark the departure of the college rector, the first verse he had made public since the Colombo charade.

Nube, che in largo umor dolce si scoglie,
　Quando Maggio cocente a noi ritorna.
　Tempra l'arsura: e i fior, l'erbe, e le foglie
Per le rive, e i pratelli erge, ed adorna:

Indi nel sen s'interna, e si raccoglie
　De la cupida terra, 'u non s'aggiorna:
　Ond'entro, e fuor lei fa di nove spoglie
Per celeste vertù grave, ed adorna.

Tal da vostra soave, alma favella,
　L'ardor calmando de' terreni affetti,
　La mia Patria, Signor, s'orna ed abbella:

E se a la pioggia de' fecondi detti
   Risponder la vedrem, cagion sì bella
   Quanto più bei non produrrà gli effetti?

(The cloud, which spreads refreshing air so widely,
When the burning month of May returns to us,
Waters the dry land, helping flowers, grass and foliage
Bloom along the river banks, making meadows thrive;

Thence it penetrates deep into the earth and gathers
Inside the thirsty ground, which never sees daylight;
So it goes in, and outside gives itself new garments
Thanks to its deep, celestial, virtue, and it adorns.

Just so your sweet and soul-inspired speech
Calms the ardour of earthly affections,
Adorns and embellishes my country, my Lord,

And if from the showers of your fertile words
We will see a response, for so fine a reason,
Won't the effects produced be even more beautiful?)

Most of Da Ponte's contemporaries admired it so much that they refused to believe it was his own work; only Colombo took it on trust, and touchingly vowed to write no more poetry himself until he fell in love. In time, Michele Colombo would go on to become a writer of some distinction; he would later recall a knife-fight between himself and Da Ponte over the favours of a beautiful Ceneda girl.

Da Ponte himself was sufficiently encouraged to resolve to devote himself henceforth entirely to Italian poetry. In less than two years, working night and day, he translated the ancient poets into Italian verse; at the same time, he made Latin versions of the Italian masters. 'I repeatedly copied them, criticized them, wrote commentaries on them, learnt them by heart.' He also tried his hand at 'all kinds of composition and metre', endeavouring 'to imitate the most beautiful of their ideas, use their most elegant phrases and select the finest passages of my habitual models ...' Above all he idolized Petrarch, 'for in his every line I seemed at each reading to find some new beauty.'

By the start of his third year at the seminary, Da Ponte was regarded as one of its most gifted pupils, his verses 'not infrequently' winning praise, even prizes. Although aware, by his own account, that much of the praise showered upon him was merely well-meaning encouragement, he began daring to hope that his 'unbounded' passion for poetry might lead to a life in literature, perhaps even earn him 'the reputation and rank of a good poet'.

Looking back at the end of his long life, and rueing his apparent failure to achieve immortality, he blamed 'Fortune' for his defeat, in that it had 'constantly thwarted my best intentions and drew me with imperious hand into the most dangerous and cruel whirlpools of life, depriving me of the means, the peace, the quiet and leisure without which in vain does the mind prepare to scale the topmost heights'.

Along with a capacity for self-pity, and an ability to blame anyone but himself for his life's vicissitudes, the young Da Ponte was developing a passion for books which would stay with him all his days. Already he had a fine collection of Latin texts, which he now hoped to supplement with the Italian authors from the well-stocked bookshop in Ceneda. Every time the teenager could scrape together a few lire, he would buy himself another Elzever edition. But his bankroll was smaller than his appetite for reading; as much as he economized on the pleasures of youth, he never had the means to acquire books as fast as he wished.

Recognizing this, the kindly Ceneda bookseller made a suggestion. His son was a shoemaker; if young Da Ponte could bring him leather or calfskin from his father's tannery, he would accept it as payment. Delighted by the bargain, Lorenzo ran home and stole three calfskins from his father's warehouse – only to be spotted by his stepmother as he was sneaking out. She promptly told his father, who paid an angry visit to the seminary. Eventually the incident came to the attention of the Bishop, who summoned young Da Ponte to explain himself. On hearing the truth of the matter, Bishop Da Ponte smiled indulgently and gave the boy the money he needed for his books.

But Lorenzo's luck was running out. The next year of his life, his nineteenth, was dogged by illness and misfortune. Struck down by malaria, to the point where his family feared for his life, he spent the best part of a year 'between illness, tears and idleness'. In the midst of this came a heavy blow indeed: the death of his patron and benefactor, Bishop Da Ponte, on 7 July 1768. Deprived of his guidance, and stricken with genuine grief for the saintly man who had so altered his life for the better,

Lorenzo was also now deprived of the funds required to live in the manner to which he had become accustomed.

As the only way he could afford to clothe himself, he began selling his precious collection of books. Worse, he would also have to abandon life at the seminary, purely for financial reasons, unless he committed himself to taking holy orders. This, in turn, would involve a sacrifice even greater than pledging his life to the church. 'The state of poverty into which my family had fallen caused me to renounce the hand of a noble and beautiful girl whom I loved tenderly, and led me to adopt a calling entirely contrary to my temperament, character, principles and studies, thus opening the way to a thousand strange chances and dangers, which the envy, hypocrisy and malice of my enemies took advantage of for more than twenty years.'

In 1766, at the age of seventeen, Da Ponte had already taken minor orders. Now as throughout his life, however, he was not going to let his holy vows get in the way of romance. According to his first biographer, Jacopo Bernardi (1871), this first girl to capture his heart was a local beauty called Pierina Raccanelli. By now, he had also enjoyed his first taste of Venice, whence he wrote to Colombo in January 1770, to say that he and his brother had been sent there to recover from another illness. It was carnival time, but the delicate state of Da Ponte's health obliged him to stay indoors with his books.

Further letters to Colombo from Venice follow that February and August. Then as dissolute as any city on earth, Venice would no doubt have introduced the hot-blooded young priest-in-the-making to the pleasures of dalliance with muses beyond the merely literary. But his forays to the capital were, as yet, only brief escapes from the dry disciplines of scholastic and clerical life. Literature remained high on his agenda, as it always would, and he now enjoyed another stroke of luck which made the sacrifices involved seem negligible.

Training for the priesthood was the only way Da Ponte could continue the education he so craved and enjoyed. And the church he proposed to enter was indeed a broad one, which would give him some standing in society, as vividly spelt out by the historian of eighteenth-century Italy, Maurice Vaussard:

Religion permeated all the outward expressions of private and public life. The clergy, excessive in number, the largest owners of landed property in every Italian state, benefiting from exorbitant privileges especially in judicial matters and holding absolute sway over people's consciences, exhibited such a large variety of prototypes ... from the highest to the humblest that it discourages any classification or overall judgment. It included sybaritic prelates and genuine saints, great men of letters and ignorant priests, dissolute or slothful monks and excellent teachers, confessors indulgent about the worst moral lapses and inflexible preachers, steeped in Jansenist maxims.

In time, Da Ponte would become the worst kind of priest. For now, knowing he was not cut out for the cloth, he was intent on pursuing the priesthood as the only way to continue his education and feed his hunger for literature. Thanks to the intervention of a kindly canon of Ceneda, Monsignor Girolamo Ziborghi, who was intent on continuing his late Bishop's mission with these members of his episcopal flock, Lorenzo and both his brothers were transferred to the seminary at Portogruaro, midway between Ceneda and Venice, to the east, nearer Trieste.

The handsome eighteenth-century seminary still stands today in the historic centre of Portogruaro, on the banks of the Lemene river, among many other ancient buildings reflecting the town's prosperity in the fifteenth and sixteenth centuries as a trading-post between Venice and Austria. The seminary's activities (and library) have long since been moved north to nearby Pordenone, but Da Ponte's name is still honoured in local history books and guides. The cranes engraved by Giovanni Antonio Pilacorte in 1494 on the Pozzetto, an ancient well, can still be seen beyond the Town Hall in the Piazza della Repubblica, just as they were when the twenty-year-old Da Ponte arrived in Portogruaro in 1770.

Four years since he had taken minor orders, Da Ponte's training for the priesthood now began in earnest. The sacrifices required were, as yet, as little to the benefits: dressed all in black, and forbidden to dance or duel, he studied philosophy and mathematics while further improving his mastery of Latin and the Italian poets. During his lessons on Euclid and Galileo, he would be studying Tasso's *Aminta* or Guarini's *Pastor fido* beneath the desk. Soon he had both by heart.

Towards the end of his first year at Portogruaro, Da Ponte gave a public recitation of a poem in praise of St Louis. Three lines in particular found favour with the Bishop of Concordia, Monsignor Gabrielli:

Ma sel ritolse il ciel, quasi sua gloria
Fosse manca e men bella
Senza la luce di quell'aurea stella.

(But Heaven reclaimed him, as if its glory
Were weaker and less beautiful
Without the light of that golden star.)

Also vice-rector of the college, Gabrielli promptly offered the twenty-one-year-old Da Ponte a post as an instructor. Briefly he hesitated, intent as he was on adding Hebrew to his linguistic skills, firmly believing that it was indispensable to greatness as a poet. Mindful of his father's poverty, however, he soon accepted the position, and found himself teaching rather than learning.

With thirty pupils in his care, and many vigilant colleagues keeping an eye on his standards, Da Ponte made sure he was well prepared for every lesson – and soon discovered he was learning as much as a teacher as he had as a pupil. Joining the seminary staff proved no handicap to his continuing self-education.

'My duties', he wrote to his friend Colombo, 'are to maintain discipline, to write the welcoming speech at the beginning of each academic year, as well as the final *accademia*, and to teach the Tuscan language to fifty-two of the top students in the seminary ... What do you think about that?' The Bishop was so pleased with Da Ponte that he continued to promote him through the ranks; soon he had risen to the post of Professor of Languages. But his rapid ascent, under the benevolent patronage of Gabrielli, was exciting jealous intrigues among his colleagues – the beginning, for Da Ponte, of a lifetime of paranoia about rivals and ill-wishers.

His 'enemies', as he called them in old age, proved 'implacable persecutors', putting it about that Da Ponte was insufficiently versed in physics and mathematics, that he was 'nothing but a chatterbox and an ignorant rhymester'. He replied initially in verse, publishing odes and dithyrambs in which, he liked to boast, 'people thought they could detect a flash of Redi's fire'. But the taunts continued; so he chose the *accademia*, at which specially written Latin, Greek and (occasionally) Italian poems were recited to mark the close of the school year, as the moment for his public revenge. Thanks to Da Ponte, the theme for the *accademia* of 1772 was 'La fisica particolare'. His verses won the praise of the Bishop, even the acclaim of the local citizenry, but served merely to inflame the back-biting of his colleagues.

After two years, he had had enough. On 17 March 1773, a week after his twenty-fourth birthday, Lorenzo Da Ponte was ordained as a priest. At the end of that academic year, wearied by the in-fighting in the seminary staff-room, he resigned his position and headed south to seek a new life in what the French poet Alphonse de Lamartine would soon call 'the permanent fancy-dress ball that was Venice'.

2

The Priest

IKE ALL great empires since ancient Rome, Venice had to go through a period of debauched abandon before its decline into mere city status; and the mid-1770s was that moment. Handsome, intelligent, amorous – and a priest – twenty-four-year-old Lorenzo Da Ponte was exchanging the tranquil, meditative foothills of the Dolomites for the temptations of the most decadent city on earth.

As the rest of Europe looked to its future via the ideas of Kant, Rousseau and Voltaire, *La Serenissima* was partying its way towards becoming merely the world's most beautiful city. The feud between the rival playwrights (and opera librettists) Carlo Goldoni and Carlo Gozzi was of much more interest than the Enlightenment to a city that thrived on intrigue. After a thousand years of independence, the Venice in which the young poet-priest arrived had its own motto: *La mattina una messeta, l'apodisnar una basseta, et le sera una donneta* – 'A little mass in the morning, a little gamble in the afternoon, a little lady in the evening'.

Day and night, meanwhile, Venice was full of music. 'In every square, street and canal', wrote Goldoni, 'singing is to be heard. The shopkeepers sing as they sell their wares; the workmen sing on quitting their labours; the gondoliers sing while waiting for their fares.' The English musician and writer Charles Burney, who visited Venice at this time, was particularly impressed by the wandering minstrels who thronged the streets and piazzas. 'If two of the common people walk together arm in arm, they are always singing, and seem to converse in song; if there is company on the water, it is the same; a mere melody, unaccompanied with a second part, is not to be heard in this city: most of the ballads in the streets are sung to a duo.'

To Foscolo, Venice was then the 'Sybaris of Europe'; to Algarotti, 'the free and blessed country of pleasure and beauty'. The city had seven theatres, two hundred cafés and numberless private casinos as well as the public ones – all open during carnival, which lasted half the year, from October to Christmas, from Twelfth Night to Lent, for two weeks from Ascension Day, again upon St Mark's Day, and (in the words of the French historian Philippe Monnier) 'whenever a Doge is elected, whenever a Procurator is chosen, on the least occasion always, on the slightest pretext'. Venetians, in the words of the eighteenth-century French traveller Jerome Le Français, were 'as attached to their religion as in the rest of Italy, but that has little influence on their behaviour. The people give way to their passions quite naturally, then go to confession and start all over again . . .'

Masks were worn by all, at carnival time and beyond, lending society a classless air, and affording a degree of licence otherwise unthinkable. From Doge to kitchen-maid, as Monnier put it in his *Venice in the Eighteenth Century*:

> With a mask over his face, a man may say and do as he pleases; for the State has sanctioned his mask, and will protect it. In his mask he seeks admittance to drawing-rooms, churches, convents, to the ball, the Palace, the casino. There he may take his ease, he may read in his armchair, but he must not forget the law of the carnival: barriers hold, authority avails, and dignity exists no more; there are no more lordlings now, nor beggars kissing their long sleeves; no more is heard of spy or nun, of *sbirro* or *zentildonna*, rope-walker or inquisitor, poor man or alien; there is but one rank, and one character, *Sior Machera*; but one costume, and one free people, garmented, steeped, confounded in delight. A scrap of white satin on the face, a black silk hood upon the shoulders; and by virtue of this comic livery, the aristocratic city becomes a democracy; and the loose garb of Laughter levels all her sons.

Any excuse for a party – religious ceremonies, military victories, VIP visits, an aristocratic wedding – saw riotous processions through illuminated streets filled with an atmosphere of permanent festivity. Shops, bars and cafés stayed open beyond usual Italian hours, thronged with revellers who partied from dusk till dawn. 'Nobleman and beggar, artisan and poet, gondolier and visiting royalty mingled under the clear winter sky, protected by their masks,' in the words of Sheila Hodges. As the French Revolution loomed, and the rest of Europe looked anxiously on, Venice's Robespierre was Giacomo Casanova, the prototype libertine, soon to become Da Ponte's friend.

But first, the Abbé had to make some conquests of his own. At 'the boiling-point of youthful spirit', as he himself put it in later years, the Jewish-born Catholic priest intent on a literary life was soon seduced by the sybaritic city's many other charms. Being 'in the full vigour of youth', by his own account, 'of a lively disposition and, by common consent, good-looking', Da Ponte found himself 'carried away' by 'customs, opportunity and example ... drawn deep into amusement and the pleasures of the senses' – to the complete neglect of literature and his other studies.

Almost immediately (if not, indeed, on one of his previous brief visits) Da Ponte fell 'violently' in love with 'one of the most beautiful, but also one of the most capricious ladies of the town'. This was Angiola Tiepolo, daughter of one of the oldest and noblest, if by now impoverished, families in Venice. For more than a thousand years the Tiepolos had figured in the records of the Republic, giving Venice two Doges; Angiola's grand-father had been ambassador to Constantinople, and her uncle Inquisitor of State, before the family fortunes had sunk to the level of the Barnabotti, or noblemen reduced to eking out a living by selling their vote in the High Council.

Married at twenty to a much older man, whom she had borne two children, Angiola had just been deserted by her husband, whom she had terrorized into belatedly becoming a priest. Da Ponte fell particularly for the dimples in Angiola's cheeks – 'as red as roses'. The rest of her was 'small, dainty and pretty, very pretty, with regular features and soft, beguiling eyes'. Despite her lack of education, Angiola was 'blessed with such charm of manner and vivacity of speech that she won all hearts and made conquests on all sides'. But she was also a neurotic, very jealous woman, with a temper violent enough to have driven her doting first husband to leave her and also take sanctuary in holy orders. Da Ponte was soon to find this out, if inadvertently, for himself.

Desperate not to lose all touch with his literary ambitions, he reserved an hour each evening for study and conversation at Venice's literary Caffè Menegazzo, known as the Caffè dei Letterati, where one night he was summoned outside by a gondolier. There was nothing unusual or un-expected about this; it was often Angiola's way of fetching him home. Wearing a half-mask, he followed the emissary to a nearby gondola, where he expected to find Angiola. Left in the dark with a female presence, he took her hand to kiss it, only to find it 'much plumper' than Angiola's. As both parties realized a mistake had been made, the unknown woman tried to withdraw her hand, but Da Ponte held on to it 'gently but firmly, earnestly reassuring her that she had nothing to fear'.

From her voice, whose accent was 'pure Tuscan', he could tell this woman was not a Venetian; when the gondolier returned with refreshments and a lantern, Da Ponte discovered that she was 'a girl of marvellous beauty and noble appearance', apparently in her mid-teens. She was Neapolitan, she told him, and her name was Matilda. Da Ponte promptly started making advances, saying 'all the things it is normal to say to a pretty woman in adventures of this kind' and begging her to let him escort her home. Matilda declined, with a show of reluctance, pleading special circumstances. But she hoped, she said, that another such opportunity would arise; she would, indeed, endeavour to ensure it.

The next few evenings he waited in vain for Matilda's summons; after a week without a messenger, that appeared to be the end of the adventure. More infatuated than ever with Angiola, but tormented by her arrogant, feckless gambler of a brother, Da Ponte left Venice for a week in the hope of getting both women out of his system. To no avail: on his return, with still no sign of Matilda, he accepted Angiola's invitation to move in with her.

But each night he returned to the Caffè dei Letterati, in the hope of another meeting with Matilda. He had all but given up hope when one evening he felt a tug on his coat in the Piazza San Marco, and turned to find her boatman – delighted to see him, with a promise to return that evening.

So again Da Ponte met Matilda, who this time took him straight home, where she proceeded to tell a long, complex tale of woe involving a weak father and a wicked stepmother, who wanted her to marry a rich but ugly, diseased old prince. When she refused, the stepmother had her shut away; but she had escaped, with the help of her nurse, and come to Venice so as to be able to hide herself behind a mask. En route she had been taken under the wing of a handsome young nobleman, who had turned out to be a reckless gambler, borrowing and losing much of her money before abandoning her. If only Da Ponte would offer her similar protection, she would share with him not merely her heart, but the considerable quantity of jewels and gold coins she had left.

Sorely tempted, Da Ponte thought of Angiola's jealousy – and hesitated. He asked for three days to make up his mind, but took a week to decide between the two women's respective charms. Another fit of jealousy from Angiola decided him; he would leave her for Matilda. He even agreed to escape abroad with her, and spent a last night beneath Angiola's roof planning flight the next day to Geneva or London.

His resolve hardened when Angiola came at him with a knife; he would leave her that night. By the time he reached Matilda's, however, there was no sign of her. He roused her maid, who told him in tears that just after he had left, officers of the State Inquisition had arrived, dragged Matilda from her bed, seized all her possessions and taken her off in a gondola.

Da Ponte never saw Matilda again. Years later, he learned that she had been shut in the convent for another six years before the death of her stepmother enabled her to take her proper place in her father's household.

What is now the Monaco Hotel, the sleek five-star establishment beside the Piazza San Marco, was Venice's main *ridotto* – or public gaming-house – during Da Ponte's years in the city. Here he spent much of the next year, having fallen back into the arms of Angiola and caught the gambling bug from her brother Girolamo. 'Every evening we went to the *ridotto*,' he recalled, 'and every evening we came away cursing gambling and the man who invented it.'

Angiola herself was an avid gambler, her dissolute brother even more so. 'Little by little I too became a gambler,' confessed Da Ponte, reluctantly obliged to treat his mistress's overbearing brother with the respect due a nobleman. 'Sometimes out of politeness, sometimes from ennui' he would give way to the young man, and furnish him with funds to take to the *ridotto*. It was not long, of course, before all three had lost every penny.

They began pawning their possessions, even their clothes, in a deluded attempt to win back their losses. Returning to his gondola one night, utterly bereft, Da Ponte was surprised to find the sympathetic boatman offering him a loan. 'Go and stake this,' he said, handing him fifty sequins, 'and learn to know the ways of the Venetian gondolier.'

Back at the *ridotto*, Da Ponte's luck turned. Soon he was 'loaded with gold'; unlike Angiola's brother, moreover, he knew when to stop. Escorting Angiola back to the gondola, he repaid the gondolier with handsome interest, and went home to count his ill-gotten gains.

So the Tiepolo dining table was piled high with gold coins when

Angiola's brother made an unexpected entrance. Grabbing it all, Girolamo insisted on dragging them both back to the *ridotto*, where he proceeded to lose the lot. A disconsolate Da Ponte withdrew to the 'Room of Sighs', an antechamber reserved for gamblers to reflect on their misfortune, only to find a masked man begging a few coins of him. Putting his hand in his pockets, to demonstrate that they were empty, Da Ponte was surprised to find one last cache of coins hidden beneath his handkerchief. He gave a handful to the stranger, who insisted that he would repay him, but only at his own house. He proceeded to write down his address on a playing card.

On his return home, Da Ponte found Angiola waiting to tell him that her brother was throwing him out. With no money left to his name, he was no use to the Tiepolo household any more. Already Girolamo had dispatched a servant to sell Da Ponte's bed, his only remaining possession. This gave him an idea.

Returning to the *ridotto* with his newly discovered gold, Da Ponte was unsurprised to find the servant who had been sent to sell the bed already gambling away the proceeds. Pretending not to notice him, Da Ponte proceeded to accumulate another great pile of gold while watching the hapless servant lose all his master's money. Then he blackmailed him into forming an alliance: in return for Da Ponte's silence, and the return of his funds, the servant would tell his master that his sister's lover had a secret: he knew how to forge money. That way, he would be received back into the Tiepolo palace – and Angiola's bed.

It worked, of course, and Da Ponte remained in residence longer than he had planned or expected – more than a year – putting up with his mistress's tantrums and her brother's constant demands, all for love of Angiola. His passion for her was such that he continued to turn down far more attractive propositions, as he had poor Matilda.

On finding that playing card in his pocket one day, for instance, he was drawn by curiosity to the address of the old man who owed him a few coins. Here he discovered that his host was really a wealthy merchant from Livorno, who confessed to having tricked him to test his character. Repaying Da Ponte with handsome interest, he told him he was also the proud stepfather of a beautiful young girl – whose hand he now offered Da Ponte in marriage, so impressed had he been by his generosity.

The fact that he was a Catholic priest never seems to have stopped Da Ponte contemplating such offers. Again he hesitated, agonizing over

Angiola; as he did so, the old man took him into the next room, to show him coffers full of gold. He had been watching Da Ponte, even pretending to be a beggar to establish that this was a good-natured, generous man. If he agreed to marry his stepdaughter, five thousand sequins would be his; upon the old man's death, another four thousand. But he must promise always to 'honour the poor'.

Still Da Ponte declined the old man's offer, haunted by his love for Angiola. They parted friends, and he later heard that the girl had made a good match with a decent young Venetian. At the time, he went away fretting that he had made the wrong decision – confirmed when he got home, where Angiola flew at him in a jealous rage. This time she threw an inkpot at him; throwing up his hand to protect his face, he sustained an injury which prevented him writing for a month. Even the sight of her lover's blood did nothing to calm Angiola's fury. That night, as he lay sleeping, she crept into his room and cut off his long hair.

This was her way of preventing him going out, which also deprived Da Ponte of the handy income he was earning as tutor to the two sons of a Venetian noblewoman. Curious about his sudden absence, his employer visited Da Ponte at home; on discovering the 'type of people' he was living with, she promptly dismissed him.

Now Angiola would allow him out only at night, and in her company. 'We went to theatres and shows, and dinner parties, spending vast amounts and earning nothing. In this way our wealth, never very great, began to vanish.' Their luck at the gaming-tables also turned, to the fury of Angiola's brother. Again he began demanding money with menaces, even armed threats, despite knowing Da Ponte had little to give him. 'Then forge some,' demanded Girolamo. 'Teach me the secret.'

To preserve his secret, and perhaps his life, Da Ponte handed Girolamo such money as he had left, with a promise to 'make' more over the next few days. Girolamo's wrath temporarily assuaged, he started to take serious stock of his parlous position. 'I began to see the danger I ran of ruining my reputation in secular life.' For some time his brother, another Girolamo, had been chiding him about the error of his ways; also an ordained priest, with a post in Venice as secretary to a nobleman, Giovanni da Lezze, Girolamo earnestly urged his brother to return to his studies, to literature. But Lorenzo 'had not the strength to free myself'. There followed an incident which drove home the truth of his brother's words, and took matters out of Da Ponte's hands.

He was used to receiving visits from a man of the cloth who had been a fellow student at the seminary in Portogruaro. Another priest fallen on hard times, also through gambling, this friend was really after the occasional free meal. On his latest visit the two enjoyed a convivial supper together before the priest went his way, as usual. Later on Da Ponte decided to go out, and asked his servant to fetch his coat. But it had gone missing. After a thorough search of the house he realized, to his surprise and dismay, that his priest friend must have stolen it.

The servant, who had never liked the visiting priest, quickly tracked the coat down to a nearby pawnbroker. Brother Girolamo redeemed it with his own money, and returned it with a sigh: 'Now see what your dissolute ways have reduced you to.' Da Ponte was left to reflect on the verities of his chosen way of life:

> Why are the principles of religion, education and honour not strong enough to curb a man's passions, and restrain him, if not from dissoluteness, at least from actions that are a disgrace to society? Can a man who comes into one's house under the cover of hospitality and friendship become so blind to right and wrong as to steal a cloak from a companion, benefactor and friend? And what has brought him to this? Gambling and women!

These last two words, as he shook his head sadly over his light-fingered fellow-priest, made Da Ponte realize with a shudder that he might as well be describing himself. 'Trembling with dread', he made a vow on the spot: to give up cards, and women, and leave Venice. That night he wrote to his brother Girolamo:

> Girolamo, I have finished with gambling and love affairs and Venice. I would leave tomorrow if I had any money. But I swear I'll be gone within three days. God be thanked – and, ah, the poor thief . . . Let us meet tomorrow morning.

His brother did not wait for morning; on receiving Lorenzo's note, he came round at once and gave him enough money to leave Venice immediately.

First thing next day, before making his escape from the Tiepolo house, Da Ponte received a note from the errant priest:

> Yesterday I acted basely. I stole your cloak and pawned it for eighty lire. The worst of it is that I went gambling and lost the money. I am

in despair about it. I would send you mine but it is old, short, poor, and not fit for this time of year. But you must meanwhile have a cloak. What is to be done? I am at your disposal.

Chuckling over the letter, Da Ponte went straight round to the priest's lodgings. Relishing his surprise when his friend saw him wearing his own coat, he had barely opened his mouth when the priest fled out of the door; chasing him down the street, he could see he was about to hurl himself in a canal. Reaching him in time to stop him, Da Ponte refrained from delivering the expected lecture, calmly and simply repeating his brother's words to him: 'See what your dissolute ways have reduced you to.' Moved by his restraint, the other priest wept and embraced him. Da Ponte gave him some money on the condition that he agreed to mend his ways, leave Venice forthwith, and return to a life worthy of a priest. His friend gave him his word.

In later years, Da Ponte learned that the priest had gone straight back to Ceneda, where he rose to become Professor of Literature in the seminary. Every year for the rest of his life, in memory of that episode, he spent much of his ample income on clothing the poor.

Da Ponte, too, briefly went home to Ceneda, honouring his promise to his brother to leave Venice after his unprofitable year there. At twenty-five, his future again appeared empty.

3

The Rebel

M IDWAY BETWEEN Ceneda and Venice, Treviso likes to boast that its canals are second only to those of *La Serenissima*. To enjoy them today, and the medieval Piazza dei Signori at the heart of Treviso's historic centre, you must struggle towards the Sile and Cagnan, the eastern branch of the River Bottenga celebrated in Dante's *Inferno*, through modern suburbs containing Venice's second airport, reconstructed in brutally civic style after eighty per cent of the city was destroyed by American bombs in 1944.

But the seventeenth-century seminary of Treviso still stands, in all its considerable Romanesque splendour, on the Via San Nicolo in the heart of the ancient city. This was where Da Ponte's luck saw him fetch up in the autumn of 1774 as Professor of Literature – but not without further mishaps en route.

From Venice he had gone straight home to Ceneda, where he spent ten days contemplating an uncertain future before the offer came up of two posts at Treviso – one for him, another for Girolamo, who had given up his job in Venice to be with his brother. But almost as soon as it had been made, the offer was withdrawn; a priest – probably the 'rival' Da Ponte had attacked in an anonymous poem – denounced him to the church authorities. The charge was that, amid other immoral acts, he had eloped with a woman from Ceneda. This was 'the one thing, as of course you know, I never even dreamt of doing,' he wrote to Colombo.

But everyone in Treviso believed it, Da Ponte forlornly told his friend.

And so I have been dismissed by the Prelate, who had previously confirmed my appointment in a letter in his own hand. You may imagine, dearest friend, how distraught I am. To see myself ruined on the very threshold of my hopes; to know that my reputation is being torn to shreds on false evidence, by a man whom, though I have never met him, I have always held in the very highest regard; to realize how very difficult it is to find any adequate defence against so powerful an assault – these are all problems which confound me as much as anything has ever done.

He pleaded with Colombo to intervene: 'My only hope lies in you, since you love me so much, and are yourself so greatly loved by this priest. You are wise, and will understand my necessity better than I can spell it out. I beg, above all, that you help me as fast as you can. A day, an hour or even less will decide my fate.'

Colombo did, it seems, intercede on Da Ponte's behalf – and success-fully, for he was reinstated as Professor of Humanities at the Treviso seminary, where his brother Girolamo took up a post as Master of Lower Grammar. But there was one more obstacle to overcome before Da Ponte could settle into his *vita nuova*.

Every day he was still receiving letters from Angiola. She had taken a new lover as soon as he had left Venice, but could not resist continuing to wield the sway she still held over him. On the first day of 1775 she wrote: 'Lorenzo, if you value my honour and my life, come to Venice at once.' She would be waiting for him at her cousin's home at 10 o'clock the following evening.

In freezing cold weather Da Ponte hurried immediately to Mestre, where he paid four strong young gondoliers a handsome sum to force a way through the frozen lagoons to Venice. As he reached for the knocker on Angiola's door, however, a hand emerged from the darkness to stay his. It was his own former servant, now in Angiola's employ, who told him the whole scheme was a trap. Stricken with jealousy, Angiola's new lover, one Dondorologi, had persuaded her to lure Da Ponte back to Venice so that he could kill him.

As it happened, the arduous journey had made Da Ponte late; it was now midnight, and the jealous lover had already given up on him and taken himself off to the *ridotto*. But Da Ponte seized this last chance to confront Angiola. Furious at her duplicity, he rejected her 'false' embraces and defiantly declared: 'May the hand of God destroy so infamous a brood!'

He ran from the room, and out of Angiola's life for good, fleeing to the nearest landing-stage and taking a gondola back to Mestre. As he returned thence to Treviso, it felt as if 'a ray of heaven's light entered my soul, enlightening my reason and healing all past wounds'.

Now Da Ponte was eager to seize the opportunity offered by Treviso of a return to respectability as a learned gentleman of letters. Rumours of his conduct in Venice were still rife on the clerical grapevine. This seemed to be his last chance to save his name and make something of his life, whether as poet or priest.

A metropolis compared to Ceneda, a dull provincial town compared to Venice, Treviso was then a retreat for Venetians from the summer stink of the canals. A vassal of Venice, as the lion over its entrance gate proclaimed, Treviso was a stuffy, claustrophobic place, peopled by petty bourgeoisie. But the city did at least house one of Italy's finest opera houses, now lovingly restored since war had damaged its original glory. The Irish tenor Michael Kelly liked the Treviso of Da Ponte's day for 'the elegant villas which surround it, belonging to noble Venetians who, during the theatrical season, pass their *vendemmias* (grape harvests) there, and have what they call their *cuganas* (riotous parties)'.

Long a centre of learning as much as leisure, Treviso now enabled Da Ponte's 'free spirit', as he put it, 'to wander once more through the sweet and lovely fields of the Muses'. The seminary boasted a fine library, stimulating colleagues, and a 'wise and big-hearted' Bishop in Monsignor Paolo Francesco Giustiani – in sum, 'a climate so pure and pleasant as to invigorate fancy and put fire in a poet's belly'. Thanks to the help of his loyal brother Girolamo, and an eminent new literary friend named Giulio Trento, a short poem in *ottava rima* called 'Il cecchino, o sia la storia del cane e del gatto' ('The Sniper'; or 'The story of the dog and the cat') helped boost Da Ponte's literary renown, shoring up his good standing with the Bishop and academic community.

He and his brother, he flattered himself, introduced higher standards to the school, thus again making him collegiate enemies as both were promoted to higher positions. At the end of their first year there, Lorenzo became Professor of Rhetoric while Girolamo took over his brother's old post and also became Master of Gregorian Chant.

His claim that he transformed the Treviso seminary is disputed by one of Da Ponte's first and most sympathetic biographers, Angelo Marchesan, who succeeded him in its Chair of Humanities one hundred and fifty years later. But he describes his quixotic predecessor as 'full of life, passion and poetry, extremely clever, with a lively imagination, quick of tongue, and very learned. All their lives his young pupils remembered their teacher, who not only fired them with the joy of studying literature but showed them such genuine affection.'

Da Ponte influenced his pupils 'so profoundly through his teaching, making the seminary walls seem less oppressive and the school benches less hard, that, even more than might otherwise have been the case, their young lives felt the need of laughter, of sunshine, and the urge to exercise their brains and bodies without constraint'.

In this dull provincial backwater, with growing ennui as much as pleasure, Da Ponte returned to the study and teaching of the Latin and Italian literature he so loved. Now twenty-six, he had finally got Angiola out of his system, and seems briefly to have deceived himself that his hedonistic days were behind him. For a while, at least, he buckled down to the literary life, whatever his feelings about the priesthood.

In less than two years, however, he was desperately bored, and found himself missing the pleasures of which Venice had given him so addictive a taste. It was as much mischief on his part as pedantry on that of the church elders that led to the next major upheaval in his life, this time changing it for ever.

As Professor of Rhetoric it was Da Ponte's duty, as at Portogruaro, to write a series of poems to be recited by his pupils at the solemn annual festival of *accademia*, in the presence of the Bishop, the local magistrate, the cathedral hierarchy and most of Treviso's prominent citizens. In 1776 Professor Da Ponte risked the wrath of the authorities by taking as his theme the subversive topic: 'Is man happier in an organized society or in a simple state of nature?' In the year of America's Declaration of Independence, with the French Revolution fermenting, and Enlightenment ideas spreading wildly across Europe, these were dangerously Rousseau-esque questions to raise.

His verses exactly met the academic requirements – four Latin and seven Italian poems in different metres, with a prose preface in Italian – but his risqué theme did not. Da Ponte's measured arguments that the state had no rights over its citizens, nor parents over their children, and that no laws served any useful purpose, caused no great fuss that day; the Bishop, church and town elders seem to have gone their ways without much hint of a scandal. And the poems were duly published.

The third, entitled 'Frottola Anacreontica', read:

S'io trivassi in colle, o in piano,
    quella Ninfa, che trovò,
    Ricciardetto a un Fauno in
      mano,
    E uccidendol lei salvò;

If I found a hill, or down a valley
That nymph, Ricciardetto,
In the hands of a fawn,

And by killing him I saved her;

Dalla Ninfa un altro dono
    Vorrei certo domandar,
    E in altr'uom da quel ch'io
      sono
    Me medesmo trasformar.

From the nymph, another gift
I would certainly like to ask:
Into a different man from the
    one I am
I would like to be transformed.

Io per lei di Briareo
    Chiederei le braccia aver,
    E la possa di Tifeo
    O d'Alcide, o d'altro fier.

And through her, of Briareo
I would like to have the arms
And the strength of Tifeo,
Or of Alcido, or of other brave
    men.

E la pelle, ch'ebbe Orlando,
    E il cavallo volator,
    E la lancia, e il specchio e
      il brando,
    E l'anello e il corno ancor.

And the skin that Orlando had
And the flying knight
And the lance and the mirror
    and the sword
And the ring and the horn, too.

E così sfidando a guerra
    Quanta gente scalda il sol,

    Del mar tutto e della terra
    Diventar Monarca io sol.

And thus challenging to war
As many people as the sun can
    warm,
Of the whole sea and land
To become the absolute
    monarch.

Quindi sparger d'ogn'intorno
    Una legge universal,
    Da quel lido u'nasce il
      giorno
    Fino al lido occidental.

Then I would spread around
A universal law
Coming from the shore where
    the day is born
To the western shore.

Una legge, onde nel mondo,

    Ogni legge avesse fin,

A law that, throughout the
    world,
Would end all other laws

Ch'ogni bene or mette a fondo
Dei dolenti cittadin.

That did not defend or give priority to
The well-being of suffering citizens.

Della Grecia i Sapienti,
I Pompili, i Ciceron,
Sbandirei come serpenti
Dalla mia giurisdizion.

The wise men of Greece
The Pompeys, the Ciceros,
I would banish like serpents
From my jurisdiction.

I fiscali, gli avvocati
Nel bordel farei garrir,

The tax experts, the lawyers.
I would make them shriek in the brothel;

E fra i pazzi e i disperati,

Among the mad and the destitute.

Lasciereigli allor piatir.

I would make them suffer.

Si può dar più strana voglia
Servo farsi a questo, a quel,

Can one have a stranger wish
Than to serve this person or that?

E cangiar, quand'altri il voglia,
Tetto, veste, e moglie, e ciel?

And to change, according to someone else's will,
Roof, clothes, wife and the sky?

Sol del cuor seguendo i moti

Only following the ways of the heart

Fora l'uom beato appien,
Che la legge ai nostri voti
Or fa forza, ed or pon fren.

Makes men truly happy.
Laws and power
Put a brake on our desires.

Tu vorresti una fanciulla
Che ti par bella e gentil,
Ma le nozze il padre annulla
Col pater del jus civil.

You would desire a woman
Who seems beautiful and kind,
But the father can cancel the wedding
With the blessing of the law.

Chi vorria da stocco o spada

Anyone would want to spend his life

Star lontan tutti i suoi dì,

Away from the sword and rapier;

Ma convien che a guerra ei vada,	But the law commands us
Che la legge vuol così.	To go to war.
Io vivrei tra il gioco e il canto,	I would like to live between games and singing
Senza invidia ad un sovran,	Without envying even a king,
Ma la legge grida intanto:	But the law meanwhile shouts:
Al lavor chi vuol del pan.	To work, those who want to earn their daily bread!
La natura dentro il petto	Nature, inside my breast,
Una legge sol mi diè,	Gave me the only law:
Di non far in atto o in detto	Not to do in action or in word
Quel che poi non piace a me.	That which I do not like.
Dunque solo in questo seno	Hence this law alone
Questa legge a me vivrà,	Will live in my heart,
E tu poi da un duro freno	And you may in harsh restraint
Cerca pur felicità.	Seek sheer happiness.

As they wound their way around the province, to a descant of spiteful tongues, these verses soon outraged the *Riformatori*, the Reformers of Studies at Padua – 'men', fumed Da Ponte, 'in more need of reform themselves than morality or judgement to reform others'. The Reformers demanded that the poet be hauled up before the Venetian Senate, where his case was heard on 14 December 1776.

At first indifferent to a scandal he regarded as absurd, insisting that his poems were no more than an academic *jeu d'esprit*, Da Ponte was soon persuaded by friends to travel to Venice to defend himself. Once back in the capital he found that the case was causing a minor sensation; he himself was something of a celebrity, with the support of a gratifying quorum of the Venetian intelligentsia. Among his leading advocates were Bernardo Memmo, a prominent intellectual who was also a scion of one of Venice's noblest families; another cultured patrician named Pietro Zaguri; and Gasparo Gozzi, brother of the celebrated dramatist Carlo.

Memmo and Gozzi were both well-connected, influential figures; Memmo was descended from a tenth-century Doge, and his brother Andrea was ambassador to the Vatican, later Procurator of St Mark, second only to the Doge in Venice. Both strove hard to sway the debate Da Ponte's way; but the authorities could not be talked out of their stern disapproval. When Gozzi went before them, to argue that Da Ponte was 'a young man with talent, which should be encouraged', the *Riformatori* replied: 'So much the worse! We must deprive him of the power to grow more dangerous.'

Da Ponte's poems were intoned to the Senate, which declared itself scandalized. A reference in the *sermone* (the seventh poem) to *corna aurate*, or 'golden horns', was taken as a personal insult to the Doge, whose ceremonial cap was horned.

> Io di censore
> O di console irato i fasci e il ciglio
> Minaccioso non temo, i fasci e il ciglio
> Miro i regi sul trono, e per le piazze
> Il cencioso mendico, a cui tal'volta
> Porgo vile moneta, onde l'imbarco
> Paghi al nicchier della letea palude.
> Il garrir de' signor, che pien d'orgoglio
> Ergon le corna aurate, un lieve fischio
> Parmi d'aura nascente, e mentre loro
> Prestano omaggio le divote torme,
> Io con equabil ciglio in me raccolto,
> Or la gru passeggiera, or per le nubi
> Qualche mostro volante, ed ora i marmi
> Di Pasquin, di Marforio intento miro.

(I do not fear the threatening brow of the censor,
Or of the enraged consul, or the fasces.
I admire the fasces and the brow
Of the king on his throne, and in the square
I give alms to the beggar, to whom sometimes
I give a mean coin, to pay the boatman
For his passage to the Lethean marshes.
The shrieking of the ruler who, full of pride,
Shakes his golden horns, is a soft whistle
On a growing breeze. While they
Enjoy the homage of loyal crowds,
I am equally content to be absorbed in myself,

Or to admire the passing stork, or some monster
Flying through the clouds, and sometimes
The marbles of Pasquin and Marforio.)

Da Ponte's friends began to worry that he might wind up in jail. As it was, he was deprived of his livelihood, if not his freedom. The sentence of the court was that Lorenzo Da Ponte be publicly admonished, deprived of his post at the Treviso seminary, and banned for life from holding any teaching position in the Venetian Republic.

Even the Bishop of Treviso was formally rebuked, and the seminary official who had approved the poems for public recital severely censured. An inquiry into 'radicalism' in schools was ordered throughout the Republic; and all copies of Da Ponte's poems, whether printed or in manuscript, were seized by the state for destruction.

It was more than mere bravado which saw Da Ponte taking a genially light-hearted attitude to the entire episode. When sentence was pronounced, he tells us, he put his handkerchief to his mouth 'to hide my laughter'. Whether intentionally or not – the evidence is ambiguous – he had managed to extricate himself from the tedium of Treviso, and indeed from seminary life.

Henceforth he could pursue his literary interests and career outside the constraints of the church. In the meantime, he decided to enjoy his new-found celebrity in Venice, and plunge back into its heady delights with all the abandon of a man making up for lost time.

Tall and slim, with an aquiline nose, a sensuous mouth and bedroom eyes, twenty-eight-year-old Lorenzo Da Ponte was handsome, witty, intelligent and charming. Men found his company as captivating as did the women of Venice, who made fools of themselves over him. Capable of extemporizing verse with remarkable skill and grace, he was soon making a name as a poet – which aided his return to prolific womanizing.

'The ability to recite or sing good, impromptu verse on any subject and in any metre is an exclusively Italian gift,' according to Da Ponte, who perfected the skill in partnership with his loyal brother Girolamo, now back in Venice as secretary to Giovanni da Lezze. One English traveller, Tobias Smollett, was particularly impressed by this uniquely Italian gift: 'One of the greatest curiosities you meet with in Italy', he wrote in his *Travels through France and Italy*, 'is the *Improvisatore*; such is the name given to certain individuals who have the surprising talent of reciting verse extempore, on any subject you propose.'

The son of Smollett's landlord, a Franciscan friar, had 'a great genius in this way. When the subject is given, his brother tunes his violin to accompany him, and he begins to rehearse in recitative, with wonderful fluency and precision. Thus he will, at a minute's warning, recite two or three hundred verses, well turned and well adapted, and generally mingled with an elegant compliment to the company.'

So accomplished did Da Ponte and his brother grow at this rare feat that they became known as 'the *Improvisatori* of Ceneda'. But Da Ponte fretted lest the practice prove harmful to the writing of really fine poetry; his extemporized verse might impress an audience, but looked decidedly mediocre on paper. On the advice of a new friend, the poet and librettist Caterino Mazzola, a graduate of the Treviso seminary, he would soon phase it out.

Taken in by his influential friend Memmo, who also financed him, Da Ponte was lionized by the leading intellectuals of the Republic, while renewing his amorous adventures. The elderly Memmo had a beautiful, twenty-year-old mistress, Teresa Zerbin, with whom he was so infatuated that he housed her entire family. After waxing lyrical over her charms, Da Ponte's memoirs recount an unconvincing story that Teresa took a dislike to him, and treated him with such cold disdain that he felt obliged to leave. More likely, he had an affair with her, and was ashamed to admit to cuckolding so genial a benefactor. The speed with which he unexpectedly left Venice suggests that he was again in fear of his life; perhaps Memmo had discovered his treachery. It was an equally curious, hasty-seeming decision to head for Padua, where his brother Luigi was a medical student as impoverished as himself.

For forty-two days, by his own account, Da Ponte lived in Padua on a diet of bread, olives and water. Ensuring, as always, that he meanwhile maintained a presentable facade, he made the acquaintance of the city's leading literati, notably Melchiore Cesarotti, Professor of Greek and Hebrew at Padua's celebrated university, and translator of Homer. For a while Da Ponte's fortunes improved when he found he could effortlessly win money from students at games of draughts and dominoes – at which he did not shrink from cheating, if necessary. But this way of life soon palled; encouraged by the kindly Mazzola, who had negotiated a truce with Memmo, Da Ponte risked returning to Venice.

There Memmo greeted him with open arms. Young Teresa had persuaded him that her disdainful treatment of Da Ponte – if that was all it
had been – was a ruse to trick the errant priest out of his immoral
ways, and restore him to the arms of his muse. Indignant at this 'base
imputation', Da Ponte valued Memmo's friendship too highly to dispute
it. But he politely declined his invitation to return to his house, and again
live under the same roof as the wily Teresa.

Memmo's friend Zaguri, the cultured patrician, had offered him a job
as his private secretary and 'companion of his studies', complete with
board and lodging. Zaguri may have had a soft spot for Da Ponte because
his younger brother, Mario, had just become Bishop of Ceneda. Da Ponte
gratefully accepted Zaguri's offer, while also becoming tutor to the children of Giorgio Pisani, an outspoken critic of the government whom he
dubbed 'the Venetian Gracchus'.

'Thus all at once,' he recalled, 'I found myself befriended and protected
by three noble and powerful personages who rivalled one another in
showing me friendship and kindness.' Through Zaguri, he met another
potent ally, whose friendship and advice he would value in Venice and
beyond over the next two decades: Giacomo Casanova.

Now fifty-two, to Da Ponte's twenty-eight, and a shadow of the phil-
anderer who had swaggered his way across Europe, Casanova was reduced
to spying for the very government that had once imprisoned him. He had
lost his youthful allure to women, but he was still a brilliant con-
versationalist and wit, a man of great charm who soon had Da Ponte
under his spell. The younger libertine wrote fawning letters to the elder,
but also held his own in conversation; while Da Ponte was in Venice they
even managed to fall out over some arcane point of Latin prosody. To
Casanova, it was because he had not praised Da Ponte's poems highly
enough; but, as he told his friend Collatio, 'a flatterer is not a friend.' The
quarrel did not prove lasting, and Casanova would prove one of the few
enduring figures in Da Ponte's eventful life.

At the time, like Casanova, he again faced a choice between literature
and love. There was little doubt which held the greater appeal for the
young Da Ponte, as he all but confesses: 'I wrote but little verse at that
time, for the work of my two posts and perhaps even more the distrac-
tions and pleasures of the city which suited only too well my age and
temperament.'

In his memoirs, Da Ponte then returns to the increasingly tedious saga of Memmo and Teresa, lavishing fulsome detail on their story to bury another he would rather forget. For all his pride in his sexual prowess, and his capacity for braggadocio, Da Ponte had no wish to tell posterity how he fell under the spell of another disreputable woman, Angioletta Bellaudi, to the point where he had to leave Venice for ever.

Not until the twentieth century were details of the episode discovered; they were first published in 1942 in an article by Fausto Nicolini entitled 'La vera ragione della fuga da Lorenzo Da Ponte da Venezia' ('The true reason for Lorenzo Da Ponte's flight from Venice'). Even then, the full details were considered so salacious that some were left smouldering in the recesses of the vast city archive, a former Franciscan monastery beside the Frari church in San Polo, where they lurk to this day.

Midway between San Marco and the Rialto, the Campo San Luca – the historic centrepoint of Venice, so designated by a tall wooden pole – today boasts a Burger King alongside the centuries-old bookshop which is its best-known landmark. Next door to the fast-food joint is a handsome eighteenth-century house where Da Ponte lived in sin with an aristocrat's wife while conducting mass in the nearby church.

This was the offence that would eventually see him banished from Venice for good. It was drawn to the attention of the authorities, in this case the *Esecutori contra la bestemmia*, in time-honoured Venetian fashion: a document denouncing Da Ponte was thrown anonymously into the mouth of a stone lion at nearby San Moisé, one of many ranged around the city for this purpose. The story it told, for all its scruffy, ungrammatical handwriting, was a highly disreputable one.

Employed as a priest at the Church of San Luca, Da Ponte had taken lodgings across the square with a woman named Laura Bellaudi, mother of one Carlo, whose wife was Angioletta. The fact that she was several months pregnant did not stop Angioletta flirting with the lively new lodger; a woman of low repute, she was known to have had 'improper' relations with a neighbour at the age of ten, and had been obliged to marry Carlo when she became pregnant by him at fifteen.

Unsurprisingly, the marriage was not a happy one; now Carlo was having an affair with a girl called Francesca Bertati, and took to using Da Ponte as his courier for secret messages. So the priest saw little harm in responding to the comely Angioletta's advances. Her sister Caterina, who also lived in the house with her own husband, one day told their mother that she had seen the lodger with his hand up Angioletta's skirt, while hers was inside his breeches. Confronted by his landlady, Da Ponte protested his innocence with truly dangerous bravado: 'May God strike me with a thunderbolt while I'm celebrating mass!' Caterina was so impressed as to decide she must have been seeing things.

Soon after, however, Laura Bellaudi herself saw Da Ponte standing naked in the doorway of his room, exhibiting himself to Angioletta through the open door of her own room opposite. She demanded that he leave her house forthwith.

But Da Ponte, so he claimed, had intercepted letters from Carlo to his lover threatening to murder Angioletta. 'The woman I hate will soon be a mother,' read one, in which he declared it his intention to be present at the birth. 'I will deliver her myself and our troubles will soon be over. If this does not work, I will put her to sleep for good.' Using these letters to terrify Angioletta, he persuaded her to elope with him.

On the agreed evening, 30 August, Da Ponte diverted Carlo to some fictional assignation in another part of the city while Angioletta packed a bag and hailed a gondola to take her to their rendezvous. But no sooner had she arrived than she went into labour; after leaving the gondola, she lay in the street until Da Ponte came looking for her. He carried her to the home of his cousin, Pietro Mariani, also a converted Jew, where she gave birth to a daughter within the hour. Next day Da Ponte and his cousin (plus, for good measure, *his* mistress) took the child to San Luca to present it to Carlo, who promptly disowned it and dispatched it to the hospital for foundlings.

Hopelessly enslaved by Angioletta, as he had been by Angiola Tiepolo, Da Ponte proceeded to live with her at his cousin's house while continuing to celebrate mass at the church of San Luca. Soon she was pregnant again, this time by him. His cousin decided this was too much, and threw them out. So by the time Angioletta gave birth to Da Ponte's child, they were shifting from one lodging to another around the San Luca district. This child, too, was consigned to the foundling hospital.

Still they continued to live together, a necessarily peripatetic existence, and still he continued to conduct mass. At one time, according to the evidence at his subsequent trial, they were living in a brothel, where Da Ponte organized the entertainments, and himself played the violin in his priest's vestments – the only clothes he now possessed. Each of them, evidently, enjoyed other affairs; Da Ponte seems not to have had any problem with Angioletta's infidelities, while she was pathologically jealous of his. On one occasion she was violently attacked by no fewer than three of Da Ponte's other lovers, armed with knives, and would surely have been killed, had he not intervened. One of the other women was seriously wounded.

In January 1779 they were visited by Da Ponte's brother Luigi and their stepmother, Orsola. The following month they all went to Ceneda, where Orsola remained while Luigi returned to Padua to finish his studies, and Lorenzo went back to Venice with Angioletta, now to the district of San Bartolomeo. Pregnant again, Angioletta tried to pass herself off as Da Ponte's sister – in vain, it seems, for she soon earned the local nickname 'the priest's whore'. He, in turn, was the subject of wild rumour; some said he went to church from an adulterous bed, others that he held mass 'with the air of a ladykiller', his long hair swept back in the latest fashion, his roaming eyes flirting with all the young female communicants.

The inevitable reprimand from the church authorities soon came in the shape of a ticking-off from the *vicario generale* of San Bartolomeo. But it made little difference. As Angioletta's pregnancy became more apparent, Da Ponte blithely continued to lead his double life, even braving the wrath of the civic authorities by writing a pugnacious poem in praise of his friend and protector Pisani, the 'Venetian Gracchus'. It was this, ironically, that was to hasten his undoing. It begins:

> Se 'l fosse anca el Pisani un impostor,
> Un prepotente, un ladro, un Lecam ... e,
> S'el stasse co le bestie buzarone,
> Col Baffo in man per so legislator;
>
> S'el gavesse anca lu come ga el sior
> Cento bardasse al fianco, e cento done,
> Per dio, tute ste cosse saria bone
> Per volerlo in Venezia avogador.
>
> Ma perché 'l segue la costituzion,
> Perché nol pol sofrir le prepotenze,
> I furti, el despotismo e l'oppression;
>
> Perché schieto el ghe parla a so celenze,
> E nel mazor consegio a l'Emo e al Tron
> El ghe dise anca lu le so sentenze,

Se ghe usa le insolenze
Dal Senato e dai Grandi del paese
De farghe fin del brogio un crimenlese:

De dirghe che ogni mese
Ga ga bastar d'aver in quarantia
El sachetin dela pitocheria.

(Even if Pisani were an impostor,
An arrogant man, a thief, an arse-licker,
If he were in the company of filthy beasts
With Baffo (a Venetian poet) on hand as his legislator;

If he had himself, like any gentleman,
One hundred dissolute, brutish boys at his side,
For God's sake, and one hundred women, all these things
Would qualify him to be a magistrate in Venice.

But since he follows the constitution,
Since he cannot bear the arrogance,
The corruption, the despotism and the oppression;

Since he talks frankly to the Excellencies,
And in the Great Council to Emo and Tron (important
    Venetian families)
Openly expressing his own personal views,

Members of the Senate, and the Greats of the country,
Got in the habit of abusing him
Telling him he was behaving like a crook:

They used to tell him that every month
All he amounted to in the Judicial Council
Was a small bag of sordid meanness.)

It goes on in this vein for some time, not shrinking from the scatological
in its venomous abuse against the authorities, before concluding:

Meteve nel pensiero,
Che questa xe Republica comun
E che la xe de tuti, e de nessun;

Che se ghe xe qualcun
Che se lamentava, el ga rason de farlo
Perché de tuto voressi spogiarlo

Contenteve mandarlo
Con un magistratuzo o un rezimento
A sfardigarse, sgonfiandose de vento.

Ma quando el xe là dentro
Dove tuti gavè una bala sola,
Feghe bon muso e no dixé parola:

Che se dopo sta scola
No pensé seriamente a qualche scampo,
Recordeve che 'l ton vien dopo el lampo.

(Keep it in mind
That this is a people's Republic
Which belongs to everyone, and to no one,

And if there is someone
Who is complaining, he has the right to do so,
Because you would like to take everything from him.

Be content to send him away
With a petty magistrate, or a regiment,
To slave away, to come down a peg,

But when he is in there (the Great Council),
Where you all have but one single vote,
Put on a brave face and do not utter a word.

And if after all this schooling
You do not seriously think of some escape-route,
Just remember that thunder comes after lightning.)

The Venice of the late eighteenth century was, it seems, less concerned about immorality than sedition. The civic authorities could turn a blind eye to a priest who continued to conduct mass while fathering children with another man's wife, but not to a poet singing the praises of a dangerous dissident. Pisani had become a powerful leader of the *Barnabotti*, that group of disaffected aristocrats intent on government reform;

Da Ponte's poem emerged not just from love of country, but from the fact that Pisani had been excluded from high office in favour of one of the most servile of the great and the good. It was, moreover, written in Venetian dialect; intelligible, and amusing, to Venetians high and low, aristocrat and working man, it was soon the talk of the town.

To prosecute a poet for liberal sentiments, however, was not a course open to the *Esecutori*, even in the case of so outspoken a poet, who had already been punished for the subversive nature of his work. So someone – probably Gabriele Doria, husband of Angioletta's sister Caterina, whose father happened to be the Chief Prosecutor's chef – was persuaded to drop that denunciation in the San Moisé lion's mouth, thus obliging the authorities to take action.

Da Ponte's trial for *mala vita* – specifically, *rapto di donna honesta* – began, in his absence, in early June 1779. Again, he seems to have made light of his difficulties, finding no reason to attend the proceedings. That July he was still living with Angioletta, now eight months pregnant again, in San Bartolomeo. She gave birth on 24 August, and the child was again dispatched to the foundling hospital. By now, Da Ponte had travelled via Treviso to Padua, where Angioletta joined him. Technically, he was still in Venetian territory. By the time he was found guilty, however, and the order issued for his arrest, he was safely across the Austrian border in Gorizia.

When Da Ponte could not be found in Venice, orders were sent to Padua that he be arrested and thrown in jail. When he could not be found there, either, an order was issued for him to appear before the Tribunal. Sentence was finally pronounced, in his absence, on 17 December; it was published in Ceneda a week later, and in Venice on 5 January the following year, 1780.

Padre Lorenzo Da Ponte was 'banished from Venice and from all other cities, lands and places of the Serene Republic for a term of fifteen years'. If he was caught defying the ban, he was to be 'imprisoned in a dungeon without light for seven years'. Tourists who have visited the notorious *pozzi*, the windowless cells beneath the Doge's Palace, with holes for food to be passed through the wall, will well understand why he had fled.

Why would the elderly Da Ponte have wanted to hide the story of his fling with Angioletta? In his memoirs, he blames his banishment from Venice on trumped-up charges of blasphemy – that he had eaten ham on a Friday, according to an embittered rival, and failed to attend mass on 'various' Sundays. His accuser 'had eaten ham with me', protests Da Ponte, less than convincingly. 'And he himself had never been to mass in his life!' And he dates his departure from Venice as 1777, rather than the true date of 1779, in a clumsy attempt to cover up the facts of his life during those two years.

What is Da Ponte trying to hide? The answer lies in the court papers, which kept their secret until a century after his death. It transpires that he had forged the letter in which Carlo Bellaudi threatened to murder his wife. In court, the warring couple admitted that all the other letters produced in evidence, however damaging, were genuine; but Carlo strenuously maintained that this one was not. Its style, moreover, is considerably more literate, and its handwriting more elegant, than the almost illiterate Carlo's.

Had Da Ponte really sunk to such depths for love of a loose woman? Whatever his other offences against his faith, against his cloth, and against womankind, this was an especially low moment in the life of the young poet-priest. It scarcely mattered now, anyway, as Carlo had come to Padua to collect Angioletta as soon as Da Ponte had slipped off across the border to Gorizia. As the thirty-year-old libertine embarked on the second of his three lives, they were settling down together again.

'I had no love left for a country that could treat both Pisani and myself with such injustice,' ran Da Ponte's official line, for public consumption. 'So I decided to leave Venice for ever. I went to see my three patrons and a few other friends, who wept as they heard of my decision but understood and approved it.

'Thus I turned my back on my ungrateful country.'

PART TWO

Europe

4

The Poet

ON 27 JANUARY 1756, as six-year-old Emanuele Conegliano mourned the loss of his mother in Ceneda, two hundred miles to the north in Salzburg Leopold and Maria Anna Mozart were celebrating the birth of their seventh and last child. Johannes Chrysostomus Wolfgang Gottlieb Mozart proved only the second of the seven to survive infancy – the other being his sister Maria Anna, called Nannerl, four years his senior.

The boy was called Wolfgang after his maternal grandfather, Wolfgang Nikolaus Pertl; Johannes Chrysostomus because he was born on the feast day of St John Chrysostom; and Gottlieb (the German for Theophilus) in honour of his godfather, Johann Theophilus Pergmayr. In later years Wolfgang himself came to prefer the Latin (or French or Italian) version of his last name, Amadeus (or Amadé or Amadeo).

The choice of that name proved, of course, prophetic. The story of Mozart's life, before and after he met Lorenzo Da Ponte in Vienna in 1783, has aptly been called 'the triumph of genius over precociousness' – a rare example, that is, of a child prodigy overcoming adversity to fulfil his early promise and beyond, way beyond, becoming one of the greatest composers of his own or any age. Despite a pushy and difficult father, unappreciative patrons and the opposition of jealous cabals, leading to constant debt, ill health and a tragically early death, Mozart's musical legacy is indisputably one of the richest we have.

When he died at the age of only thirty-five, Mozart had been a professional musician for more than thirty years. There was some musical talent on his mother's side of the family, the Pertls, none at all in the genes of his father Leopold, who was nevertheless a better-than-average violinist and composer, a Kapellmeister in the employ of the Prince-Archbishop of Salzburg. In the year of Wolfgang's birth Leopold published his *Versuch einer Gründlichen Violinschule*, a treatise on the violin which is still required reading for students of eighteenth-century music. He was naturally delighted when his son showed musical gifts at a very early age, composing his first work when he was five and playing before the Bavarian Elector and the Austrian Empress.

Mozart's parents were described as 'the most handsome couple in Salzburg', but their son Wolfgang as 'small, thin, pale of complexion, and devoid of any distinguishing characteristics'. Before Mozart's fourth birthday, however, it was clear to Leopold that his son was an extraordinary musical prodigy. 'Learned by little Wolfgang in his fourth year,' wrote his father in the score of some minuets. And yet more touchingly, in the score of a scherzo by G. C. Wagenseil: 'Little Wolfgang learned this piece on 24 January 1761, 3 days before his fifth birthday, at night between 9 and 9.30 o'clock.'

Wolfgang's sister, Nannerl, also proved a gifted keyboard player, eventually to earn renown as a teacher rather than composer. Sensing profits in their potential, Leopold took his children to Paris and London in 1763, visiting numerous European courts en route. Seven-year-old Wolfgang astonished audiences all over Europe with his precocious skills; he played for the French and English royal families, had his first music published and wrote his first symphonies. After all of three years away from Salzburg, the family Mozart returned home late in 1766; but nine months later father and son were off again, this time to Vienna, where Leopold's hopes of having an opera by his ten-year-old son performed were frustrated by jealous intrigues.

At the end of this period the composer Johann Adolph Hasse wrote to a friend in Venice:

> I have made the acquaintance here of a certain Mr Mozard (*sic*), *maestro di capella* of the (Arch)bishop of Salzburg, a man of spirit, astute, experienced; and I think he well knows his way in the world of music and also in other things as well. He has a daughter and son. The former plays the harpsichord very well and the latter, who cannot be more than twelve or thirteen, even at that age composes and is a *maestro di musica*. I've seen compositions which appear to be his, and certainly they are not bad and not such as I would expect to find from a boy of twelve ... The boy is good-looking, vivacious, gracious and

very well mannered; when you make his acquaintance, it is difficult not to like him. Certainly he will become a prodigy if, as he grows older, he continues to make the necessary progress ...

In 1769 the Mozarts returned to Salzburg, where the following year fourteen-year-old Wolfgang was enrolled among the Konzertmeister. He proceeded to write three operas in three years for the court of Milan, then under the Habsburg rule of Archduke Ferdinand, Governor and Captain-General of Lombardy, from whom he hoped to obtain an appointment. Ferdinand was sufficiently impressed by *Mitridate, re di Ponto, Ascanio in Alba* and *Lucio Silla* to want to give their teenage composer a job; but his mother, the Empress Maria Theresa, talked him out of it in a stern letter of 12 December 1771, advising against employing 'useless people' of his kind.

So in 1773 the Mozarts *père et fils* paid another visit to Vienna, in the hope – again frustrated – of securing Wolfgang a position; while there he wrote a set of string quartets and, on his return, more symphonies. Apart from a journey to Munich for the premiere of his opera *La finta giardiniera* early in 1775, at the age of nineteen, Mozart spent the period from 1774 to mid-1777 in Salzburg, where he worked alongside his father as Konzertmeister at the Prince-Archbishop's court. His works at this time include masses, more symphonies, all his violin concertos, six piano sonatas, several serenades and divertimentos, and his first truly mature piece, the 'Jeunehomme' piano concerto, K. 271.

In 1777, seeing limited opportunity in Salzburg for a composer as gifted as young Wolfgang, Leopold resolved to continue his efforts to find him a post elsewhere. Obliged by his court duties to remain behind in Salzburg, he sent his wife with Wolfgang to Munich and Mannheim; but again Wolfgang was offered no position. During his four-month stay at Mannheim, composing works for piano and flute, he fell in love with a young singer named Aloysia Weber.

Mozart's father then dispatched mother and son to Paris, where Wolfgang had some minor successes – notably with his 'Paris' Symphony, deftly designed to please local taste. But job prospects there were also poor, not least because he was beginning to show almost too much confidence in his abilities; so Leopold ordered his son home to Salzburg, where the loftier (and better-paid) post of court organist now awaited him. Aloysia, meanwhile, had moved to Munich, where he visited her on the way home; when she told him her affections had moved on, her younger sister Constanze consoled him with great tenderness.

Mozart returned to Salzburg slowly and alone; his mother had died in Paris. The years 1779–80 were spent in Salzburg, playing in the Cathedral and at court, showing the first signs of his true stature with sacred works and serenades, symphonies and concertos. But opera remained his supreme ambition, and there was no demand for it in Salzburg, where the nearest he managed was the incidental music to *Thamos, König in Aegypten* (K. 345).

Then came his chance, with a commission from Munich for an *opera seria*. Mozart went there to compose it in late 1780, writing letters to Leopold which are richly informative about his approach to music for the stage. To a libretto by the poet-priest Giambattista Varesco, chaplain to the Archbishop of Salzburg (modelled on a seventy-year-old libretto by André Campra, itself based on a recent tragedy), this innovative work, *Idomeneo*, proved a success – but not a lasting one; apart from a private performance in Vienna, it was never again performed in Mozart's lifetime, lay unpublished until 1797, and did not really achieve its current high standing until after the Second World War.

In *Idomeneo* Mozart depicted serious, heroic emotion with unprecedented richness, vivid orchestral writing and an abundance of profoundly expressive orchestral recitative. As Professor H. C. Robbins Landon has written, 'There is absolutely nothing in the whole range of Mozart's music (or anyone else's) to suggest the muted power of the great Act III quartet, wherein Mozart displays the conflicting emotions of his principal characters; it is the high point of a work during the course of which Mozart strove to create real flesh-and-blood figures onstage.'

Only with reluctance had Mozart's employer, Prince-Archbishop Colloredo of Salzburg, granted him permission to absent himself in Munich for his opera. Now, in March 1781, he summoned his young employee to Vienna, where the Salzburg court was in residence on the accession of the new emperor, Joseph II. Immediately Mozart was plunged into a maelstrom of daily concerts for his employer's guests, the local nobility and visiting VIPs. Frustrated and unappreciated, he looked back on his time in Munich as the happiest of his life.

Da Ponte, too, happened to be in Vienna during the mourning for the Empress Maria Theresa – but only for three days, en route to Saxony. By the time he met Mozart there at Baron Wetzlar's, more than two years later, he had been in Vienna a year. But he had arrived by a circuitous route.

After fleeing Venice, with just three books (Horace, Dante and Petrarch) and the clothes he stood up in, Da Ponte at first took refuge across the Austrian border in the small town of Gorizia, some twenty miles north of Trieste. Like Treviso, Gorizia was a popular summer resort for Italian patricians, and so a cultural centre blessed with fine (if private) libraries and a handsome theatre. Here, in the autumn of 1779, he would have heard operas by Cimarosa, Paisiello and Salieri.

At thirty, however, the amorous Abbé was still young enough for matters of the heart to take precedence over all others. Despite the stern rule of Maria Theresa – much less tolerant than Venetian society of licentious ways, especially from a priest – Da Ponte immediately embarked on a fling with the landlady of the first inn he entered:

> She was very beautiful, young, with a fine complexion and very viv-
> acious. She was dressed in the German fashion: on her head a cap with
> gold lace, around her alabaster neck a fine Venetian chain winding at
> least thirty times and falling in crescent loops upon her bosom, which
> it tantalizingly part-covered. A tight-fitting small jacket showed off
> her shapely figure with wanton elegance, and silk stockings des-
> cending to rose-coloured shoes displayed to the covetous eye the
> dainty shape of a tiny foot.

The fact that neither spoke the other's language soon worked to Da Ponte's advantage, not least because his hostess seemed to possess an equally adventurous spirit. At first she took his attempts to convey his hunger for amorous advances, which she eagerly reciprocated. But for once Da Ponte was primarily intent on eating; when he saw a passing tray of chicken, intended for another guest, he fell upon it – to the point where his hostess finally grasped what he was saying, and prepared him a meal which climaxed in a scene reminiscent of Fielding's *Tom Jones*. With the blade of her pocket-knife she peeled a pear and divided it, one half for each of them, then gestured to him to do the same. It was not long before she fetched a German–Italian dictionary and picked out the words 'Ich liebe Sie'. Da Ponte in turn found the word for 'sleep', and they duly repaired to his room.

Over the coming week he was surprised that, for all the strict moral regime of Maria Theresa, he was visited by a succession of women prepared to sell rather more than the ribbons and handkerchiefs in their baskets. After ten days, unsurprisingly, he was broke. For all the inn-keeper's protestations – she even hid some gold coins beneath his pillow, which he returned to her 'with kisses and tears' – it was time to move on, with the proud boast: 'I have never taken financial advantage of women.' They remained friends, and he was deeply dismayed to hear, just seven months later, that she had died of inflammatory fever at the age of only twenty-two. 'I shed many tears for that beautiful and charming young woman. She deserved to be a princess rather than an innkeeper. She was, without exception, one of the finest women I have ever known . . .'

From his latest inamorata Da Ponte had learned an extensive German vocabulary of romance and lovemaking, which was 'of the greatest use to me in the course of my youthful conquests in that town and elsewhere'. But the time had come to find sources of income as well as amorous amusement. Penniless, and stranded in Gorizia, Da Ponte researched the local aristocracy in shameless search of a potential patron.

One of the wealthiest and most eminent residents of Gorizia, and indeed of all Germany, was the Count Guidobaldo Cobenzl, father of the diplomat who had recently negotiated the truce between Prussia and Austria enshrined in the Peace of Teschen, which ended the 1778–79 War of the Bavarian Succession.

Da Ponte hastily composed an ode in honour of the treaty, entitled 'La gara degli uccelli' ('The war of the birds'), ensuring it contained fulsome praise of the Empress and Cobenzl *fils*. Then he took it round to present to the Count, who received him 'with the greatest courtesy'. After reading the work over, he 'appeared to approve it highly' – highly enough to have it printed and circulated, thus winning its author much praise and many wealthy patrons: 'I cannot recall without a lively feeling of gratitude such names as Strasoldo, Lanthieri, Cobenzl, Attems, Tuns, Coronini and Torriani.'

According to Casanova, who had recently passed through Gorizia, Count Cobenzl was 'wise, generous, extremely erudite and without pre-tensions'. But he disagreed with Da Ponte about such figures as Count Luigi Torriani, whom he accused of 'cruelty, disloyalty, treason, pride, sensual brutality, hate and jealousy'. Torriani's eldest son could tell a good anecdote; apart from that, he was 'an ugly and shady individual, a libertine, a braggart, a liar, brazen, spiteful and indiscreet'. Casanova's stay with the Torrianis ended in a fist-fight with the Count over a woman; they agreed to resolve the matter in a duel, but Torriani (according to Casanova) was too cowardly to turn up.

No doubt they had different priorities – Casanova was less easily impressed by a title, or in need of board and lodging – but these were the families who made life in Gorizia very pleasant for Da Ponte. After leaving the inn, he had been able to afford nothing grander than a small rented room in the home of a grain-merchant; now he was taken into the household of Count Torriani, whose wife he described as 'an angel of goodness rather than a woman', not least because she commissioned him to write a play for a visiting theatre company. With no experience in the genre, and no wish to damage his literary standing by writing anything substandard, he contented himself with translating a German text – which was duly performed, but proved a flop, lasting only two nights. Later he translated a French play, by a dramatist then in vogue named J. F. de la Harpe; *Il Conte di Warwick* met with more success, and was later performed in Trieste.

Cobenzl, Torriani and the other local families in Da Ponte's list were the stalwarts of L'Accademia degli Arcadi, an association of aesthetes sworn to upholding the purity of the Italian language, its literature and culture, and to defending their native tongue from the attempts of the Viennese to stifle it. The Gorizia branch, formed soon after Da Ponte's arrival, called itself L'Accademia letteraria degli Arcadi Romano-Sonziaci, taking its name from the local river. It would meet at its members' country houses for poetry readings and concerts, often held alfresco. They adopted noms-de-plume of an equally pastoral character, Da Ponte's being Lesbonico Pegaslo, under which he wrote numerous poems. One such, 'La gratitudine o sia la difesa delle donne' ('Gratitude, or A defence of women'), he dedicated to Torriani.

The president of the Gorizia Academy was his patron, Count Cobenzl, and its founder-secretary a soldier-turned-printer and historian named Giuseppe de Colletti. As so often in his long life, the temperamental Da Ponte took against this apparently blameless figure, whom he believed to be jealous of his literary prowess. He would later hurl all sorts of accusations against the Gorizian Arcadia's secretary – that he was 'mad, fanatical, licentious, a liar, flatterer, hypocrite and totally devoid of true poetic taste'. Da Ponte's memoirs grow tedious in their abusive assaults upon

Colletti, suggesting ulterior motives. Certainly there is no evidence that Colletti was anything other than a model citizen, and a dedicated literary man, who would later start a Trieste branch of the Accademia, found the town's first public library and launch its respected newspaper *L'Osservatore Triestino*. At the time, Da Ponte conducted a vendetta against him, working out his irrational rage in a subversive satire entitled 'Il Capriccio', which (if he is to be believed) caused much sniggering in noble circles.

One of the poem's admirers, Count Rodolfo Coronini, gave Da Ponte a generous commission to translate one of his own Latin works, the *Liber primus fastorum Goritiensium*, into Italian (in which it became the *Fasti Goriziani*). In the process, Da Ponte inserted verses of his own, praising the virtues of his noble patrons and singing the praises of their exquisite houses and gardens. This was published in 1780, as were several more of Da Ponte's poems including his fine pastoral allegory 'Il cecchino, o sia la storia del cane e del gatto'.

Their publisher was a printer named Valerio de Valeri, who appears to lurk at the heart of the puzzling disaffection between Da Ponte and the apparently blameless Colletti – who, in truth, seems to have been more of an irritating busybody than a positively malign force. De Valeri had taken Da Ponte into his home after hearing him complain that his latest landlord was in the habit of continually beating his wife. Eager to steal his rival Colletti's business, not least the publication of works by Gorizia's latest literary lion, Valeri told him that Colletti was putting it about that Da Ponte could not possibly have been the true author of 'La gara degli uccelli'.

If this were true, Colletti was probably expressing surprise that such a gifted poet should have produced something so second-rate. But Da Ponte rose to Valeri's bait, and wrote the attack on Colletti which gave him a local bestseller; it was the talk of Gorizia for weeks. For his part, Colletti was either too high-minded, too Christian or perhaps simply too naive to take offence. He continued to behave with perfect civility towards his tormentor.

It was in the midst of all this that Da Ponte's old friend from Venice, Caterino Mazzola, passed through Gorizia en route to Dresden, the opera-loving capital of Saxony, where he had been appointed poet to the court theatre. The news Mazzola brought with him from Venice was mixed. Their mutual friend Pisani, Da Ponte's patron and benefactor, had been elected Procurator of St Mark; only three months later, however, he had been arrested and imprisoned in Verona for 'revolutionary activities'.

For all his success in Gorizia, where he had spent a relatively contented six months, Da Ponte told Mazzola that he had become bored with its small-town provincial life – and homesick for larger, livelier Venice and all its delights. He had been secretly nursing hopes of a return, if Pisani's party were to come to power. Now that seemed impossible, he asked Mazzola to bear his name in mind if a suitable appointment were available in Saxony.

Two months later, a letter from Mazzola duly arrived with the news that an excellent position was awaiting him in Dresden. Grateful for the generosity of his aristocratic friends in Gorizia, and suddenly suffused with regrets about moving on, Da Ponte explained to his fellow Academicians that this was an opportunity he could not pass up.

The little border town gave him a generous send-off. Torriani organized a whip-round on his behalf; and before he left Gorizia, on New Year's Day 1781, Cobenzl gave Da Ponte a letter of introduction to his son the diplomat, now right-hand man to the Austrian Chancellor, Prince Kaunitz, in Vienna.

And so it happened that, en route to Dresden, Da Ponte passed through Vienna at the very moment Mozart was arriving. But a city in mourning is a dull one, and he stayed only three days. He wrote a sonnet 'Per la morte di Sua Maesta l'Imperatrice Maria Teresa', and took the chance to pay his respects to the Count's son, Johann Philipp Cobenzl, who gave him a warm welcome. Clearly flattered by Da Ponte's poem singing his praises, the diplomat also wished him *bon voyage* with a pocket-book containing 'travelling expenses' of 100 florins.

So Da Ponte arrived in Dresden in high spirits. But they were immediately dashed by the look on Mazzola's face when he called to enquire about this new position. 'Are you on your way to the theatre in St Petersburg?' asked his friend, who professed himself surprised to see him.

The letter informing Da Ponte about the vacant post in Dresden, it suddenly became clear, had not come from Mazzola. He thought he detected as much coldness as cordiality in his friend's manner; clearly Mazzola, far from helping Da Ponte to a job in the same city, was none too keen on having a rival poet there. Tongue-tied by the awkwardness of the situation, Da Ponte felt unable to make direct mention of the letter;

he tiptoed his way around the subject, to the point where he satisfied himself that Mazzola had no knowledge at all of any such document.

So it must have been a forgery. But by whom? Someone who wanted him out of Gorizia. Da Ponte immediately decided that it must, of course, have been Colletti. The next day he summoned the courage to raise the matter with Mazzola, who confirmed that he had indeed written him a letter, but not the one he had received. The true letter had given him a progress report on Mazzola's attempts to find him a post, but said there was nothing suitable as yet. Turning it all over, Da Ponte recalled that he had confided to Colletti his hopes of a post in Dresden, to which Colletti had expressed regret that Gorizia would lose him. Rank hypocrisy, decided Da Ponte. Colletti must have intercepted Mazzola's letter, copied his friend's signature, and inserted the forgery in the envelope bearing the Dresden address and postmark.

All contemporary accounts of Colletti suggest he was far too honest, if not innocent a figure to have gone to such lengths to dispose of a man whose work, in truth, he admired. But Da Ponte believed him guilty, on no evidence at all, to his dying day. Almost fifty years later, when a friend of Colletti's protested at Da Ponte's account of him in his memoirs, he replied: 'There is much I could say about Colletti, but this letter is too long as it is without dragging dead men into it.'

So the forged letter remains a mystery, and presumably always will. But Da Ponte's penchant for paranoid suspicion of rivals was equally misplaced in the case of Mazzola, who now turned out to be a true friend. There was no question that he was in any way to blame over the letter; even before Da Ponte's arrival, he had sought an appointment with the Prime Minister to put forward his name for the vacant post of secretary to the Elector's brother, Prince Antony.

Now that Da Ponte was in Dresden, Mazzola pursued these enquiries on his behalf with renewed energy, but to no avail. So he was generous enough to offer Da Ponte a share of his considerable workload for the court theatre, which boasted one of the best opera companies in Europe. Da Ponte began by translating or composing arias, duets and sometimes whole scenes for the works upon which Mazzola was engaged. Soon he had translated an entire libretto by the French dramatist Philippe Quinault, *Atis and Cybele*, set by Lully in 1676.

Mazzola was sufficiently impressed to urge Da Ponte to consider a career as a librettist, given the current vogue for Italian opera. 'You well know', replied Da Ponte, 'that the drama is in such a bad way in Italy that it is a courageous man who would take up that line of work.'

They both knew he was right. Italian opera-house managers spent most of their money on singers, obliging librettists to work for a pittance or seek decently paid employment abroad. All the best poets, from Metastasio to Mazzola himself, had long since left Italy. Those that remained were not capable of writing a play that was, in Da Ponte's judgement, 'tolerable, much less fit to be acted'.

For a while he worked on as the kindly Mazzola's assistant. He made other good friends in Dresden, notably a Jesuit priest named Father Michael Hueber, a fellow devotee of Italian literature, in whose honour he composed seven penitential psalms, *Setti salmi*. He also befriended an Italian painter with an attractive wife ('though nearly forty') and two very beautiful daughters – with both of whom he fell 'deeply in love'.

Mazzola was now suggesting that Da Ponte earn his living by using his skills as an *improvisatore*, an entertainment then in vogue in Dresden. Da Ponte politely declined, seeing it as a step down from his true calling – but also recognizing, without any of his usual rancour, that Mazzola was still concerned about losing work to this potential rival. Da Ponte had no wish to fall out with a friend who had proved so generous; and his latest amorous adventure was to give him one of several good reasons to oblige Mazzola, if inadvertently, by leaving town.

Not content with admiring both the painter's beautiful daughters, Da Ponte had taken to flirting with his wife, who did not seem averse to his advances. 'If you were not married, Signora,' he whispered in her ear, 'I should think it very dangerous to come and see you.' So infatuated was he with both daughters, meanwhile, that he could not choose between them. Rosina or Camilla? He was happy only when he was with them both. 'I believe that if the laws had allowed it, I would have betrothed myself to both of them at the same time.'

Soon the situation grew so complex that their mother felt obliged to issue Da Ponte with an ultimatum. Whatever her own feelings for him, her daughters were each as much in love with the handsome Italian poet as was he with them. Other potential suitors were becoming jealous, and looking elsewhere. It was a responsible mother's duty to act. He must choose between the two girls, and make his intentions clear. And he must do so by the following morning.

At this moment, as her words sank 'like so many daggers' into Da

Ponte's heart, the decision was taken out of his hands by the girls' father, who brought them into the room to say goodbye. He was taking them away for a while. Neither could look Da Ponte in the eye before their father led them from the room. He never saw them again.

Back home, he wept bitter tears, wailing 'O Rosina, O Camilletta, O Camilletta, O Rosina, what's to become of you?' Into the midst of this pathetic scene walked Mazzola, whose laughter at first outraged Da Ponte, then brought him back to his senses. He gave him further reason to compose himself by handing over two letters, one with tragic news, the other merely unwelcome.

The first was from his father, informing him of the death in Padua of his brother Luigi, aged only twenty-seven. Luigi had been just about to receive his degree in medicine. Da Ponte had heard that he was unwell, but the news still came as a heavy blow, not least because Luigi had been supporting his father and the rest of the family, who would now be helpless. As Da Ponte relapsed into tears, Mazzola read him the second letter, in an apparent attempt to cheer him up. Addressed to Mazzola from a friend in Venice, it read: 'It is said here that Da Ponte has gone to Dresden to hijack your post as court poet. Be careful, dear friend. This Da Ponte, as you well know, is a dangerous man!'

Mazzola saw it as a joke, but Da Ponte took it in earnest. He bore his friend no ill will, and could see how generous it had been of Mazzola to endanger his own work by sharing it with him. But the subtext remained the same: there was not enough work in Dresden for two Italian poets. All three of that day's developments – the departure of his two beloveds, his brother's death and the realization of his good-natured friend's generosity – combined to determine him to move on from Dresden.

That night he wrote a note to Father Hueber informing him that he was leaving town. By morning he had decided to seek work in Vienna, and booked himself on a carriage to Prague. There followed an emotional farewell with Hueber, who pressed upon him a basket of provisions for his journey and a fur coat, complete with hat and muff, hidden in which were two devotional books (Boethius and Thomas à Kempis) and twelve gold coins worth a hundred florins. 'Go, dear Da Ponte,' said his Jesuit friend. 'My heart tells me that all will go well for you.' As he spoke, Hueber's face 'seemed to shine with a sacred light'.

Da Ponte then went to take his leave of Mazzola, who seemed as surprised by his sudden departure as he had been by his unexpected arrival. 'Thank you, dear friend, for everything,' said Da Ponte, adding rather pointedly: 'I am leaving Dresden for Vienna. Please be sure to write and tell your friends in Venice.' They parted in tears.

As Da Ponte waited for his carriage to arrive, Mazzola rushed up with a parting gift which was to prove even more valuable than Father Hueber's gold coins: a letter of introduction to Antonio Salieri, court composer to Emperor Joseph II, and one of the most celebrated composers of the day.

'Friend Salieri,' it read. 'My well-beloved Da Ponte will bring you these few lines. Do as much for him as you would for me. His heart and his talents deserve it. He is, besides, *pars animae dimidiumque meae*' (part, even the half of my soul).

5

The Librettist

THE ATMOSPHERE in Vienna had changed as radically as rapidly in the year since Da Ponte's last, brief visit, when Joseph II had succeeded his formidable mother as sole Emperor. As if sensing that his own reign would be short, after fifteen years as her junior partner in a co-regency, forty-year-old Joseph had swiftly implemented many reforms in the spirit of the Enlightenment, from Jewish emancipation, religious tolerance and the relaxation of many censorship laws to refinement of the Viennese love of music and dancing. In all, Joseph issued more then six thousand edicts during the ten years of his reign, all designed to implement his belief that the state existed to provide 'the greatest good for the greatest number'.

On his arrival at the turn of 1781–82, Da Ponte immediately paid a visit to Salieri, the court composer, two years his junior but already a renowned composer and a particular favourite of the Emperor, with great influence in musical and court circles. Courteously, Salieri said there was nothing he could do to help immediately; he would be in touch if and when an opportunity arose.

Da Ponte did not know any Germans, or even speak their language. What was he to do? For some months he kicked his heels, sponging food and lodgings off the large Italian community in Vienna. Through one of these, he procured an introduction to the great Metastasio, whom he had so admired since childhood. Now eighty-four and notoriously reclusive, Caesarean Poet to the Imperial court for some fifty years but latterly unproductive, his work long out of fashion, this was not an easy man to meet. But the canny Da Ponte had dedicated a pastoral poem, 'Filemone e Bauci', to a German nobleman known to the poet, who would also have approved its Ovidian theme and Metastasian style. In April 1782 the great man received his young admirer warmly and took an interest in his work, paying him the singular compliment of reading its first few lines aloud at one of his literary salons, before inviting Da Ponte to declaim the rest. From the foremost poet of the day, whose libretti had been set by composers from Handel to Mozart, this was praise indeed, which would help make Da Ponte's name in Vienna.

But it was to prove the only time he met Metastasio, who died just a few days later – 'of grief', according to Da Ponte. In the wake of his mother's death, the Emperor had cancelled all the state pensions she had handed out with notorious abandon, making them subject to his own review. Metastasio took this so personally that it proved a mortal blow; too late arrived a letter from the Emperor, among the first he wrote, reassuring Metastasio that he was of course exempt from the decree, and reinstating all his pensions. This was not an issue that would ever cause Da Ponte any such anguish, as he himself was quick to point out.

Broke, unemployed and desperate, friendless and for once without a woman, the thirty-four-year-old Da Ponte had reached a new low. Ruefully he thought of the forty days in Padua when he had lived off olives and water, readying himself for another such 'second Lent'. As the money he had brought from Dresden dwindled, he moved from handsome lodgings in the centre of Vienna to the suburb of Vidden, where he took a room in the house of a tailor. But even the briefest of associations with Metastasio had won him a reputation as good company, as well as a gifted poet; among those who saw his potential was a cultured young man whose name he does not reveal, a great lover of Italian opera generous enough to finance his basic needs for several months.

Da Ponte had been in Vienna a year and more, hoping in vain to hear from Salieri, when the Emperor made the fateful decision to restore Italian opera to the Imperial Theatre, the Burgtheater. An accomplished musician himself, a player of keyboard, cello and violin blessed with a fine bass voice, Joseph had long taken a close personal interest in the Burgtheater's management; after his mother's death, he had himself replaced Italian opera with German *Singspiel*, comic opera with spoken dialogue. But standards had recently slipped; and one of the company of French actors employed alongside the German singers had mustered the nerve to complain to the Emperor about the quality of his wine. 'It is quite good enough for me,' replied Joseph, 'though perhaps not for you and your companions.

Back in France, I dare say, you will find wine more to your taste.' Thus ended the Viennese residency of the French comedians, to be replaced by Italian singers.

When he heard the news, Da Ponte's first thought was that the new Italian arrivals would be needing libretti. Remembering Mazzola's suggestion that he should try writing for the stage, he consulted Salieri about applying for the job of Caesarean Poet, vacant since Metastasio's death. No doubt Salieri had heard of the late poet's warm approval of this would-be successor, who had also come highly recommended by their mutual friend Mazzola. The court composer proved encouraging. Da Ponte was not yet eminent enough for the post of Caesarean Poet; but there might now be a need for an Italian poet attached to the Imperial Theatre, specializing in Italian libretti. Perhaps thinking of his own future needs, Salieri put Da Ponte's name forward to the Grand Chamberlain and director of the court theatre, the all-powerful Count Orsini de Rosenberg, who in turn mentioned Da Ponte's name to the Emperor himself.

Soon Da Ponte found himself summoned to the Imperial presence:

> I had never before spoken to a King, so I could not appear before him without fear and trembling, even though everyone had told me he was the kindest and most affable of princes. But his smiling face, his pleasant voice, and above all the extreme simplicity of his demeanour and his attire, which were not at all what I had expected of a monarch, not only reassured me, but almost made me forget I was standing in the presence of an Emperor.

Joseph plied Da Ponte with questions about his homeland, his work, and why he had come to Vienna. His answers were naturally vague and evasive, but the Emperor seemed satisfied. At length he asked Da Ponte how many plays he had written. 'None, Sire,' he replied, with a smile as disarming as his candour. 'Good, good!' said Joseph. 'Then we shall have a virgin muse.'

Da Ponte was thus appointed Poet to the Imperial Theatres, with a handsome salary of 1,200 florins a year, the right to print and sell the libretti of all operas performed at the theatre (which the audience purchased to read during the performance), and a royalty for those he wrote himself. 'My heart was full of gratitude, joy, respect and admiration,' he wrote. 'Without doubt, it was the sweetest and most joyful moment of my life.'

All too aware of his inexperience, Da Ponte began his new job by paying a visit to Giambattista Varese, a *soi-disant* poet with a celebrated collection of some three hundred Italian texts. A notorious miser, Varese merely laughed when Da Ponte asked if he could borrow some. 'This collection, Sir, is worth a fortune,' he replied. 'There is no other like it in all the world. You would never believe what trouble and expense it has cost me. One day it will be as valuable as a famous necklace. No, no, do not imagine that I will let one single volume leave this room. They are jewels, Sir, great treasures!'

After further such protestations – including Varese's insistence that he would rather have an ear cut off, or all his teeth pulled out ('and he had a good many teeth,' noted Da Ponte) – the miser was persuaded to let his visitor look through some of these treasures under his vigilant eye. Da Ponte's patience ran out after barely twenty:

> Poor Italy! What stuff they were! They had no plot, no characters, no interest, no scenic effects, no charm of language or style, and though they were written to make people laugh, one would rather have thought they had been written to make people weep. Not a line of all those wretched pastiches showed any charm, or any display of fancy or elegant turn of phrase which in any way would make one want to laugh. They were so many accretions of tiresome conceits and stupidity and buffoonery.

So this was what he was up against. Da Ponte's main responsibility was the editing and adapting of the libretti of other poets, at least one a month – a considerable workload, as we know from Mozart's letter to his father of 6 May 1783, soon after they had met at Baron Wetzlar's party: 'We have a new poet here, Abbé Da Ponte, who has a huge amount to do in revising pieces for the theatre.' The first to pass through his hands, appropriately enough, was by his friend and benefactor Mazzola, *La scuola de' gelosi*, set by Salieri. The first Da Ponte wrote himself would also be for Salieri.

Among the performers now drawn to Vienna by the return of Italian opera was the Irish tenor Michael Kelly, whose memoirs describe Salieri as 'a little man with an expressive countenance' and eyes 'full of genius'. Salieri's biographer, Ignaz von Mosel, calls him a 'methodical, active, religious-minded, benevolent and peculiarly grateful man, easily irritated, but as quickly pacified'. For all the notoriety now attaching to his name through Peter Shaffer's play-turned-film *Amadeus* – which explores his paranoid delusions, late in life, that he had murdered his more gifted rival Mozart – Salieri was, by all accounts, a clever, witty and versatile man, capable of great kindness to his friends, though also of malice towards his enemies. Da Ponte himself calls him 'most accomplished and able'. 'He was a very pleasant man,' concludes Kelly, 'and much esteemed at Vienna.'

Upon offering Salieri a variety of texts, Da Ponte was dismayed to find that he chose 'the one that was perhaps least likely to prove attractive and interesting on the stage'. This was *Il ricco d'un giorno* ('Rich for a Day'), based on a text by Giovanni Bertati. Soon Da Ponte was finding his new calling much harder than he had imagined:

> My difficulties were endless. The subject did not furnish enough characters and variety of incident to make an interesting plot that would last about two hours. My dialogues seemed dull, the scenes contrived, the sentiments commonplace, the action halting and the effect lifeless. In short, I felt as if I were no longer capable of writing either prose or verse, and that I had undertaken a labour of Hercules with the powers of a child.

He took an eternity over the first act before confronting the most difficult section, its finale. Known as the *chiusa* (closure), or *stretta* (literally, 'drawing-together'), this was conventionally a small, self-contained comedy involving all the main characters, designed to show off the skills of composer and cast, requiring all sorts of linguistic fireworks from the librettist to be transformed into music of infinite variety and richness. When Da Ponte finally finished the project, he felt so dissatisfied that he shut it away in a drawer for two weeks. Upon finally looking it over again, he found it 'even worse and more lifeless than ever'. But the time had come for him to show it to Salieri, who had already begun to compose the score, and was badgering Da Ponte daily for more text.

To Da Ponte's surprise and delight, Salieri did not seem to share his disappointment. 'It is well written,' declared the court composer, 'but we must see how it works on the stage. It has some very good songs and scenes which I like very much, but I shall need a few small alterations made, purely for the musical effect.'

Exit a relieved Da Ponte, only to find that Salieri's 'few small alterations' entailed shortening or lengthening most of the scenes, introducing new duets, trios and quartets, changing metres in the middle of a song, adding choruses, cutting almost all the recitative – 'and thus such plot and interest as the drama possessed, so that when it was staged I think there were barely a hundred of my original lines left.'

His task complete, Salieri went off to Paris to work on another opera, *Les Danaïdes*, pending *Il ricco*'s first performance. During his absence, in April or May 1784, there arrived in Vienna two potentially dangerous rivals to Da Ponte and himself, the poet Casti and the composer Paisiello.

The name of Abbé Giovanni Battista Casti was celebrated throughout Europe; he was close to Count Rosenberg, whom he had met in Florence at the court of the Emperor's younger brother, Leopold. The author of stylish but bawdy verse, with a private life to match, he had been unwelcome in Vienna during the reign of Maria Theresa; now, in the wake of her death and Metastasio's, he had come to angle for the post of Caesarean Poet. Casti was useful to Rosenberg 'comme bouffon et comme pourvoyeur des filles', according to Casanova, who loathed him as 'a fool and a pimp ... an impudent, worthless fellow whose only merit was a knack for versification'.

Composer of the hugely successful *Barber of Seville*, adapted by Giuseppe Petrosellini from the play by the French dramatist Caron de Beaumarchais, Giovanni Paisiello also arrived in Vienna with a formidable reputation. He was a particular favourite of the Emperor. For all his doubts about Casti's private life, Joseph found the poet entertaining, and asked him to collaborate with Paisiello on a new opera. This they managed in short order, producing *Il re Teodoro in Venezia* in time to be staged ahead of Salieri-Da Ponte's *Il ricco d'un giorno*.

In his capacity as theatre poet, Da Ponte was pleased to get first sight of Casti's text. Unable to wait until he got home, he hurried to a café and read it through twice:

> It did not want purity of language, beauty of style, charm and harmony of verse, or wit, elegance and animation; the arias were beautiful, the ensembles delightful, the finales poetic. Yet the play was not alive, interesting, comic or actable. The action was feeble, the characters tedious, the denouement improbable and almost tragic. In short, the parts were excellent but as a whole it was ill-proportioned. It was as if a jeweller should spoil the effect of many precious stones by not knowing how to assemble them in the right order and symmetry.

Consoled, at least, that *Il re Teodoro* was no better than *Il ricco d'un giorno*, Da Ponte reached a momentous conclusion about the art that would make his name: 'I knew then that it was not enough to be a great poet (for Casti was certainly that) to write a good libretto.' It was necessary, he decided, to 'acquire a great deal of practical knowledge, to get to know the actors and make their parts fit them, to observe on the stage other people's mistakes and one's own, and after they have been hissed at by two or three thousand people to know how to correct them; all of which things, however useful, are nonetheless very difficult of execution, for sometimes one is hindered by expense, sometimes by meanness, and sometimes by self-esteem'.

So did he do his duty as superintendent poet, and demand changes of Casti? No. 'I did not dare tell anyone what I thought, being sure that if I did they would have stoned me or shut me up as a lunatic. Casti was more infallible in Vienna than the Pope in Rome.'

He decided to let time, 'the judge of all things', decide. But time was not on Da Ponte's side, in more ways than one. When *Il re Teodoro in Venezia* was performed in August 1784, it was such a success that Salieri temporarily withdrew *Il ricco d'un giorno* and hurried back to Paris. Of Casti's and Paisiello's triumph, Da Ponte mused, 'How could it be otherwise?' Even he conceded that 'the singers were excellent, the sets superb, the costumes magnificent, the music heavenly'. Da Ponte seethed as he watched Casti, 'with a grateful smile, acknowledge the applause intended for the singers, the set and costume designers and the conductor as if it were all for him'. But he noted sourly that the 'fair-minded' Emperor, while the Casti–Rosenberg set kept exclaiming 'What a good libretto!', countered with 'What fine music!'

Nursing his wounded pride, and apprehensive about his future as long as Casti was around to threaten it, Da Ponte took his own advice and made sure that he got to know two of the leading lights of the Italian opera company, both stars of *Il re Teodoro*, the Irish tenor Kelly and the English-born soprano Nancy Storace. Both became lasting friends, and would lead the cast of several of his own works.

But the first night of *Il ricco d'un giorno*, in December 1874, was a disaster. Storace had been taken ill, and replaced by another singer 'about as suitable for the part as a dove for an eagle's' – but that was the least of it. As Da Ponte himself admitted, 'the book was positively bad, and the music not much better.' Salieri had returned from Paris 'with his ears full of Gluck' and 'screechings as of the possessed'; he was composing music which was 'wholly French, while the beautiful and popular melodies that he had been wont to produce in such abundance he had left behind in the Seine'.

Such was the booing and barracking that it was all the singers could do to finish the first performance, which constantly threatened to grind to a halt. The verdict of one present, the opera-loving Count Zinzendorf, a former governor of Trieste who kept detailed diaries, was that Salieri's score had been 'stolen from all over the place'. But the Casti faction pinned the blame squarely on Da Ponte – now joined by Salieri, who vowed that he would have his fingers cut off before he worked with Da Ponte again.

No doubt Salieri had in mind the power of Count Rosenberg, the only artistic figure in Vienna with more musical muscle than himself, and so close to Casti as now to demand of the Emperor that Da Ponte be sacked. 'No doubt he has Casti in mind,' Joseph told the Venetian ambassador, Sebastiano Foscarini. To Rosenberg himself, when he suggested that 'We shall be wanting another poet', Joseph replied simply: 'First, I'd like to see another opera by Da Ponte.'

And to Da Ponte himself, when they chanced to meet as the Emperor took his morning walk, Joseph said: 'You know, Da Ponte, your opera is not so bad as they try to make out. You must summon up your courage and give us another.'

But that would take him a while yet. The following year and more were a fallow period for Da Ponte. He wrote home to his friend Zaguri, who would understand, that he passed the time like a true Venetian: 'I eat and drink and write and think.' He composed snatches of verse, including an Ode to the Emperor, some sonnets and an Italian translation of the Latin prayers said at mass.

In his suspicion of gossip and intrigues against him – some of them anti-Semitic, for a version of his origins had somehow caught up with him – he found a staunch ally in a fellow Venetian, Casanova, now in Vienna as secretary to Foscarini. 'The hours which my goddess, Minerva, allows me for pleasure,' he wrote to Zaguri, 'I pass with Casanova, feeding now the mind, now the heart ... and talking of you, gentle signore, as of someone precious and noble.'

Da Ponte had been estranged from Casanova for more than three years, since that falling-out in Venice over a fine point of Latin metre.

Now he had a dream that he encountered his old acquaintance on the Graben, one of Vienna's main streets – and the next day it came true. 'When I went to the Graben, I saw in the distance an old man who stared at me as if he knew me. Suddenly he hurried towards me with cries of joy, shouting: "Da Ponte, my dear Da Ponte, how pleased I am to see you!" – the very words he had spoken in my dream.' Now it was Da Ponte's turn to lend Casanova money, and occasionally to take him in. Their friends Zaguri and Memmo, as he put it, 'loved all that was good in Casanova and forgave the bad. They taught me to do the same.'

His professional woes were meanwhile compounded by personal ones, as his latest amorous adventure nearly cost him his life. A fellow Italian by the name of Doriguti, who was a tenant in the same house as Da Ponte, fell madly in love with a pretty girl who also lived there. Her way of fending off Doriguti was to tell him that she loved Da Ponte – whose affections, for once, in truth lay 'elsewhere'. But Doriguti became determined to see off his apparent rival.

When they met by chance in a café one day, Doriguti asked Da Ponte 'with an apparent show of sympathy' why he seemed so quiet and thoughtful. Not knowing what had passed between him and the girl, but aware that he was a medical man, Da Ponte truthfully replied that he had a painful swelling in his gums after the extraction of a tooth. The Emperor's own physician, Brambilla, had advised further surgery. 'Wrong, wrong, wrong!' exclaimed Doriguti. 'Give me a sequin, and I will cure your swelling without surgery.'

Da Ponte duly obliged, and Doriguti disappeared, soon to return with a small phial of liquid that eased the swelling within a week. On seeing him applying it with a cloth, however, the woman who cleaned his room snatched it from his hand, shrieking that it was 'aqua fortis' – or nitric acid, which she used for cleaning his silk stockings. A little more would have killed him. As it was, most of his teeth fell out, and he lost his appetite for a year and more. It was a miracle, to his friends, that he survived. In vain did he seek vengeance on Doriguti, scouring Vienna for him 'like a madman'. But his nemesis had fled.

Lucky to be alive, his morale low and his health permanently damaged, Da Ponte might now have dwindled into obscurity had it not been for the arrival in Vienna of the Spanish composer Vicente Martín y Soler, fresh from considerable success in Florence. He came as a protégé of the Spanish ambassador's wife, who was said to be on 'the most intimate terms' with the Emperor – who in turn encouraged Martín to try to rally the theatre poet in whom he still kept faith, despite the carping of his detractors and his recent lack of productivity.

Naturally anxious to avoid another failure, Da Ponte proposed to 'Martini' that they adapt an already successful play, to pre-empt criticism about plot and characterization. Specifically he suggested Goldoni's comedy *Il burbero di buon cuore*, which had enjoyed great success in an Italian version adapted from his French original, *Le bourru bienfaisant*, written to celebrate the marriage of Louis XVI (then the Dauphin) to Marie-Antoinette. A comedy of errors in the traditional manner, about a curmudgeonly old man with a good heart, it was the perfect vehicle for Da Ponte to perfect the art of filleting popular drama for the operatic stage, reshaping scenes and remodelling characters to suit the demands of a cast of some half-dozen principals, plus chorus and stage business to satisfy an easily bored audience.

Casti made sure that he was present when Da Ponte read the text to Count Rosenberg for his approval in the autumn of 1785. The play was not suitable, Rosenberg protested, for *opera buffa*; it would not make people laugh. Evidently he repeated his complaint to the Emperor, who put it to Da Ponte. 'We must wait and see, Your Majesty,' the poet replied. 'For my part, it will be better if it makes them cry.' Understanding his meaning, Joseph answered: 'I hope it will.'

The first night of *Il burbero* on 4 January 1786 was a triumph for all concerned. Even the recitative won applause from much of the audience, including the Emperor himself. As he left the theatre after the performance, Joseph whispered to Da Ponte: *'Abbiamo vinto!'* ('We have won!') Those two words, to Da Ponte, were 'worth a hundred volumes of praise'.

Next morning he presented himself at the office of Count Rosenberg, whom he found whispering conspiratorially with Casti. Asked what he was doing there, Da Ponte said, 'I have come to hear the verdict of the Director of the Theatre.'

'You have already had your verdict from our very easily pleased public,' replied Rosenberg. 'Whether they are right or wrong ... who knows?'

As he said this, Rosenberg and Casti smiled 'acidly', and bade him good day. It was an unpleasant moment, enough to leave Da Ponte feeling uneasy, for all the public triumph of *Il burbero*. 'These two enemies, I said to myself, are too powerful, and the Emperor's favour will not be enough to save me from their traps.' Thinking it better to leave than to be dismissed, he decided to offer his resignation.

But as soon as he walked into the Emperor's presence, Joseph greeted him with: 'Bravo, Da Ponte. I like both the music and the words.'

'Your Majesty,' he replied, attempting modesty, 'the Director seems to think otherwise.'

'It isn't the Director,' said Joseph, 'it's Casti, who speaks for him. But this is a triumph for you. You've made him cry. Now go home, pluck up your courage, and give us a second opera with Martín's music. You must strike while the iron is hot.'

There followed another false start with the mediocre composer Giuseppe Gazzaniga, a 'pastiche' (as even Da Ponte admits) of a French comedy called *L'aveugle clairvoyante*, which was 'played three times and then heard of no more'. Casti continued to carp behind his back, but Joseph's faith in Da Ponte redoubled his confidence.

'It gave me the courage not only to face the assaults of my enemies, but also to regard their efforts with disdain,' he recalled years later. 'It was not long before numerous composers approached me for libretti. But there were only two in Vienna whom I considered worthy of my respect: Martín ... and W. Mozart.'

6

Le nozze di Figaro

O N THE face of it, Mozart and Da Ponte were singularly ill-matched. Behind his equally carefree exterior, Mozart hid an essential seriousness that Da Ponte as yet lacked. Much of Da Ponte's life so far had been play; all of Mozart's had been work. By the time the illiterate fourteen-year-old Da Ponte had been received into the Catholic church, the seven-year-old Mozart was already giving concerts, winning awards and writing early masterpieces. How ironic, in the light of their respective talents and posthumous reputations, that the struggling Viennese Mozart should have been so thrilled to find his 'able poet' in the wayward but much better-known Abbé Da Ponte.

From such less than kindred spirits, perhaps, are the greatest artistic partnerships formed. The works that each wrote with others fall short of the standards of the three works they wrote together, which have stood the test of time as mighty operatic masterpieces. And Da Ponte made an indispensable contribution; without his 'true phoenix', Mozart might not have reached the full heights of which he was capable, in the genre which meant most to him.

The English musicologist Nicholas Till calls it a 'complementary' partnership, with Da Ponte's 'robust realism tempering Mozart's more idealistic inclinations'. He also argues that there is a sense in which Da Ponte can be seen as Mozart's spiritual twin. 'For all his would-be Casanovan bravado, Da Ponte was, like Mozart, a man in search of identity, security and acceptance.'

It was two years since they had first met at the home of Baron Wetzlar. Mozart had enjoyed some success with his German *Singspiel, Die Entführung aus dem Serail*, but the Emperor's sole response had been: 'Too

fine for our ears; and too many notes, my dear Mozart, too many notes!' –
to which the composer's sardonic reply had been: 'Just as many notes,
Your Majesty, as are necessary.' Joseph preferred the less complex music
of Salieri, Paisiello and Martín y Soler, telling Rosenberg that 'Mozart's
music is much too difficult to sing'. He is also quoted as saying that
Mozart had 'only one fault in his works for the stage, and his singers have
often complained of it: he deafens them with his full accompaniment'.
Mozart may not have known of this; but he did know that he had to write
Italian opera to stand a chance of popular success in Vienna.

We have no details of Mozart's second meeting with Da Ponte – or,
indeed, whether they discussed collaboration at the first. Who, after all,
was this young Mozart? Like the Emperor, Da Ponte still considered
Martín y Soler the better – and more commercial – composer. But on 7
May 1783, while Da Ponte was wrestling with the text of Salieri's *Il ricco
d'un giorno*, Mozart wrote to his father that the poet, for all his 'huge
amount of revising to do for the theatre', had promised to write him a
text. 'But who knows whether he will keep his word – or will even want
to? For you know what these Italian gentlemen are like: very civil to your
face ... enough, we know all about them! If he is in league with Salieri, I
will never get a word out of him. But how dearly I should love to show
what I can do in Italian opera!'

Uncertain of Da Ponte, Mozart goes on to mention Giambattista
Varesco, the poetic priest with whom he had worked on *Idomeneo* –
'provided he isn't angry with me because of the Munich opera!' Mozart had
changed so much of Varesco's text that his relations with the Archbishop's
chaplain had grown strained:

> Basta, you probably know whether this could be arranged or not. He
> could start putting down some thoughts, and when I come to Salzburg
> we could look at them together. The most essential ingredient is this:
> it has to be, on the whole, very *comical*; and include, if possible, *2
> equally good female roles* – one would have to be a Seria, the other a
> Mezzo Carattere – but in *quality* – both roles would have to be
> absolutely equal – the third female part can be entirely *buffa*, and so
> could the male roles.

This could be a blueprint for *Le nozze di Figaro*. Two months later, on
5 July, Mozart tells his father: 'An Italian poet here has recently brought
me a libretto that I may well use, if he agrees to trim and adjust it to suit

my wishes.' In a postscript, he asks: 'Don't forget to keep nudging Varesco. Who knows whether I'll like the opera of the Italian poet here?'

It is strange that Mozart does not name Da Ponte, having already told his father a little about him. But the letter shows signs of haste, like so much of Mozart's correspondence, and he may well have decided it was not worth telling Leopold more about the Italian until he had determined to collaborate with him. The work to which he refers here is Da Ponte's *Lo sposo deluso* ('The disappointed bridegroom'), subtitled *La rivalità di tre donne per un solo amante* ('The rivalry of three women for one lover') – for which Mozart wrote an overture, an opening quartet, two arias and a trio (K. 430) before abandoning it.

Da Ponte makes no mention of it in his memoirs. Nor does he of *Per la ricuperata salute di Ophelia*, a celebratory aria they wrote together to mark the return to health of Nancy Storace, who had dismayed the Emperor by being unable to sing for several months. Joseph had commissioned an *opera buffa*, *Gli sposi malcontenti*, from Nancy's brother Stephen Storace, apparently as a way of getting her into his bed; it was during the first performance, perhaps for psychological reasons, that she lost her voice. The piece written to celebrate her recovery was sung at the piano by 'the three famous Kapellmeister Mozart, Salieri and Cornetti' – this last unidentified, presumed to be their nickname for the composer Alessandro Cornet.

At this time, in early 1785, Da Ponte and Mozart also collaborated on *Davidde penitente*, K. 469, an oratorio whose music Mozart took from the Kyrie and Gloria funeste of his C minor Mass, K. 427, to which he added two new arias: 'A te, fra tanti affanni' and 'Tra l'oscure ombre'. The text was a free translation by Da Ponte of Psalm 51.

'Although he was blessed with talents greater, perhaps, than those of any other composer in the world, past, present or future,' Da Ponte wrote of Mozart, 'he had been prevented by the plots of his enemies from exercising his divine genius in Vienna, remaining unknown and obscure – like a precious stone which, buried in the bowels of the earth, hides the true brilliance of its splendour.'

He goes on: 'I can never remember without satisfaction and joy that Europe and the whole world owe the exquisite vocal music of this remarkable genius largely thanks to my own perseverance and determination.'

It is a gross claim, of course, made with the benefit of early-nineteenth-century hindsight, for Mozart's lasting reputation would not be made until he and Da Ponte had gone their separate ways, and the impoverished poet needed an immortal name to cling to in his frequent moments of desperation. But Da Ponte was almost as good at being in the right place at the right time as he was at being in the wrong place at the wrong time. Mozart needed a librettist, and Da Ponte responded with exactly the skills needed to bring out the best in the as yet unacknowledged genius.

In defiance of operatic tradition, Mozart considered that the words should be the 'obedient daughter' of the music. If he took an unusually proactive role in the shaping of his libretti, Da Ponte gave him a stronger narrative structure, better-drawn characters, more wit and more elegant verse than any of his other collaborators. Da Ponte's poetic gift combined with his sense of theatre to make the perfect match for Mozart's musical genius.

'I readily perceived that the greatness of his genius demanded a subject that should be ample, elevated and abounding in character and incident,' Da Ponte writes of Mozart. It was 'while we were talking about it one day' – presumably in mid-1785, after those first brief but bitty collaborations – that Mozart asked Da Ponte if he could 'easily' adapt the revolutionary play by Pierre-Augustin Caron de Beaumarchais, *The Marriage of Figaro* – a sequel to *The Barber of Seville*, which had recently enjoyed such success in Vienna in Paisiello's operatic version, to a libretto by Giuseppe Petrosellini.

The son of a master clockmaker, born in Paris in 1732, Beaumarchais had swiftly risen to various roles at the French court, while pursuing careers as a financial speculator, spy, gun-runner, litigant and, ultimately, playwright and man of letters. After an inauspicious start with *Eugenie* (1767), he enjoyed huge success with *The Barber of Seville* (1775) and its sequel *The Marriage of Figaro* (subtitled *La folle journée*, or 'The crazy day'), first publicly performed in Paris on 27 April 1784 to great acclaim, enjoying some seventy sold-out performances.

In *The Barber* Figaro is a barber-cum-factotum who helps the Count Almaviva win his love, Rosina, from the amorous clutches of her guardian, Don Bartolo. In *Figaro* he has become the valet of Almaviva, who has designs upon Figaro's own fiancée, Susanna, maid to his wife Rosina. Given a servant standing up to his aristocratic master, who plans in this instance to rescind his abolition of *droit de seigneur*, this was the play of which Napoleon would later say: 'C'était la Revolution déjà en action.' If we take this at face value, the resulting ironies are numerous, as succinctly summed up by the late John Wells: 'Beaumarchais, watchmaker to Madame de Pompadour, secret agent to Louis XVI, creat(ed) a piece of dramatic machinery credited with the destruction of a society that commissioned it, only to be turned by Mozart and Da Ponte into a work of art in which we recognize the most perfect flowering of the civilization it is alleged to have destroyed.'

Only a few days before Mozart and Da Ponte set to work, the Emperor had expressly forbidden the German theatre company in Vienna, run by Mozart's friend Emanuel Schikaneder, to perform Beaumarchais's play. 'I hear that the well-known comedy *Le mariage de Figaro* is said to have been proposed for the Kärntnertor Theatre in a German translation,' wrote Joseph, three days before it was due to open, to Count Johann Anton Pergen, President of the Government of Lower Austria, in a note preserved in the Vienna state archive. 'Since this piece contains a great deal that is objectionable, I shall expect the Censor either to reject it altogether or at least require such alterations to be made that he can be held responsible for the performance of the play and the impression it may make.' The production was abandoned; when the text was published in Vienna later that year, the translator dedicated his work to the memory of the two hundred ducats that the Emperor's ban had cost him.

As Da Ponte blithely puts it, the project thus presented 'a great difficulty'. This was a banned play. Given his faith in Mozart's abilities, and his knowledge of the Emperor, Mozart's patron Baron Wetzlar immediately assumed that the work could never be performed in Vienna. He offered to pay both librettist and composer, and arrange for performances in London and France. But they – 'I', says Da Ponte – declined the Baron's generous offer, and agreed to work on it in secret. *Le nozze di Figaro* was to be written as a speculative venture.

It was with this work that opera would come of age. When Da Ponte was born, Handel reigned supreme; four years after his death, Wagner would make his debut. Da Ponte and Mozart were twin pillars of that huge and vital transition, transforming opera into an emotionally manipulative artform exploring central human issues in a potent, accessible but above all realistic manner, via characters the audience could recognize, and with whom they could identify – transforming it into the genre, to paraphrase Walter Pater, 'to which all art aspires'.

Opera buffa was Da Ponte's speciality, Mozart's aspiration. Popular in

Vienna because it encapsulated bourgeois taste as opposed to aristocratic pretension, it portrayed people from everyday life more than abstract ideals – the man or woman familiar from the family or the street rather than gods, heroes or classical archetypes. With different characters of whatever social status sharing similar views and aspirations, *opera buffa* reflected the Enlightenment ideal of the similarity of all human beings, regardless of birth or rank. As yet, however, it was regarded by the cognoscenti as an inferior form to *opera seria*. This was soon to be shown up as mere snobbery.

Buffa observed the Aristotelian unities of time and space; all three Mozart–Da Ponte operas take place within twenty-four hours, without leaving the town or even (in two cases) the house in which they are set. A happy ending, or *lieto fine*, was also required, reconciling the warring characters and restoring the status quo. Many of the criticisms to which the three Mozart–Da Ponte operas have been subjected by later critics fail to acknowledge these eighteenth-century rules.

By fusing *seria* characters and other elements with the comic, by introducing socially significant themes and morals into a genre that was hitherto mere entertainment, Mozart and Da Ponte between them turned *opera buffa* into an infinitely more mature genre – transforming, as it has been put by the musicologist Patrick Steptoe, 'an enjoyable but trivial entertainment into one celebrating the richness and diversity of human experience'.

It cannot be doubted that Mozart was the senior partner in the enterprise; but the superiority of the three Mozart–Da Ponte operas to any other works by either man suggests a perfect synergy, that the librettist brought to these works the theatrical and poetic qualities the composer could not find elsewhere. 'It was perhaps only a matter of time before these two veritable geniuses would converge,' as the conductor Jane Glover has recently put it.

That Mozart was calling the shots is evident from the high index of ensembles in the three Mozart–Da Ponte operas, as compared with Da Ponte's (or indeed anyone else's) previous work. 'Arias consistently make up a smaller portion of the whole in Mozart's operas compared with the libretti written for other composers,' as Steptoe has calculated. In *Le nozze di Figaro* and *Don Giovanni*, arias comprise some fifty per cent of the musical numbers (fourteen out of twenty-eight and thirteen out of twenty-four respectively, in their original versions) as opposed to nineteen arias in thirty numbers (sixty-three per cent), and nineteen in thirty-two, in the best-known operas Da Ponte wrote for other composers.

This is even more true of the third and last Mozart–Da Ponte collaboration, *Così fan tutte*, where only twelve of the thirty-one numbers are solo pieces. 'The composer's will must be in evidence here,' writes Steptoe, 'since Da Ponte clearly had no personal predilection for ensemble. These differences indicate that Mozart must have felt himself "talented enough to make sound suggestions".'

He had certainly made his views clear in that same letter to his father of 13 October 1781, two years before he had met Da Ponte, in which he argues that 'the poetry must be altogether the obedient daughter of the music'. Mozart goes on to express a deep distaste for rhyme – which, of course, he was now obliged to suppress:

> Why do Italian comic operas give such pleasure everywhere – in spite of their miserable libretti – even in Paris, where I myself witnessed their success? Because there the music reigns supreme; when one listens to it, all else is forgotten. Why, an opera is sure of success when the plot is well worked out, the words written solely for the music and not shoved in here and there to suit some miserable rhyme (which, God knows, never enhances the value of any theatrical performance, be it what it may, but rather detracts from it) – I mean, words or even entire verses, which ruin the composer's entire conception. Verses are certainly the most indispensable element for music, but rhymes – solely for the sake of rhyming – the most detrimental. Those high and mighty people who set to work in this pedantic way will always come to grief, both they and their music.
>
> The best thing of all is when a good composer, who understands the stage and is talented enough to make sound suggestions, meets an able poet, that true phoenix. When that is the case, there need be no fears as to the applause even of the ignorant. Poets always remind me of trumpeters with their professional tricks! If we composers were always to stick so faithfully to our rules (which were very good at a time when no one knew better), we should be concocting music as unpalatable as their libretti.

Da Ponte would make his own views clear more than three decades later, when his life had changed beyond recognition, and he was looking back on his collaboration with a Mozart whose name had by then begun to achieve the international recognition it never enjoyed in his own lifetime. 'If the words of a dramatic poet are nothing but a vehicle to the notes, and an opportunity to the action,' asked Da Ponte in 1819, 'why does a composer of music not more speedily take a doctor's recipes, a bookseller's catalogue, or even a spelling book, instead of the poet's verses, and make them a vehicle to his notes, just as an ass is that of a bag of corn?'

As Mozart argued the supremacy of the music, Da Ponte understandably (if less convincingly) puts the case for the libretto:

> Mozart knew very well that the success of an opera depends first of all on the poet; that without a good poem an entertainment cannot possess the merit of invention, design and a just proportion of the parts; that a composer who is, in regard to drama, what a painter is in regard to the colours, can never do that with effect, unless excited and animated by the words of a poet, whose province is to choose a subject susceptible of variety, incident, movement and action – to prepare, to suspend, to bring about the catastrophe; to exhibit characters interesting, comic, well supported and calculated for stage effect; to write his *recitativo* short, but substantial, his airs various, new and well situated; in sum, his verses easy, harmonious and almost singing of themselves, without all which requisites, the notes of the most sublime and scientific composer will not be felt by the heart, the passions remaining tranquil, and unmoved, their effect will be transient, and the best of airs, after a short time, will be heard with no more attention or pleasure than a trio or a sonata ...
>
> I think that poetry is the door to the music, which can be very handsome, and much admired for its exterior, but nobody can see its internal beauties if the door is ill-proportioned.

If we can take Da Ponte's and Mozart's respective views as read, we know little of their modus operandi – not least because there are no letters between them, as they were presumably living near each other in the heart of Vienna. We know where Mozart lived while writing *Le nozze* – a first-floor flat at No. 5 Domgasse, just behind St Stephen's Cathedral, now the Mozarthaus, refurbished for the celebrations of the 250th anniversary of his birth in 2006. But no amount of research in the Vienna archives can turn up any address for Da Ponte, at any stage of his decade and more in the city. If he had been living in the impoverished suburbs at this point, however, there would presumably have been some surviving correspondence.

But we can analyse what Da Ponte did with Beaumarchais's text, presumably at Mozart's instructions, beyond turning prose into the most refined, elegant verse. First, he cut down the roles of Marceline, Bartholo and the music master, Bazile. In Beaumarchais, Bazile bears some *tendresse* for Marceline, which causes a few diversions in Acts II and IV; these were removed, leaving Basilio a mere vassal of the Count, with little character and few desires beyond foppish mischief-making. Marcellina is similarly reduced, her great Beaumarchais speech about male expectations being distilled into her only solo aria, Act IV's 'Il capro e la capretta' – which is usually cut from modern performances.

Where Beaumarchais was presenting a range of variegated characters with complex, often confused motives, Da Ponte needed to simplify them into less multi-faceted people, moving the plot forward at greater speed. His Countess is less ambiguous than in Beaumarchais, where her husband's infidelities provoke an overt desire to respond to Chérubin's advances. And what librettist before him (or composer before Mozart) ever left his prima donna out of Act I? The first time we see the Countess in the opera, lamenting happier days in 'Porgi amor' at the opening of Act II (with overt musical echoes of Paisiello's Rosina in his *Barber of Seville*), sets her character for the piece; she is distressed about her husband's conduct, but not enough to contemplate taking other lovers herself. Throughout the work, both Da Ponte and Mozart show great understanding of, and empathy towards, the female characters – who really run the show.

Similarly, the Count is a more one-dimensional character in Da Ponte: shallow, arrogant, capricious, unrepentant until he is caught *in flagrante* and given no other choice than to seek the pardon he has just denied others (moving Mozart, in the process, to supreme musical heights). Beaumarchais's Count carries more of the dignity of the Spanish aristocrat, with more awareness of his own inadequacies, not so easily outsmarted by Figaro. The confrontation between master and servant in Beaumarchais's Act II scene v is dropped from the opera, where Da Ponte has Figaro constantly second-guessing the Count.

Figaro himself is less disreputable, more endearingly honest in Da Ponte – who, alas, felt obliged to drop the great Act V tirade against social injustice given him by Beaumarchais, which begins:

> Oh woman, woman, woman! What a feeble creature you are! No living animal can be untrue to its nature. Is it yours to be deceitful? ... No, Your Lordship, you won't have her, you will not have her! Just because you're a great nobleman, you think you're a great genius! Being an

aristocrat, with money, a position, public office – how arrogant they make a man! What have you ever done for all these privileges? You took the trouble to be born – nothing more! That apart, you're a rather ordinary man. But I, just one of the crowd, I've had to use more craft, calculation and skill just to stay alive than has been spent governing the whole of Spain for all of a century!

It runs on in this vein for quite some time, several pages in book form, but all that remains in Act IV of the opera is Da Ponte's elaboration on the opening rant against women's fidelity, 'Aprite un po' quegl' occhi, uomini incauti, e sciocchi'. The aria ends with the line 'il resto nol dico, già ognuno lo sa', which Mozart followed with solos for the *corni*, or French horns – a deliberate musical pun on the horns of a cuckold.

In this castration of Beaumarchais's grandstanding speech, no doubt Da Ponte had the Emperor's ban on the play in mind as much as the need to keep moving the plot forward; and Figaro's aria, with its punning horns, would have suited the Emperor's ambivalent feelings towards women. But the revolutionary spirit of Beaumarchais's original is retained in Figaro's addressing the Count in Act I – at first behind his back, then a second time in front of the Countess – as 'Signor Contino'. You may pay the piper, he sings, but I'll call the tune, Signor Contino. That sneering diminutive catches the spirit of Beaumarchais.

In the original play, Figaro rails against not just the privileges of heredity, but also censorship, the law, sexism and gambling – all topics acceptable for satire in the Vienna opera house, again suggesting that pragmatism as much as discretion was guiding Da Ponte's selection of material. It seems probable, as Steptoe points out, that 'much of the social and class tension of Mozart's and Da Ponte's opera was defused by its conformity with current fashions'. The modifications made by Da Ponte were 'largely consequences of the problems presented by the original play'. Beaumarchais's text was too long, involved and discursive for the *opera buffa* format. Da Ponte resolved these difficulties 'by shearing away subplots, aspects of character, and topical allusions that were not essential to the basic imbroglio of love and jealousy . . . The features which tightened his libretto as operatic material simultaneously softened the political force of the play.'

Buffo convention, for instance, also required that each act end with a grand finale, which required Da Ponte to alter and embellish Beau-marchais significantly. In the play Act II ends quietly, with the Count and

Susanna plotting their next move; Da Ponte follows Beaumarchais closely until the entry of Marcellina, Bartolo and Basilio, to present their case against Figaro, then expands into the expected 'tutti allegro' and 'prestissimo' sections concluding twenty minutes of seamless ensemble music climaxing in a glorious septet.

Da Ponte (and/or Mozart?) also invented the whole business of the pin that seals the letter, but gets lost before it can be returned, becoming so central a theme of the work's second half that it is said that Queen Elizabeth II, on being told she was again going to see *The Marriage of Figaro* at the Royal Opera House, declared: 'Oh no, I've seen that one. It's the one about the girl who loses the pin.'

The girl who loses the pin is Barbarina, daughter of Antonio the gardener and cousin of Susanna, who is given a short but exquisite aria on the subject at the opening of Act IV – in the distinctive key of F minor, uniquely for the opera. The pin is nowhere in Beaumarchais; it is almost as if Mozart and Da Ponte invented it, and all the shenanigans incumbent on its temporary loss, as a justification for giving Barbarina this lovely if out-of-place little 'whimper', as the eminent critic Sir Frank Kermode argued in a 2005 lecture. 'Beaumarchais's Fanchette (the French original of Barbarina) does enter at roughly the same moment,' he avowed.

> However, she is looking not for a pin but for (Beaumarchais's) Suzanne. Far from having lost the pin, she immediately shows it to Figaro. So all the business of Barbarina losing the pin, and Figaro filching another pin from Marcellina and telling Barbarina he has found the lost one is not in the play. Fanchette is cheeky to Figaro, then goes off to complete her errand. Nothing in the least disturbing has happened to her. In other words Da Ponte/Mozart invented an extra bit of plot and decided, at this stage in an already sufficiently complex intrigue, to add another flourish, the lost pin; and all so that Mozart could write for Barbarina this little anxious cavatina of thirty-five bars.

It might be added that Barbarina, who tells us that she too had been wooed by the Count, feared what kind of punishment he might inflict on her over the lost pin. The exquisite aria and its unique key, in other words, are Mozart–Da Ponte's way of blackening Almaviva's character yet further.

At times, Da Ponte elaborates on hints in Beaumarchais with

memorable results; at others, the scale and importance of his arias correspond with the original. To take two examples from Act I, set to some of Mozart's best-known music, we can see what poetry Da Ponte makes out of a few words of Beaumarchais's prose. In the play, Chérubin says:

> Je ne sais plus ce que je suis; mais depuis quelque temps je sense ma poitrine agitée; mon coeur palpite au seul aspect d'une femme; es mots *amour* et *volupté* le font tressaillir et le troublent. Enfin le besoin de dire a quelqu'un *je vous aime* est devenu pour moi si pressant, que je le dis tout seul, en courant dans le parc, à ta maîtresse, à toi, aux arbres, aux nuages, au vent qui les importe avec mes paroles perdues.

(I don't know what's come over me. For some time now I've felt these strange feelings in my chest; my heart palpitates at the mere sight of a woman; words like 'love' and 'desire' make it leap and miss a beat. In fact my need to say 'I love you' to someone has become so pressing that I say it when alone, running in the park, or to your mistress, to you, to the trees, to the clouds, to the wind which carries them off with my lost words.)

This becomes Da Ponte's first aria for Cherubino:

> Non so più cosa son, cosa faccio,
> Or di foco, ora sono di ghiaccio;
> Ogni donna cangiar di colore,
> Ogni donna mi fa palpitar.
> Solo ai nomi d'amor, di diletto.
> Mi si turba, mi s'altera il petto,
> E a parlare mi sforza d'amore
> Un desìo ch'io non posso spiegar.
> Parlo d'amor vegliando,
> Parlo d'amor sognando,
> All'acqua, all'ombra, ai monti,
> Ai fiori, all'erbe, ai fonti,
> All'eco, all'aria, ai venti,
> Che il suon dei vani accenti
> Portano via con sé.
> E se non ho chi m'oda,
> Parlo d'amor con me.

(I don't know who I am, what I'm doing,
For at first I'm on fire, then I'm freezing;
Every woman can make me change colour,
Every woman makes me palpitate.
Simply words like 'love' or 'pleasure'
So disturb me, so make my heart tremble,
And I'm forced to keep speaking of love
By a longing I cannot explain.
I speak of love when I am waking,
I speak of love when I am dreaming,
To the flowers, to the grass, to the mountains,
To the echo, the air and the winds,
Which carry my empty words
Away with them.
And if there is no one to listen,
I speak about love to myself.)

And at the end of Act I, Beaumarchais's Figaro says:

Adieu, mon petit Chérubin. Tu vas mener un train en vie bien différent, mon enfant: damn! Tu ne rôderas plus tout le jour au quartier des femmes; plus d'échaudes, de goûters à la crème; plus de main-chaude, ou de colin-maillard. De bons soldats, morbleu! basané, mal vêtus; un grand fusil bien lourd; tourne à droite, tourne à gauche, en avant, marche à la gloire; et ne va pas broncher en chemin, à moins qu'un bon coup de feu ...

(Goodbye, my little Cherubin. You're off to lead a very different life, my boy: by God! No more creeping around the women's quarters all day; no more doughnuts and cream buns; no more games of 'It' or blind man's buff! Good old soldiers, by Jove! Weather-beaten, ragged-clothed; a great big heavy musket; right turn; left turn; forward march, off to glory; and don't go breaking step, unless you're fired at ...)

This becomes Da Ponte's celebrated aria for Figaro:

Non più andrai, farfallone amoroso,
Notte e giorno d'intorno girando,
Delle belle turbando il riposo,
Narcisetto, Adoncino d'amor.
Non più avrai, questi bel pennacchini,

Quel cappello leggero e galante,
Quella chioma, quell'aria brillante,
Quel vermiglio donnesco color.
Fra guerrieri, poffar bacco!
Gran mustacchi, stretto sacco,
Schioppo in spalla, spada al fianco,
Collo dritto, muso franco;
Un gran casco, un gran turbante,
Molto onor, poco contante;
Ed invece del fandango
Una marcia per il fango.
Per montagne e per valloni
Con le nevi, e i sollioni,
Al concerto di tromboni
Di bombarde, di cannoni,
Che le palle in tutti i tuoni
All' orecchio fan fischiar.
Cherubino, alla vittoria,
Alla gloria militar.

(No more, amorous butterfly,
Will you flutter around by night and day,
Disturbing the peace of the ladies,
Little Narcissus, Adonis of love.
No more will you wear these fine feathers,
Or this cap so light and jaunty,
These curls, that air so dashing,
Those cheeks of women's colour.
But with soldiers, by Bacchus!
Big moustaches, tight knapsack,
Gun on shoulder, sword at side,
Head held high, brave expression,
A big helmet, or grand turban,
Lots of glory, little money.
Instead of dancing the fandango
You'll be marching through the mud,
Over mountains, through valleys,
In the snow, or burned by the sun,

Born Emanuele Conegliano, the young Lorenzo Da Ponte (right) took his name from the Bishop who baptized him in 1763 in the cathedral of his home town, Ceneda, pictured today (below). He was then educated in the seminary beside it (below right). Now part of Vittorio Veneto, Ceneda takes due pride in its most famous son (inset).

As a young Catholic priest in Venice, Da Ponte celebrated Mass in the Chiesa San Luca (today, left) while living in sin in this house in the nearby Campo San Luca (below).

Da Ponte first became friends with Casanova (right) while spending too much time gambling in the *ridotto*, as painted by Pietro Longhi (below).

Da Ponte arrived in Vienna in 1781 with a letter of introduction to the court composer Antonio Salieri (left), thanks to whom he was appointed theatre poet by the Emperor Joseph II, pictured with his brother and eventual successor, Leopold II (below).

In 1783 Da Ponte met the
young, unemployed Mozart
(in an unfinished portrait by
Joseph Lange, who intended to
portray him at the keyboard).

(Above) Mozart's family – father Leopold, deceased mother (in the painting on the wall), Wolfgang and his sister Nannerl. In 1783 he married Constanze Weber (left, painted by Joseph Lange).

In 1785–6, in his house at No. 5 Domgasse, near St Stephen's Cathedral (today the Mozarthaus, left), Mozart and Da Ponte wrote their opera *The Marriage of Figaro*, based on the play by Beaumarchais (below, painted by Jean-Marc Nattier), which includes Figaro's celebrated aria 'Non più andrai'.

Da Ponte could not be present when
Mozart conducted the first performance
of their opera *Don Giovanni* at the Tyl
Theatre in Prague (above), today the
Estates (right) on 29 October 1787. The
work was not such a success in Vienna,
where Da Ponte received semi-annual
royalties as theatre poet at the
Burgtheater.

To the sound of blunderbusses,
Of bombardments, and of cannons,
With the thunder of every shot
Making your ears whistle.
Cherubino, on to victory,
On to military glory!)

It has been suggested (by Steptoe) that Da Ponte even borrowed from his arch-rival Casti, that he modelled Cherubino's Act II aria on Lisetta's song 'O giovinette innamorate' in the first act of Casti's piece for Paisiello, *Il re Teodoro*, so successful in Vienna in 1784. Again, however, comparison with Beaumarchais's prose is instructive. Beaumarchais's song, to guitar accompaniment, about a horseback rider mourning his lost love, becomes the famous:

Voi che sapete	You who know
Che cosa è amor,	What love is,
Donne, vedete	Ladies, look
S'io l' ho nel cor.	If that's what's in my heart.
Quello ch'io provo,	All that I'm feeling
Vi ridirò;	I'm going to tell you,
E per me nuovo,	For me it is new,
Capir nol so.	I don't understand it.
Sento un affeto	I have a feeling,
Pien di desir,	Full of desire,
Ch'ora è diletto,	Now it is pleasure,
Ch'ora è martir,	Now it is pain,
Gelo, e poi sento	Freezing one moment
L'alma avvampar,	Then all on fire,
E in un momento	And in a moment
Torno a gelar.	Turned back to ice.
Ricerco un bene	I seek a blessing
Fuori di me,	Outside of myself,
Non so ch'il tiene,	I don't know who holds it,
Non so cos'è.	Nor what it is.
Sospiro e gemo	I sigh and I groan
Senza voler,	Without wishing to.
Palpito e tremo	I flutter and tremble
Senza saper.	Without knowing why.

Non trovo pace	I cannot find peace
Notte, nè dì,	By night or by day;
Ma pur mi piace	But yet it pleases me
Languir così.	To languish thus.

In six weeks, so Da Ponte says, he had finished his work. Recent scholarship confirms that Mozart may also have finished a shorthand version of the 'short score' (without instrumentation) of this very long opera – the full score runs to 592 pages – in six weeks; but he took more like six months, from October 1785 to April 1786, to orchestrate and complete it, presumably getting Da Ponte to make adjustments and write new material as he progressed.

During this period Mozart also wrote two of his greatest piano concertos, the A major K. 488 and the C minor K. 491, a one-act *Singspiel* called *Der Schauspieldirektor,* and additional music for an amateur performance of *Idomeneo.* By the time he had finished *Figaro* – apart from the overture, written as usual at the very last minute – the Burgtheater happened to be in need of a new Italian opera. Only now that the piece was complete, to both their satisfaction, did Da Ponte inform the Emperor what he and Mozart had been up to.

'What?' exclaimed Joseph. 'Don't you know that Mozart, although excellent at instrumental music, has written only one opera – and that nothing very great?'

'Without Your Majesty's favour,' replied Da Ponte at his most unctuous, 'I too should have written only one play in Vienna.'

'That's true,' mused the Emperor. 'But I've forbidden this *Marriage of Figaro* in Vienna to the German company.'

'Yes,' replied Da Ponte, in a clearly pre-rehearsed response. 'But as I was writing a play to be set to music, and not a comedy, I have had to omit a good many scenes and shorten a great many more – and I've omitted and shortened whatever might offend the refinement and decorum of an entertainment at which Your Majesty presides.'

While Joseph thought this over, Da Ponte added: 'As for the music, as far as I can judge, it is remarkably beautiful.'

'Very well,' said the Emperor. 'If that is so, I'll trust your taste as to the music, and your discretion as to the morals. Have the score sent to the copyist.'

Da Ponte hurried to tell Mozart the good news. He was still there when a servant arrived from the Imperial Palace with orders that the composer attend the Emperor immediately, with the full score. When Mozart played him some extracts, Joseph was delighted – even, in Da Ponte's word, 'astounded' – and agreed, to the horror of Salieri, Rosenberg and Casti, to sanction *Le nozze di Figaro* for performance.

'Joseph had exquisite taste in music, as indeed in all the arts,' purrs Da Ponte. 'The great success of this opera throughout the civilized world was soon to show that he was not mistaken in his judgement.'

But that was written thirty years later, again with the benefit of hindsight. At the time, the cabal opposing Mozart and Da Ponte saw its chance when its fifth columnist, Francesco Bussani, who was playing both Dr Bartolo and Antonio the gardener, noticed that there was a ballet in the score – towards the end of the third act, when Susanna gives the Count a note arranging a rendezvous while a chorus of village maidens presents his wife with posies of flowers.

Bussani, who was also stage manager, in charge of wardrobe and costumes – 'he knew', in Da Ponte's words, 'something of every profession except that of gentleman' – rushed to inform Rosenberg, who at once summoned Da Ponte.

'So the Signor poet has introduced a ballet into *Figaro*?'

'Yes, Your Excellency.'

'Doesn't the Signor poet know that the Emperor does not wish to have ballets in his theatre?'

'No, Your Excellency.'

'Well, Signor poet, I am telling you so now.'

'Yes, Your Excellency.'

'And I am further telling you that you must take it out, Signor poet.'

This patronizing repetition of 'Signor poet' was beginning to irritate Da Ponte, who says he felt as if the Count were saying 'Signor Donkey'. But Da Ponte's 'Your Excellency', he thought, had an innuendo of its own. He replied simply: 'No, Your Excellency.'

'Have you the libretto with you?'

'Yes, Your Excellency.'

'Where is the ballet scene?'

'Here, Your Excellency.'

'Well, this is what we shall do with it,' said Rosenberg, tearing out the two relevant sheets of paper and throwing them on the fire. Handing the rest back to Da Ponte, he added: 'You see, Signor Poet, that I can do anything!' With that, he bid him a second 'Vade'.

The news reduced Mozart to despair. 'He wanted to plead with the Count, give Bussani a thrashing, appeal to the Emperor, recall the score – in truth, I had quite a task to calm him.' Da Ponte begged the composer to give him two days to sort out the problem, knowing that this would take them to the day of the dress rehearsal; he then paid the Emperor a visit especially to make sure that he would be present.

As indeed he was, with Casti and most of the Viennese nobility, as the work proceeded to universal approval until the end of the third act. 'All that could be seen was the Count and Susanna gesticulating, while the orchestra remained silent, so it looked like a puppet-show.'

'What is the meaning of this?' the Emperor asked Casti, who was sitting behind him.

'You must ask the poet,' replied Casti with a malicious smile.

Da Ponte was summoned, but instead of replying gave the Emperor his manuscript, in which he had restored the missing scene. Joseph read it and asked why there was no dancing. Da Ponte remained silent, implying there had been some disagreement. So the Emperor turned and asked Count Rosenberg, who replied that the theatre had no dancers.

'Are there none at other theatres?' asked the Emperor.

'Yes, Sire,' replied Rosenberg.

'Very well, then, let Da Ponte have as many as he wants.'

In less than half an hour twenty-four ballerinas and extras had arrived, and the end of the act was repeated.

'That's better,' cried the Emperor, and Da Ponte's triumph was complete.

The first night of *The Marriage of Figaro* took place at the Burgtheater on 1 May 1786. 'In spite of all the other composers and their partisans muttering "We shall see" and "We shall hear", in spite of the Count and Casti and the devil himself, it met with general success,' reported Da Ponte. 'The Emperor and others of real discernment considered it sublime, almost divine.'

Even Casti declared that the libretto had 'its good points'. What were they, asked Da Ponte? He was ever ready to speak ill of Casti, who apparently replied: 'These two lines, for instance, are very pretty':

Non più andrai, farfallone amoroso,
Notte e giorno d'intorno girando.

So, according to Casti, all the merit of the play 'consisted in a few good lines, or, at most, a few good songs'. After all, as even Da Ponte acknowledged, it was only an adaptation of Beaumarchais's play. But, as he also wrote years later, 'if a writer of a theatrical piece does not deserve to be praised, or even noticed, when the subject of his composition is known, what praise is due to Shakespeare for all the pieces taken by him from Boccaccio, and Bandello's novels; what praise to Voltaire for his *Merope*; to Alfieri for his *Antigone*; to Metastasio for his *Semiramide*; to Monti for his *Aristodemo*; and to all those poets who, in common with them, not only wrote tragedies and dramas on well-known subjects, but wrote them after having seen the performances of pieces on the same subjects?'

Some years later Da Ponte was given Beaumarchais's own view of his work, after Salieri had shown it to the playwright in Paris. Writing to Da Ponte, Salieri quotes Beaumarchais as saying: 'I admired the art of the Italian poet, in contracting so many *colpi di scena* in so short a time, without the one destroying the other. Had I altered thus a comedy of another author, I would not hesitate a moment to call it my own work.'

Da Ponte himself distils precisely what he had done. 'A comedy of 230 pages 8vo. in prose, I have reduced to 51 12mo. in verse, and sixteen *dramatis personae* to eleven: this is calculated by my *friend Observer* a few retrenchments!'

In a preface to the published edition, he wrote:

The length prescribed by custom for dramatic performances, the established number of characters generally considered practicable, as well as certain other sensible attitudes and conventions regarding the manners, the place and the audience, were the reasons why I did not make a translation of this excellent comedy, but rather a copy, or, so to speak, an extract.

For this purpose I was obliged to reduce the sixteen characters of the original to eleven, two of which can be played by the same person, and to omit not only one whole act, but many delightful scenes, and many witty turns of phrase which are scattered throughout it. In their place I have substituted canzonettas, arias, choruses and other thoughts and words susceptible of being set to music: things that can be managed only in poetry, never in prose.

In spite of all the zeal and care on the part of both the composer and myself to be brief, however, the opera will not be one of the shortest that has been performed on our stages. We hope that adequate excuse for this may be found in the variety of dramatic strands by which the drama is developed, the size and scope of the same, the number of musical pieces necessary in order not to keep the performers idle, to avoid the boredom and monotony of the long recitatives, to paint faithfully and in varied colours the diverse passions that are aroused. Above all, we hope to have realized our special purpose: to offer a new type of entertainment, as it were, to a public of such refined taste and seasoned judgement.

The cast included Francesco Benucci as Figaro (later to be Leporello in the first Viennese performances of *Don Giovanni* and Guglielmo in *Così fan tutte*), Nancy Storace as Susanna, Luisa Laschi as the Countess, Stefano Mandini as the Count and the twelve-year-old Anna Gottlieb as Barbarina. Michael Kelly, who played Basilio and Don Curzio, has left a charming description of the first rehearsal with full orchestra:

Mozart was on the stage with his crimson pelisse and gold-laced cocked hat, giving the time of the music to the orchestra. Figaro's song 'Non più andrai, farfallone amoroso' Benucci gave with the greatest animation and power of voice. I was standing close to Mozart, who, *sotto voce*, was repeating "Bravo! Bravo, Benucci!"; and when Benucci came to the fine passage "Cherubino, alla vittoria, alla gloria militar", which he gave out with stentorian lungs, the effect was electricity itself, for the whole of the performers on the stage, and those in the orchestra, as if actuated by one feeling of delight, vociferated "Bravo! Bravo! Maestro! Viva, viva, grande Mozart!" Those in the orchestra I thought would never have ceased applauding, by beating the bows of their violins against the music-desks. The little man acknowledged, by repeated obeisances, his thanks for the distinguished mark of enthusiastic applause bestowed on him.

As for the Act II finale – twenty minutes of seamless ensemble which stand as one of the finest, most thrillingly sustained passages in all opera: 'The same meed of approbation was given ... That piece of music alone, in my humble opinion, if he had never composed anything else as good, would have stamped him as the greatest master of his art.'

The delightful third-act sextet, in which Figaro discovers that Marcellina and Bartolo are his long-lost parents, was Mozart's own favourite piece in the work. He asked Kelly, who was playing the stuttering judge, not to stutter during this ensemble; young as he was, Kelly demurred, insisting he could stutter in such a way that he would not interfere with the other parts. According to Kelly, Mozart reluctantly yielded, but later thanked him for his persistence:

> Crowded houses proved that nothing ever on the stage produced a more powerful effect; the audience were convulsed with laughter, in which Mozart himself joined. The Emperor repeatedly cried out 'Bravo!' and the piece was loudly applauded and encored. When the opera was over, Mozart came on the stage to me, and shaking me by both hands said: 'Bravo! young man; I feel obliged to you; and acknowledge you to have been in the right, and myself in the wrong.' There was certainly a risk run, but I felt within myself I could give the effect I wished, and the event proved that I was not mistaken.

Kelly also confirms that the first night, conducted by Mozart from the continuo keyboard, was greeted with great enthusiasm by a packed house:

> All the original performers had the advantage of the instruction of the composer, who transfused into their minds his inspired meaning. I shall never forget his little animated countenance, when lighted up with the glowing rays of genius – it is as impossible to describe as it would be to paint sunbeams ...
>
> At the end of the opera I thought the audience would never have done applauding and calling for Mozart, almost every piece was encored, which prolonged it nearly to the length of two operas, and induced the Emperor to issue an order on the second representation that no piece of music should be encored. Never was any thing more complete than the triumph of Mozart and his *Nozze di Figaro*, to which numerous overflowing audiences bore witness.

On the first night, as Kelly says, numerous encores were demanded. Five pieces were encored at the second performance on 3 May, and seven at the third on 8 May, with one duet sung three times. The next day the Emperor wrote a memorandum to Rosenberg: 'To prevent the excessive duration of the operas, but without prejudice to the fame often sought by opera singers from the repetition of vocal pieces, I deem the enclosed notice to the public (that no piece for more than solo voice was to be encored) to be the most reasonable expedient. You will therefore have some posters printed to this effect.' The same rule was extended to the German *Singspiel* company.

Kelly's version runs slightly differently, suggesting that even encores of solos were banned:

> One morning, while we were rehearsing in the grand salon of the palace, His Majesty accompanied by Prince Rosenberg entered the salon, and addressing himself to Storace, Mandini and Benucci, said: 'I dare say you are all pleased that I have desired there shall be no more encores; to have your songs so often repeated must be a very great fatigue, and very distressing to you.' Storace replied: 'It is indeed, Sire, very distressing, very much so.' The other two bowed, as if they were of the same opinion. I was close to His Majesty, and said boldly to him: 'Do not believe them, Sire, they all like to be encored. At least, I am sure I always do.' His Majesty laughed, and I believe he thought there was more truth in my assertion than theirs.

After conducting the first two performances of *Figaro* from the harpsichord, Mozart handed the baton to the conductor-composer Joseph Weigl, then only twenty, who led the remaining performances. Two days after the premiere, the publisher Torricella advertised full and piano scores in the *Wiener Zeitung*. On 11 July a review in the *Wiener Realzeitung* began with a topical reference to the ban on the play, paraphrasing the Figaro of *The Barber* as saying, 'That which cannot be said these days will be sung.' It went on to declare that 'Herr Mozart's music was generally admired by connoisseurs at the first performance, if I except those whose self-love and conceit will not allow them to find merit in anything not written by themselves ... Now, after several performances, one would have to side either with the cabals or with the tasteless to maintain that Herr Mozart's music is anything but a masterpiece of art. It contains so many beauties, and such a wealth of ideas, as can proceed only from a born genius.'

The Hungarian poet Franz Kazincky wrote that 'the joy which this music causes is so far removed from all sensuality that one cannot speak of it. Where could words be found that are worthy to describe it?' But that inveterate operagoer Count Zinzendorf declared himself 'bored' by the work, and Mozart's music 'singular: hands without head'.

The latter view prevailed. *Figaro*'s success in Vienna proved modest and transitory. Within six months it had been eclipsed by *Una cosa rara*, Martín y Soler's setting of another Da Ponte libretto, whose first performance that November saw *Figaro* dropped a month later, after only nine performances in Vienna, where it was not performed again for two years.

In Prague that winter, however, it proved a triumph, single-handedly restoring the flagging fortunes of the Bondini Company. In January 1787 Mozart accepted their invitation to go to the second city of the Habsburg empire to see for himself. The whole place had gone 'Figaro-mad', he reported excitedly in a letter to his Viennese friend Baron Gottfried von Jacquin. 'Nothing is being played, sung or whistled but *Figaro*. No opera is drawing the crowds like *Figaro*. Nothing, nothing but *Figaro*. Certainly a great honour for me!'

Pasquale Bondini, manager of the Prague theatre, seized the moment to commission another opera from Mozart and Da Ponte.

7

Don Giovanni

'MY FRIEND the poet', wrote Michael Kelly of Da Ponte thirty years later, 'had a remarkably awkward gait, a habit of throwing himself (as he thought) into a graceful attitude by putting his stick behind his back and leaning on it; he had also a very peculiar, rather dandyish way of dressing; for, in sooth, the Abbé stood mighty well with himself and had the character of a consummate coxcomb; he had also a strong lisp and broad Venetian dialect.'

Kelly put these observations to good use in a *pièce d'occasion* written by Casti for Salieri with the unambiguous title of *Prima la musica e poi le parole*, written for a celebration at Schönbrunn on 7 February 1786, where it was performed alongside a one-act comedy by Mozart called *Der Schauspieldirektor*.

'The first night of the performance,' Kelly continues, Da Ponte 'was seated in the boxes, more conspicuously than was absolutely necessary'. As usual, on the first night of a new opera, the Emperor was present, and a packed house:

> When I made my *entrée* as the amorous poet, dressed exactly like the Abbé in the boxes, imitating his walk, leaning on my stick, and aping his gestures and his lisp, there was a universal roar of laughter and applause; and after a buzz round the house, the eyes of the whole audience were turned to the place where he was seated. The Emperor enjoyed the joke; the Abbé was not at all affronted, but took my imitation of him in good part, and ever after we were on the best of terms.

Judging from later evidence, it seems that Da Ponte was putting a brave face on an acute embarrassment. Forty years later, he was still hurting. In 1826, the year of Kelly's death, he would publish a direct assault on his impersonator:

> The jests and the romantic nonsense which you wrote, or *had written for you*, in your ridiculous book (which was ghost-written), are so worthless that it is a waste of time for a man of any sense to give himself the trouble of denying them; I know that a man of your *mimicking* nature believes he can say anything and everything, however false, because what he says will make people laugh: I shall take care, however, to make it clear to others, and above all to those who do not know you, even if not to you yourself, that everything you have said about me in your crazy book contains not one syllable of truth, and that if it had been the truth you would have been the last to publish it.

Da Ponte would later have reason to resent Kelly, who failed to offer him any assistance at another difficult moment in his life. For now, he contented himself with the rank self-deception that this stage creature was in fact an impersonation of his arch-rival Casti – who now did him the best possible turn by leaving Vienna.

Eighteen months earlier Casti had written an opera named *Poema Tartaro*, a satire on Russia which was particularly brutal about Catherine the Great. At the time it had amused the Emperor, who held Catherine in low regard; but now he was looking to forge an alliance with Russia, to which Casti's presence in his court might prove a minor obstacle. So Joseph suggested to the poet that he might care to absent himself for a while, handing him a generous subsidy for the purpose. A seasoned traveller, Casti had anyway been contemplating a visit to the Near East. He was gone within a fortnight, and would not return to Vienna during Joseph's lifetime.

With Casti gone, Da Ponte had no real rivals in Vienna; and the success of *Figaro* had composers beating at his door. For Stephen Storace, who again had the Emperor's leave to approach Da Ponte, he quickly adapted Shakespeare's *The Comedy of Errors*, using a French translation entitled *Les Méprises*; Storace's *Gli equivoci* was premiered on 27 December 1786, and well received. Kelly and Storace's sister Nancy both sang leading roles, Kelly attesting that Da Ponte had made the play 'operational' via the subtlety of his adaptation. In 1936, in *The Monthly Musical Record*,

Alfred Einstein wrote that: 'Da Ponte ... knew his trade. To follow step by step the methods by which Da Ponte converts Shakespeare's five acts into two would be tantamount to writing a short study of the dramatic technique of the opera-libretto – a technique from which many a librettist of the twentieth century could learn much.'

But Da Ponte had also promised his friend Martín another libretto before writing *Figaro*. So close were they now that 'Martini' agreed to enter a conspiracy. To have some fun with his detractors, Da Ponte asked Martín to keep it a secret that he was writing him an opera; Martín entered into the spirit of the joke to the extent of pretending to be angry with him for failing to deliver, and to be setting a text sent him from Venice. No one but Da Ponte's patron, the Emperor, and Martín's, the Spanish ambassadress, were let in on the secret.

To please the Spanish ambassadress, Da Ponte chose a Spanish play to adapt for Martín: a comedy called *La luna della sierra* by Luis Vélez de Guevara (not, as he says in his memoirs, Calderón). As Da Ponte puts it, while insisting he made the theme his own: 'The story of the play is very simple. The Infante of Spain falls in love with a beautiful girl of the mountains, but she is in love with a mountaineer, and being most virtuous, resists all the prince's advances before her marriage and after. So I called the opera *Una cosa rara*: "A Rare Thing", or "Beauty and Honesty".' This he supplemented with Juvenal's celebrated line: 'Rara est concordia formae atque pudicitiae.'

Never in his life, he says, did he so much enjoy writing anything so fast; he finished his work in a month, as did Martín. When rehearsals began, however, the singers found much to complain about: they had too much or too little to sing; this part was too high, that too low; much of it was too difficult, and so on. As none knew that Da Ponte had written the libretto, the brunt of their discontent fell on Martín; one of the singers even gratified Da Ponte hugely by telling him that 'You could learn a great deal about *buffo*-writing from this libretto'.

Finally they went on strike – the whole row, in truth, probably stemming from the fact that the composer had been romancing the *primo buffo*'s mistress. When the news came to the Emperor's ears, he sent for Martín and Da Ponte, who 'made bold' to tell him that 'Never had the talents of the singers been displayed to better advantage than in this play of mine, nor perhaps had Vienna ever before heard music so charming, so delightful, so fresh and so universally appealing'. The Emperor asked to see the libretto, which fell open at the end of the first finale, with the line: 'What's done is done and cannot be changed.'

'Nothing could be more to the purpose,' cried the Emperor with a smile. He then wrote a note to Rosenberg: 'Dear Count, Tell my singers that I have heard their complaint about Martín's opera, and that I am very sorry about it, but "What's done is done and cannot be changed".'

The first performance of *Una cosa rara*, less than six months after *Figaro* on 17 November 1786, was the biggest triumph operagoing Vienna could remember. The recalcitrant singers were stunned by their ovations, and everyone wondered who had written the text. Only Kelly guessed; and he was happy to keep the secret. *Figaro* was forgotten as Viennese ladies dressed and did their hair '*à la Cosa rara*'. When Da Ponte was finally identified, he enjoyed the high point of his career, wallowing in praise, and watching his work travel swiftly across Europe. Over the next half-century it was translated into several languages while *Figaro* struggled to gain a foothold in the repertoire. Only Mozart, at this stage, had confidence in *Figaro*'s future, prophetically announcing that Martín's music was 'really very pretty ... but in ten years nobody will take any notice of it'.

1786 was proving an *annus mirabilis* for Da Ponte, at the height of his powers at the age of thirty-seven. Twenty-two Italian operas were staged at the Burgtheater that year, ten of them new, six of them by Da Ponte – including one still regarded as among the greatest ever written. As theatre poet, he would also have supervised the texts – and, in Salieri's absence, the staging – of most others. It has been called 'a staggering achievement, the apex of his Vienna period'.

But success, as so often, was followed by a few failures. Although in unprecedented demand, Da Ponte agreed to a request from Salieri that he write a libretto for Vincenzo Righini, who ran the theatre with him during Salieri's absences in Paris. 'In view of his good offices in recommending me as poet,' Da Ponte wrote to Salieri, rather patronizingly, 'it seemed the honourable thing to please him.' Righini's *Il demogorgone ovvero il filosofo confuso* proved an abject failure, closing after four performances; a more accurate title, in Da Ponte's own view, would have been "The composer and the poet punished in turn" ... Righini's friends put the blame on the words; I blamed the music and the composer's worthless ideas, which suffocated my poetic soul.'

A similar fate befell his *Bertoldo*, adapted from a minor poet named

Gaetano Brunati for the journeyman composer Francesco Piticchio. 'Da Ponte,' the Emperor implored him after its disastrous first night, 'write plays for Mozart, for Martín, for Salieri! Don't write again for this Potacci, Petecchi, Pitocchi, Peticchi ... whatever he's called.' Joseph rammed his point home with a judicious taunt: 'Casti was cleverer than you; he wrote plays only for a Paisiello or a Salieri ...'

Joseph knew his court composer. The success of *Una cosa rara* saw Salieri, who had vowed to lose his fingers before collaborating with Da Ponte again, switching sides in the constant cabals and asking the Abbé to make an Italian translation of his French success *Tarare*, a Beaumarchais setting then highly successful in Paris. Martín, naturally enough, was also keen to capitalize with all speed on the success of *Cosa rara*. And Mozart, from whom Prague's National Theatre had commissioned another opera, was also impatient for a new idea.

To Martín Da Ponte proposed one of his very few original libretti, *L'arbore di Diana*; and to Mozart he suggested a reworking of the old legend of Don Juan. When the Emperor asked whether he had taken his advice, Da Ponte replied: 'All too literally, Sire. I am writing for all three at once.'

'You won't succeed!' laughed Joseph.

'Perhaps not, but I shall try,' replied Da Ponte. 'At night I shall write for Mozart, which will be like reading Dante's *Inferno*. In the morning I shall write for Martín, which will be like reading Petrarch. And in the evening for Salieri, who will be my Tasso.'

He settled down to his three tasks with a bottle of Tokay to his right, an inkstand in front of him, and a box of Seville tobacco to his left.

Ambitious as his plan was, it was further complicated by the buxom beauty of the sixteen-year-old serving-girl, his landlady's daughter, briefed to supply his every need. Soon she was satisfying more needs than her mother had bargained for. 'I should have wished to love her only as a daughter, but ...' recalled Da Ponte, who found himself ringing the bell to summon the girl in the next room with increasing frequency, 'especially when my inspiration cooled ...'

> She would bring me a biscuit, or a cup of coffee, or just her own pretty face, always cheerful, always smiling, custom-built to inspire poetic fancy and clever ideas. With only brief breaks, I worked twelve hours a day for two months, and for the whole of this time she stayed in the

next room, sometimes reading a book, sometimes sewing, so as to be ready to come to me as soon as she heard my bell.

Sometimes she would sit near me without moving, without opening her lips or twitching an eyelid; she would look at me steadily, smile sweetly, sigh and sometimes appear to be on the verge of tears. In short, this young girl was my Calliope for three operas, and for all the verses I wrote for the next six years ...

On the first such day, if Da Ponte is to be believed, 'between the Tokay, the Seville tobacco, the coffee, the bell and the young Muse, I wrote the first two scenes of *Don Giovanni*, two scenes of *L'arbore di Diana* and more than half the first act of *Tarare*' (whose title he changed to *Axur, rè d'Ormus*). 'In the morning I took these scenes to the three composers, who could hardly believe their eyes. In sixty-three days the first two operas were quite finished, and nearly two thirds of the last.'

A few pages later in Da Ponte's memoirs, perhaps unsurprisingly, there is a significantly different version of the genesis of *L'arbore di Diana*. A few days before he gave the first few pages to Martín, he tells us, he was visited by the composer and a mutual friend, who asked when they would be able to see some of the libretto. 'The day after tomorrow,' replied Da Ponte.

'So the subject has been chosen?'

Bluffing, for he had given it no thought, Da Ponte replied, 'Of course,' even telling them the title. 'So there is a synopsis ready?' Playing for time, Da Ponte replied, 'Don't worry about that.' Dinner was just being served, and he invited his guests to stay, promising to show them the synopsis after they had eaten. Leaving them with his muse and his brother – Paolo, a music student, was staying with him at this time – Da Ponte disappeared next door and dashed off a synopsis in half an hour. It pleased his guests 'enormously'.

However haphazard its composition, *L'arbore di Diana* proved the first of the three to be performed, premiered on 1 October 1787 to mark the wedding of Joseph's niece, the Archduchess Maria Theresa, to Prince Anton Clemens of Saxony. 'Voluptuous without being lascivious' was Da Ponte's own verdict on his allegory about Cupid, Diana and an apple tree which turns black and sheds its fruit when an unchaste woman walks beneath it; at the end, to spare Diana's blushes in her pursuit of Endymion, it is uprooted and replaced by a Temple of Love.

This first original piece he had ever written proved almost as popular as *Una cosa rara*, not least with the Emperor, who saw it as a covert tribute to his recent measures against monasticism, and rewarded Da Ponte with a bonus of a hundred sequins. As the work followed *Cosa rara* across Europe, and Count Rosenberg asked Da Ponte where he had found his inspiration, the theatre poet was riding high enough to give his boss a blunt reply: 'Up the backsides of my enemies.'

On 18 October 1786 the Mozarts had a third child, Johann Thomas Leopold, who died within a month. By January Mozart and his wife were in Prague, staying with the family of his Viennese patron and friend Count Thun while savouring the huge success of *Figaro*. He also gave concerts, including the first performance of a new symphony thereafter called the 'Prague', and a pianoforte recital at the National Theatre, where *Figaro* was playing. So frenzied was his reception that he was obliged to improvise on the piano for a further half-hour, finally responding to requests for '*Figaro!* Something from *Figaro!*' with an impromptu set of variations on 'Non più andrai'.

By the time he and Constanze returned to Vienna in mid-February, Mozart was ready to work on his new commission from Bondini's National Theatre. As he got down to *Don Giovanni*, Mozart was trying to brush up his English, with a view to visiting London, where his friends Kelly and Nancy Storace had returned; it was now that he famously wrote in another friend's album, in English: 'Don't never forget your true and faithfull friend.' He also agreed to take on a new pupil in composition, a sixteen-year-old who had come to Vienna especially to study with him, Ludwig van Beethoven.

On 28 May, his father Leopold died in Salzburg. Prevented by an illness of his own from being at his father's deathbed, Mozart showed more emotion about the death of his pet starling. He continued to work on *Don Giovanni*, and was also writing such works as *Eine Kleine Nachtmusik*, K. 525, the Sonata in C for piano duet, K. 521 and the Violin Sonata in A, K. 526, as well as most of his songs.

By September, he was ready to travel to Prague with Constanze, who was pregnant again, leaving their three-year-old son with foster-parents outside Vienna. Mozart was needed for the rehearsals of his new opera, due to open on 14 October, also to celebrate the wedding of Maria Theresa and Prince Anton. But the piece was not ready in time, and the newlyweds were instead feted at another performance of *Figaro*. (It has been suggested that this was deliberate, as *Don Giovanni* was not suitable for performance before newlywed aristocrats; but much the same might be said, in truth, of *Figaro*.)

'You will probably think that my opera has been performed by now,' Mozart wrote from Prague to Baron Gottfried von Jacquin on 15 October. 'If so, you would be somewhat mistaken. In the first place, the stage personnel are not as smart here as those in Vienna, when it comes to mastering an opera of this kind in a very short time. Secondly, I found on my arrival that so few preparations and arrangements have been made that it would have been completely impossible to produce it on the 14th, that is, yesterday. So yesterday my *Figaro* was performed in a fully lighted theatre, and I myself conducted.'

On 9 October, immediately after the Vienna premiere of *L'arbore di Diana*, Da Ponte arrived in Prague to join Mozart in completing *Don Giovanni*. He took rooms in the rear of an inn called 'Zum Platteis' (The Flatfish), very near Mozart's in the Kohlenmarkt. Legend suggests that they leaned out of their upper-storey windows to talk to each other across the narrow alleyway between their apartments; certainly, they were very close to the theatre where their work was to be performed. Most of the music was written by the time Da Ponte arrived; only the second-act finale, the duet for Zerlina and Masetto ('Giovinetta che fate all'amore') and Masetto's protest aria ('Ho capito') remained to be finished.

But rehearsals were still in progress, with Mozart yet to write the overture, when Da Ponte was recalled to Vienna by the Emperor after only eight days. During that week, he tells us, he 'directed' the singers. Although we can assume the text was finished before Mozart left for Prague, Da Ponte was no doubt also making insertions and amendments to the composer's wishes.

In the final scene of *Don Giovanni*, to cap his famous (and some would say revolutionary) ball-scene cry of 'Viva la libertà', the Don sings a less political mantra: 'Vivan le femmine, / Viva il buon vino! / Sostegno e gloria / D'umanità!'. In his *Cours familier de littérature* the French poet Alphonse de Lamartine quotes Da Ponte's daily routine while writing *Don Giovanni*, and concludes: 'C'est ainsi que Don Juan devait être écrire, par un aventurier, un amant, un poète, un homme de plaisir, et de désordre inspire du vin, de l'amour et de la gloire, entre les tentations de la débauche et le respect divin pour l'innocence, homme sans scruple, mais non sans terreur des vengeances du ciel. D'Aponte (*sic*) a l'impénitence près, écrivait le drame de sa propre vie dans le drame de Don Juan.'

Da Ponte was chronicling his own life? To some extent, perhaps, but also that of a friend who now came back into it. Casanova was in Prague at the time, negotiating with the publisher Ritter Johann Ferdinand Schönfeld over his utopian novel *Icosameron*; recent scholarship suggests that, as Da Ponte was summoned back to Vienna, he handed over the completion of his task to his old friend. In the library of his last home at Dux in Bohemia, long after his death, Casanova's handwriting has been found on drafts of the second act 'escape scene' from *Don Giovanni* – which could well re-enact one of his own escapades in the alleyways of Venice.

There was another postponement of the first night when one of the singers fell ill; even so, legend has it that Mozart did not get round to writing the overture until 28 October, the night before the first performance. A synthesis of several accounts has him locked in a room at one of the homes of his friends the Duscheks – either the 'Zu den Drei Goldenen Löwen' in the Kohlenmarkt Court, now in Prague's old town, or their rural seat of Bertramka, then outside the town, now its Mozart museum – while Constanze alternately plied him with punch, which made him drowsy, and told him stories, to keep him awake. It was finished at seven the next morning, just as the copyist arrived.

Each year to this day, on 29 October, there is a performance of *Don Giovanni* at the recently restored Estates Theatre in Prague to commemorate the huge success of its premiere there, conducted by Mozart, in 1787. 'Connoisseurs and musicians say that Prague has never heard the like,' reported the Prague *Oberpostamtszeitung*. 'Herr Mozard (*sic*) conducted in person: when he entered the orchestra, he was received with threefold cheers, which erupted again when he left it. The opera is, moreover, extremely difficult to perform, and all admired the excellence of the performance in spite of this, after such a short period of study and rehearsal. Everyone on the stage, and in the orchestra, strained to thank Mozart by rewarding him with a fine rendering ... The unusually large attendance applauded its unanimous approval.'

An opera 'with no equal in the whole musical world' had completed its first stage performance, according to the contemporary historian Alfred Meissner. 'The maniacal heathen who defied God and all his angels had gone into his eternal fiery grave. A world of desire, arrogance, fear, lamentation and despair, as only Mozart could depict it, was presented to the audience and rewarded with endless applause. It was on that evening that Mozart pronounced the now famous words "My Praguers understand me", words that will always honour that generation.'

Meissner also describes the buzz among the audience as the sheet music for the overture was passed out to the orchestra at the very last minute, even as Mozart was arriving to conduct it. Given no time to rehearse this potent piece of music, the orchestra sightread it so well that Mozart is said to have whispered to the musicians near him during the introduction to the first act: 'Some of the notes went under the music-stands, it is true, but on the whole that went brilliantly.'

When Da Ponte later claimed that he had chosen the legend of Don Juan as 'a subject especially suited to Mozart's genius', he omitted to mention that in February 1787, while Mozart was away in Prague, news reached him in Vienna of the premiere in Venice of Gazzaniga's opera *Don Giovanni Tenorio o sia Il Convitato di pietra*, to a libretto by Bertati. Da Ponte immediately sent for a copy.

Mozart's and Da Ponte's *Don Giovanni*, sub-titled *Il dissoluto punito*, is a retelling of the Don Juan legend dating back to a 1630 romp by Tirso de Molina, *El burlador de Sevilla*, which had since fallen out of fashion. After versions by Molière (1665), Shadwell (1676) and Goldoni (1736), among many others, the legend of the seducer dragged down to hell had been reduced to mere vaudeville by the mid-eighteenth century; until not long before, it had been the subject of a pantomime in Vienna on All Souls' Day. Even thirty years after Mozart's and Da Ponte's celebrated version, Byron felt obliged to call his (unfinished) poem *Don Juan* an attempt to 'strip the tinsel off the sentiment'.

Although regarded with distaste by the Viennese cognoscenti, the tragi-comic theme appealed to the darker, not to say coarser side of Mozart's sense of humour. And, of course, he and Da Ponte were writing this for Prague, which was past its glory days, and whose opera audiences were less sophisticated than Vienna's. So Da Ponte made no attempt, unlike some predecessors, to 'rationalize' the story. The talking statue or 'stone guest', much derided in recent years, still comes to dinner; Don Giovanni is literally dragged down to hell.

In truth, Da Ponte's version of the Don Juan legend was not as original as he claimed; he leaned heavily on Bertati's version for Gazzaniga, among other recent reworkings of a very old theme. But Bertati's was a one-act libretto, revolving entirely around the licentious Don; where he had been reducing a source in *Figaro*, Da Ponte was expanding one in *Don Giovanni*. By filling out the other characters, Da Ponte made an old tale very much his own. In Bertati, the peasant girl Maturina (Da Ponte's Zerlina) is a major character, but her fiancé disappears early, as indeed does Anna. Da Ponte created the twin sets of lovers, Zerlina and Masetto, Anna and Ottavio, to pursue their own subplots as well as interacting with Giovanni; similarly, Elvira and Leporello have a long diversion ensuring that the action does not flag while Giovanni is offstage.

Apart from the cemetery scene and the climactic banquet, most of the Bertati material was recycled in Act I, moving some critics to bemoan the static nature of Da Ponte's second act, where each character seems to take turns to sing a solo aria amid the ensemble development. The idea of Don Giovanni and his servant swapping identities – the 'disguise' motif – was a stock *buffo* device; but Da Ponte, no doubt on Mozart's instruction, ensures that it leads to a glorious sextet. In the final scene, Bertati gave Elvira an aria about retiring to a convent after she has failed to persuade the Don to repent, then his servant (Pasquarello) another celebrating the city in which the opera is being performed (in his case, Venice). Da Ponte wisely dispensed with these – 'generating', according to Patrick Steptoe, 'the momentum and contrast that he achieved so successfully in *Le nozze di Figaro*'.

At the end of the first act comes but one of Mozart's great innovations in this work, the musical (and mathematical) miracle of having three orchestras playing simultaneously onstage during the ball scene: a minuet in G in 3/4 time, joined by a Contredanse in G in 2/4 time, then a German dance in 3/8 time. But Mozart's main achievement, perhaps, was to introduce real terror to the opera stage for the first time; by bringing trombones from the choir loft to the pit, he turned them into the instruments of hell, as the ghost of the Commendatore arrives to demand Don Giovanni's repentance, in vain, then drag him down below.

It was Da Ponte who insisted on a comic element to the tragedy, despite Mozart's initial doubts. They called it a *dramma giocoso*, a dramatic piece with some laughs. As he had in *Figaro*, Da Ponte again also borrowed from his arch-rival Casti. The catalogue aria in *Don Giovanni* is closely modelled on the list of accusations read by the chief of police to the disgraced Teodoro in *Il re Teodoro*.

In the final scene, just before the entry of Elvira, soon followed by the 'stone guest', Da Ponte and Mozart indulge in some private jokes, suggesting that, for all his licentious youth, Da Ponte may have seen himself as Leporello to Mozart's Don Giovanni, or Boswell to his Johnson. The band entertaining the dining Don strikes up a tune from his post-*Figaro* hit with Martín y Soler, which Leporello salutes with '*Bravo, Cosa Rara!*' There follows a parody of Sarti's *Fra i due litiganti* (1782) – '*Evvivano "I Litiganti!*",' exclaims Leporello – suggesting that the librettist of Sarti's forgotten opera, usually credited as anonymous, may well have been Da Ponte himself, not least because the next onstage tune is the first line of *Figaro*'s celebrated aria from *Le nozze*, 'Non più andrai, farfallone amoroso'. Leporello greets this familiar melody with the words: 'Questa poi la conosco pur troppo' ('That's a piece I know all too well'). The death of Mozart's father as he was composing *Don Giovanni* also appears to have informed this most theatrical of operas – as did the death of Shakespeare's father while he was writing *Hamlet*. In each case, the writer appears to be as haunted by the ghost as are the characters in the work.

The first night in Prague on 29 October 1787 was a triumph; Da Ponte again missed it, having returned to Vienna for the opening of his piece for Salieri. The Archduchess had left Prague before the first night of *Don Giovanni*, but Italian royalty was present at the first night, as Mozart wrote to Da Ponte: 'Our opera of *Don Giovanni* was performed last night before a glittering audience. The princess of Tuscany, with her entire entourage, was present. The success of our work was as complete as we could wish. Guardasoni came into my room this morning enraptured with joy. "Long live Mozart, long live Da Ponte," said he: "as long as they shall exist, no manager shall know distress."

'Adieu! my dear friend,' concluded Mozart's letter to Da Ponte. 'Prepare another opera for your friend Mozart!'

8

Così fan tutte

AXUR, RÈ D'ORMUS, Da Ponte's opera for Salieri, was premiered on 8 January 1788 as the climax of the three-day wedding celebrations of the Emperor's nephew, Maximilian, Prince-Archbishop of Mayence, to Elizabeth of Württemberg. Joseph had formed an especial bond with the intelligent, handsome Elizabeth, but the marriage would end tragically in barely two years; in February 1790, as Joseph lay dying, Rosenberg had the unenviable task of informing him that Elizabeth had given birth to a stillborn child, then within a few hours died herself.

The wedding was one of the last hurrahs of the crumbling Austro-Hungarian empire. One of the most splendid festivals seen in Vienna throughout Joseph's reign, it was also its swansong; his health was beginning to fail, amid political upheaval throughout Europe, which was soon to change for ever with the storming of the Bastille.

Overwhelmed by problems, not least war with the Turks, Joseph had less time for such pleasures as opera. Visits to his front-line troops meant that not until 15 December 1788, six months after its premiere, did he see *Don Giovanni* – which had proved too dark and sophisticated to please the essentially frivolous Viennese.

The Emperor sensed this in advance, as far away as the front, where he was sent reports on the progress of rehearsals by Rosenberg. Even he had to admit that the music was 'exceptional', said Rosenberg, to which the Emperor sardonically replied: 'Your taste is beginning to grow reasonable!' But Joseph goes on to muse that it would not surprise him if the opera failed in Vienna; he knows what the people like there, and the best thing for them would be to give them a year off, with no opera at all, to make the public 'more moderate in its expectations'.

Mozart had written *Don Giovanni*, he said, 'not at all for Vienna, a little for Prague, but mostly for myself and my friends'. To gratify the Vienna principals, and adjust to their different strengths, he inserted 'Mi tradì' for Donna Elvira and 'Dalla sua pace' for Don Ottavio, plus a duet for Zerlina and Leporello which is rarely performed today; he also deleted the sextet, conventionally drawing the moral of the story, with which the work closes. But still *Don Giovanni* did not please the hedonistic Viennese, who went to the opera more to laugh than to be made to think.

One account of a party at the house of an unidentified Prince R. reveals the ambivalent Viennese response to the opera:

> Most of the musical connoisseurs of Vienna were present, also Joseph Haydn. Mozart was not there. There was much talk about the new work. After the fine ladies and gentlemen had talked themselves out, some of the connoisseurs took up the work. They all admitted that it was the valuable work of a genius and was of an unlimited imagination, but for one it was too full, for another too chaotic, for a third too unmelodic, for a fourth it was uneven. Etc. In general one cannot but admit that there is something true in all these opinions. Everyone had spoken by now, except only Father Haydn. Asked at last for his opinion, this modest artist replied: 'I cannot settle the argument. But one thing I do know' – he added with great conviction – 'and that is that Mozart is the greatest composer that the world now has.' The ladies and gentlemen were silent after that.

The Emperor, too, maintained confidence in Mozart in the face of the general doubts. 'The opera is divine,' Joseph would eventually say to Da Ponte of *Don Giovanni*, 'perhaps even more beautiful than *Figaro*, but it's not food for the teeth of my Viennese.' 'We'll give them time to chew it,' Mozart told Da Ponte when he passed on this remark. But *Don Giovanni* closed, never to be performed in Vienna again in Mozart's lifetime. Joseph nevertheless appointed Mozart his Imperial and Royal Court Composer after the death of Gluck – if at a significantly lower salary. There was time for one more collaboration between Da Ponte and Salieri, *Il talismano*, adapted from Goldoni and coolly received, before the end of the 1788 season saw the Emperor reluctantly close down the opera – too costly and inappropriate, he believed, while the nation was at war.

Faced with ruin, Da Ponte hatched a plan to keep it going at no cost to the Emperor. He rounded up a list of subscribers, headed by the wealthy

Baron Gondar, and got Joseph's permission to keep the theatre open, with a full programme of operas, underwritten by wealthy Viennese opera-lovers. The singers and musicians were delighted – Da Ponte was a hero – but a jealous cabal at court, notably the musical directorate, did their best to thwart him. Again, to their dismay, Joseph interceded in Da Ponte's favour.

'It can't be done,' Rosenberg and Thorwart, the theatre's deputy director, told Da Ponte, 'it can't be done!' But Joseph scribbled a note to Rosenberg on the back of Da Ponte's plan of action: 'Count: Tell Thorwart that it *can* be done, and that I will keep the theatre personally, according to the plan of Da Ponte, whose salary is to be doubled.'

Now the plots and intrigues directed against Da Ponte intensified as he embarked on yet another love affair, perhaps his most intense yet – with a singer called Adriana del Bene, known as La Ferrarese, whose complaisant husband turned a blind eye to her string of lovers. A recent arrival in Vienna, she had made her debut there as Diana in Da Ponte's opera for Martín, *L'arbore di Diana*. Born in Ferrara circa 1755, she had studied at the Venice conservatoire and made a reputation around Europe for her dramatic versatility and the remarkable range of her voice. The English writer Charles Burney reports that La Ferrarese 'sang very well, and had an extraordinary compass of voice, as she was able to reach the highest E of harpsichords, upon which she could dwell a considerable time, in a fair, natural voice'. Mozart would soon be exploiting this to great effect.

Other contemporary accounts suggest that Adriana was not much of a singer, nor indeed a beauty; in England, where she had appeared, she was dismissed as 'a very moderate performer'. Mozart told his wife that 'Madame Allegranti is far better than Madame Ferrarese, which, I admit, is not saying much'. Joseph himself said of La Ferrarese: 'She has a rather weak contralto voice; understands music very well, but has an ugly face.'

He was wrong about her voice, which was soprano, now heard in a string of works written for her by the poet openly known to be her lover. 'Without being especially beautiful,' says Da Ponte himself, 'she entranced me with her singing; so, since she showed considerable interest in me, I ended up falling in love with her.' Never much of a musical authority, he continues: 'Her voice was a delight, her method original and wonderfully affecting; her figure was not especially pleasing nor her acting that good, but with two ravishing eyes and a seductive mouth, there were few operas in which she did not please immensely.'

La Ferrarese swiftly became popular with Viennese audiences, if not her fellow singers and the theatre management. Like Da Ponte's Venetian lovers Angiola and Angioletta, Adriana was highly strung, with a violently jealous disposition, which did her no favours. Nor did the first two Da Ponte works in which she appeared, *Il pastor fido* and *La cifra*, both by Salieri, and both soon forgotten.

When *Figaro* was revived, on 20 August 1789, Da Ponte and Mozart wrote two new arias for Ferrarese's Susanna; her Act IV aria 'Deh vieni' was replaced by the rondo 'Al desio, di chi t'adora' (K. 577) and she sang the short 'Un moto di gioia mi sento nel petto' (K. 579) in place of Susanna's Act II 'Venite inginocchiatevi'. Neither piece carried the sparkle of its predecessor. But Mozart wrote to his wife, who had gone for her health to the nearby spa of Baden, that they 'ought, I think, to be a success, provided she is able to sing them in an artless manner, which I very much doubt'.

This revival was well received, and is said to have 'reminded the Emperor of Mozart's existence'. If you believe, that is, the dubious legend that Joseph himself suggested the plot of *Così fan tutte* to Da Ponte and Mozart, based on 'incidents which had actually occurred in or near Vienna'. Joseph certainly commissioned the opera, which makes it the only Italian opera commissioned from Mozart in Vienna. But the Emperor was ill at the time, and distracted by the war with Turkey and civil unrest elsewhere around the empire. There is no mention of the piece in his memoranda to Rosenberg, which suggests that the Imperial involvement was minimal.

As with the Vienna revival of *Figaro*, it was for La Ferrarese that Da Ponte came up with the idea for his third and last great collaboration with Mozart: *Così fan tutte*, sub-titled *La scuola degli amanti*, the only original libretto among the fifty or more he wrote apart from *L'arbore di Diana*.

Vienna had recently been enjoying a vogue of 'Scuola' pieces; as well as Salieri's *La scuola de' gelosi* (1780), English plays such as Sheridan's *School for Scandal*, Hugh Kelly's *School for Wives* and Whitehead's *School for Lovers* had all been played in translation. Da Ponte had originally offered a version of the text to Salieri, but the court composer had soon abandoned setting it on the grounds that it was 'unworthy of his musical invention'. There is some evidence that Da Ponte originally named the work by its subtitle, only for Mozart to prefer the phrase sung by the three men towards the climax of the piece, which he had already used in the Act I trio of *Figaro*.

Although adapted from no single source, *Così fan tutte* is based by Da Ponte on a rich mélange of themes and traditions. The 'wager theme', or the notion of a man betting on and testing the fidelity of his beloved dates back to the thirteenth century via Boccaccio's *Decameron*, Shakespeare's *Cymbeline* and many other versions in sixteenth-century European literature. More often than not, the venture proves fatal to the relationship. Obliged to provide a *lieto fine*, Da Ponte defies convention by returning the lovers to their original suitors at the end, amid a celebratory coda from Mozart, though many latter-day directors understandably take a different view.

The worldly-wise Don Alfonso bets his young friends Ferrando and Guglielmo that they cannot trust the fidelity of the girls to whom they are betrothed, Dorabella and Fiordiligi. The two men must obey his instructions for twenty-four hours – during which they pretend to be dispatched to war, return disguised as Albanians, and woo the other's girlfriend; after initial rebuffs, each is successful to the point of marrying them, after which they promptly return as their real selves. By the conventions of *opera buffa*, there is then a happy ending, with the lovers reunited with their original partners. To later eras this seemed awkward and unconvincing, no doubt contributing to the opera's fall into obscurity for many years.

In much of this Da Ponte goes against the traditions of the 'wager theme'. The tale of an uncertain husband disguising himself, and laying (usually fatal) siege to his own wife, was reworked by such other Da Ponte icons as Boccaccio and Ariosto. That Da Ponte had in mind Cantos 42 and 43 of Ariosto's *Orlando furioso* is evident from the names of its characters Fiordiligi, Doralice and Fiordespina; he calls his Fiordiligi and Dorabella 'sisters from Ferrara' in a covert tribute to his lover Adriana, La Ferrarese, and their maid Despina. Da Ponte also seems to have drawn on Cervantes's *La novella del curioso*, in which a man loses his wife to the friend he has asked to test her virtue.

The feigned departure, return in disguise and success of the seduction by the 'pretend' lovers goes back to Da Ponte's beloved Ovid, and the myth of Cephalus and Procris – as the art historian Ernst Gombrich pointed out in 1954. 'There is the same fervour of rejection, the same insistence just to the point when fidelity gives way,' wrote Gombrich in the *Journal of the Warburg and Courtauld Institutes.* 'What is original in *Così fan tutte* is that here the plot turns round the nature of human passion itself. Da Ponte has perceived that Cephalus's test, whether cynical or not, can be viewed as an experiment about human nature.'

As with his two previous operas for Mozart, Da Ponte breaks with operatic tradition by opening the proceedings in the middle of a conversation, almost in the middle of a sentence, in high theatrical style. 'La mia Dorabella capace non è', protests Ferrando, drawing the audience immediately into the action with the assumption that Don Alfonso has already expressed the doubts about female fidelity which he later repeats. Da Ponte may have picked up the notion from Beaumarchais, whose Figaro is also in mid-measurement of the space for his marriage bed as the action opens, but it is nevertheless a device reeking of the sense of theatre he shared with Mozart, with whom he lifted the *buffa* tradition onto an entirely new plane.

Da Ponte's other crucial innovation in *Così* was to recast the 'wager' tradition with two sets of lovers, thus affording himself scope for a far greater range of contrasting emotions and human responses. He perhaps had in mind his arch-rival Casti's recent libretto for Salieri, *La grotta di Trofonio*, in which two very different sisters are mismatched with two very different suitors. He may also have learned from Choderlos de Laclos's recent (1782) novel *Les liaisons dangereuses*, with its daring portrayal of women as determined sexual predators.

But he was also drawing on the Rousseau-esque, Enlightenment ideas of his youth, which had since invaded the European imagination. To Nicholas Till, *Così fan tutte* bears 'all the hallmarks of the Rousseauist programme of education, in that it addresses the question of whether men and women are best educated to moral maturity through reason or feeling, or whether there is a sphere of moral truth that exists beyond either of these'.

Like Rousseau, after all, Da Ponte 'appears to have suffered guilty anxiety for his rejection of both the faith of his forefathers and the paternal embrace of the Catholic church. Unlike Casanova, he was not a true adventurer relishing his footloose quest for new horizons of pleasure, but a man in search of certainties.'

To Patrick Steptoe, *Così* is 'Da Ponte's finest text, well structured and paced, with a timely variation of sentiment and humour ... Da Ponte tailored his verse on a minute scale to integrate with Mozart's style. His most impressive achievements lie in the manner in which each number is paced, giving Mozart the opportunity to exploit all the dramatic possibilities of classical musical forms.'

Dorabella's 'Smanie implacabili' is, as Steptoe puts it, 'a parody of exaggerated passion as well as of *opera seria* grandiloquence'. Similarly, as Otto Jahn has pointed out, 'Ferrando's vapid sentiment was intended to inspire ridicule rather than sympathy.' In his use of Moorish disguises and the recently discredited Dr Mesmer, Da Ponte was also showing 'a detailed knowledge of recent history and theatrical fashion'.

A sublime number even by Mozart's standards is the celebrated Act I trio in which Don Alfonso joins the distraught girls in waving their lovers off to war, wishing them gentle breezes to match their fortunes. Da Ponte's concise, limpid poetry perfectly matches the mood Mozart seeks to conjure:

Soave sia il vento,	Gentle be the breeze,
Tranquilla sia l'onda	And tranquil the wave
Ed ogni elemento	And every element
Benigno risponda	Benignly respond
Ai vestri desir.	To your wishes.

Criticisms of *Così*, long regarded as both immoral and unconvincing, revolve largely around the quest for realism at the expense of the *opera buffa* tradition. The happy ending was incumbent upon Da Ponte, however improbable.

Mozart's first biographer, Franz Xaver Niemetschek, suggests that the composer was 'commanded' to write the piece by Joseph, and could not refuse because he needed the money. Why else would Mozart have set so louche and immoral a libretto? 'Everyone wondered why that great intellect could so have demeaned himself by wasting his sweet and heavenly melodies on such a worthless and trashy libretto. But it did not lie in his power to refuse the commission ...'

Even Mozart's wife Constanze disapproved of the morality of the piece. 'She did not admire the plot of *Così fan tutte*,' reported her English musician friend Vincent Novello, long after Mozart's death, 'but agreed with me that such music would carry any piece through ...'

*

When Joseph returned to Vienna from his military travels in November 1789, it was clear to all that he was far from well, perhaps dying. Da Ponte and Mozart knew what would happen to their opera if Joseph died before it was ready, so they worked at full speed even by their own remarkable standards. By the end of December, vocal rehearsals had begun; on 29 December, when Haydn was returning to Vienna from Esterhazy, Mozart wrote to their mutual friend Michael Puchberg:

> Tomorrow evening there can be nothing at our house – I have too much work ... Thursday (31 December), however, I invite you (but just you alone) to come to me at 10 o'clock in the morning, for a small opera rehearsal. Only you and Haydn are invited. Then I'll tell you a *viva voce* about all the cabals of Salieri, which however have come to nothing ...

Salieri was irritated that Mozart was setting the Da Ponte text he had himself rejected. But the cabals against Mozart and Da Ponte were really, as always, fuelled by jealousy. In the existing political climate of Vienna, according to the musicologist Michael Robinson, Mozart was 'an outsider':

> a man who although recognized as possessing exceptional talent did not have the right qualifications (because not an Italian, and not recognized by the Italian musical world as its equal) to become pre-eminent among the opera composers commissioned by the court. How was he to establish his rightful place among them? Naturally he had to show that he understood all the conventions of Italian comic opera and work within these conventions. But this was not enough. Not only had he to compose like an Italian; he had to do better than most Italians to obtain equal status with them.

H. C. Robbins Landon sums up the consequences: 'Between 22 April 1783, when the Italian opera opened again, and 25 January 1790, the eve of the third Mozart–Da Ponte opera, *Così fan tutte*, fifty-nine *opere buffe* were performed in Vienna. Among the German composers represented, Mozart was by far the most successful, with twenty performances of *Le nozze di Figaro* and fifteen of *Don Giovanni*, but in terms of popularity Mozart lagged far behind the most successful composers of Italian opera: Sarti (ninety-one performances), Martín y Soler (105), Cimarosa (124), Salieri (138) and Paisiello (166).' During Mozart's lifetime, moreover, not one of his Italian operas was given complete in England, France, Russia, Spain, Portugal or Italy.

On 20 January 1790, a few weeks after filling in Haydn and Puchberg on Salieri's plots against him and *Così*, Mozart writes again to Puchberg: 'Tomorrow is the first orchestral rehearsal in the theatre. Haydn will go with me – if your affairs allow of it, and if perhaps you would like to attend the rehearsal, you need only have the goodness to come to me tomorrow morning at 10 o'clock and we will go together ...'

La Ferrarese – at best a mediocre singer, as acknowledged by everyone but Da Ponte – was the original Fiordiligi in this comedy of amorous errors, in which Da Ponte's innate cynicism is tempered by the themes of love and forgiveness in Mozart's sublime music. First performed at the Burgtheater on 26 January 1790, it went down well in Vienna; even Count Zinzendorf, who had been 'bored' by *Figaro*, said, 'The music by Mozart is charming, and the subject rather amusing.'

But *Così* fared less well with posterity, which has considered its subject-matter vulgar, frivolous, absurd or plain immoral. For a century and more it was bowdlerized to suit nineteenth-century morality; in Germany bastardized versions were performed under such titles as *Love and Temptation; Women's Constancy, or the Girls from Flanders; The Wager, or The Love and Artfulness of Women*. Even in Vienna itself, only a dozen years after its premiere in 1802, it was revived as *The Two Aunts from Milan, or The Disguise*. It premiered in London in 1811, in barely recognizable shape, under the title *Tit for Tat, or the Tables Turned*. The opera was not performed in New York until 1922.

Not until the 1930s did a celebrated Glyndebourne production by Carl Ebert, conducted by Fritz Busch, win *Così* its rightful place in the Mozart–Da Ponte pantheon alongside *Figaro* and *Don Giovanni*. The English conductor Sir Thomas Beecham described the score as 'a long summer day spent in a cloudless land by a southern sea'; and by the 1970s the musicologist Richard Rickett spoke for many, perhaps a majority, when he wrote: 'From a purely musical point of view, *Così fan tutte* is arguably Mozart's finest opera.'

But so limited was the success of *Così* in his lifetime that Da Ponte barely mentions it in his memoirs. While boasting that it was his words which had enabled Mozart's music to ring round the world, he stubbornly uses his own original title when naming *La scuola degli'amanti* – 'an opera that holds third place among the three sisters born of that

most celebrated father of harmony' – only in the context of his love for
La Ferrarese.

Joseph II never saw the opera he had commissioned. By the time of its
first night, on 26 January 1790, he was dying. In the early hours of
20 February, Da Ponte was among a group of loyalists waiting in an
antechamber when the end came.

Perhaps the most intelligent of all the Habsburgs – 'without the
eccentricity of a Ludwig of Bavaria or the egomania of a Louis XIV', in
the words of the Harvard historian Aram Bakshian Jr – Joseph had been
'the ideal patron for a clever, gifted artist like Da Ponte ... So long as
Joseph lived, Lorenzo was a significant figure in the artistic life of Vienna.'
His demise could only spell trouble for Da Ponte.

A complex, enlightened man, but an unpopular monarch, Joseph was
mourned by few – but Da Ponte was foremost among those few. As he
composed an ode on the Emperor's death, he might well have been
concerned for his future; but he could not know that his enemies at court
were already persuading Joseph's successor – his brother Leopold, the
former Archduke of Tuscany, a typically embittered younger sibling with
few fond memories of his brother – that the Imperial Poet had been
plotting against him.

It was an unlikely scenario, justified mainly by Da Ponte's conspicuous
devotion to Joseph, which did him no favours with the new Emperor,
understandably impatient to be rid of his predecessor's favourites. Da
Ponte had made enough enemies to render null and void an ingratiating
Ode he addressed to the new Emperor – who had no time to read it,
anyway.

There was a brief diversion in 1791, when Prince Adam Auersperg
commissioned Da Ponte to write a cantata to mark the visit of the King
of Naples to Vienna. The result was *Il tempio de Flora*, to music by Joseph
Weigl; performed in the garden of the Prince's palace, this standard
eighteenth-century confection about Venus and Apollo seems to have
gone down well, for the Prince rewarded Da Ponte handsomely.

He could have benefited from another commission for the same occasion, but his habitual hauteur instead made him a powerful new enemy.
The Neapolitan ambassador, the Marquis de Gallo, had also commissioned
a cantata for his monarch's visit – from the Abbé Sertafini, to music by
the second-rate Piticchio. When Serafini's work proved inadequate, the

Marquis turned to Da Ponte, who was happy enough to carry out the commission – but disgusted by the pay, which he gave back to the servant who had brought it. Embarrassed by his own meanness, the ambassador gave Da Ponte a gold watch, which he in turn gave to La Ferrarese, the muse who had 'inspired' his verses. For this, the Marquis never forgave him.

Thanks to the closure of the opera for two months of court mourning, *Così fan tutte* enjoyed only four performances; there were just five more when it reopened in April, before it fell out of the repertoire. When La Ferrarese's contract became due for renewal, she had made so little impact in Vienna that only one man was keen on renewing it: her lover, Da Ponte, who argued her case high and low, infuriating those few who were not already his enemies. Adriana's own personality did not help. Even Da Ponte conceded that she had 'an impulsive, violent disposition, rather calculated to irritate the malevolent than to win friendships'.

So much fuss did Da Ponte make that the row came to the notice of the new Emperor, who had more important matters to deal with than operatic gossip. Outraged by reports of Da Ponte's affair with La Ferrarase, fed to him by the librettist's enemies, Leopold II is said to have declared: 'To the devil with this disturber of the peace!'

Now, as Ferrarese's contract was not renewed, the Emperor was told that Da Ponte was engaging in black propaganda: writing anonymously to the new singers engaged for the following season, trying to discourage them from coming to Vienna by telling all sorts of dark untruths about the state of the city in general and its opera in particular. The truth of the matter remains uncertain; what is quite clear is that Da Ponte had never been so universally unpopular in Vienna, and that he had lost his greatest ally, Joseph, in his battles with the theatre directorate. Now he had incurred the displeasure of his successor.

Realizing his days in Vienna were numbered, Da Ponte began to cast around Europe for another job. His friend Martín, who had gone to Russia two years before as Director of the Italian Opera in St Petersburg, suggested he join him there. Da Ponte accepted with alacrity, and handed in his notice to the Imperial Theatre. It was almost up, anyway. But there were a few months to go, and his resignation was not immediately accepted; by the time the bureaucracy had agreed to his release, the post in St Petersburg had been filled.

Now Da Ponte tried to persuade Mozart to go with him to London, where Italian opera flourished under the management of their friends Stephen Storace and Michael Kelly. Though seriously tempted, Mozart was preoccupied by a new comic opera he was writing with his masonic friend Emanuel Schikaneder, *Die Zauberflöte*, and asked for a while to think it over.

It is unclear whether, in the end, Da Ponte resigned or was fired from his job as poet to the Imperial Theatre. There is some evidence that he was given five months' salary in lieu of notice. Uncertain which way to turn, he hung around in Vienna for a while, seemingly paralysed. When his opera *Axur* was revived with a new cast, he went along to see it – only to find himself forbidden entry to the theatre where he had worked for the best part of ten years. The order came, he was told, from its deputy director, Thorwart.

Friends like Prince Adam Auersperg offered to intercede on his behalf, but even Da Ponte by now realized there was little point. His heady decade in Vienna was over, in the least dignified style possible. Rosenberg had been replaced as Director of the Imperial Theatre by Count Ugarte, who disliked him even more. His vain campaign for La Ferrarese had alienated many of the singers and theatre staff. Now, it seems, bruised by being barred from the theatre, he wrote an ironic letter in the most florid blank verse to Leopold, flavouring his complaints with the boldness of a new Figaro: 'My destiny does not depend on you; with all your power, you have no rights over my soul . . .'

Leopoldo, sei re, Giustizia imploro,	Leopold, you are King, I beg Justice,
Grazia non vo'. So che la prima è questa	Mercy I do not desire. I know that this is prime
Di tue virtù; ma buon voler sovente	Among your virtues; but goodwill is often
Non basta all'uom, ed uom tu sei, soggetto	Not enough for men, and you are a man, subject
Com'altri a frode, anzi più ch'altri ancora,	Like all men to deceit, perhaps even more than others.
Se nessun come te, perchè re sei,	Nobody like you, because you are King,
Schiera d'adulator circonda è cinge,	Is surrounded by such a multitude of sycophants,

E di fallaci consiglier, che il vero

Cercan velar o colorire in parte

Col vil pennello d'interesse. Avvezzo

All'arti di regnare, è ver, tu aguzzi.

Il linceo sguardo e il rapido intelletto

All'esame dei cor; ma troppi sono

Gli insidiator, son troppi, a me lo credi,

E forse più chi men ti par. Or odi

Quel che un labbro sincero, il più sincero

Che vanti il regno tuo, del solio al piede

Impavido depone, e sprezza poi

Quanto da opinione e da fortuna

Nascer può di sinistro. Il mio destino

Non dipende da te, chè non ha dritto

Tutta la tua possanza e tutta quella

Dei possibili re sull'alma mia.

S'io non sentomi reo, se coscienza

Non parla contra me, posso adorarti,

Posso amar il tuo nome e tue virtudi,

Ma temerti non posso. Or cangia aspetto,

And treacherous advisers who are

Trying to conceal the truth or partly

Colour it with the vile brush of interest.

You are used to the art of governing, it is true,

You have sharpened your lynx-like look and quick mind

In the examination of hearts; but too many,

Too numerous are the tempters, trust me,

And perhaps more than you may believe. Now listen

To what these sincere lips, the most sincere

That your kingdom can boast, lays at your feet

Fearlessly, and scorns the evil

That comes from opinions and from fortunes

Born of evil. My fate

does not depend on you,
     Because all your power,

and all the powers of possible kings,

Have no rights over my soul.

If I do not feel guilty, if my conscience

Does not speak against me, I can love,

I can adore your name and your virtues,

But I cannot fear you. Now change your appearance,

Spoglia la maestà, che spesso il corso
Dell'eloquente verità ritarda.
E resti l'uom, resti l'uom sol. Son corsi
Dieci anni omai che del Danubia l'onda
Io bevo. Al tuo Giuseppe affatto ignoto
Il mio nominee non fu. Proterva schiera
A' mei danni tentò qual ch'ora cerca,

Leopoldo, con te. Macchia non prende
Aurea onestà. Trionfator rimasi;
Mi sostenne l'eroe; fu scudo ei solo
Dell'innocenza mia: non già di quella
Che scaltra prende l'apparenza e il nome,
E sotto un manto ingannator asconde
Cabala, invidia, tradimento, frode,
Mal talento, calunnia, a regi e a regni
Egualmente fatal; ma della vera

D'angelo no, ma d'uom. Con questa guida
A te vengo, a te parlo ed ho diritto
Che tu mo'oda e mi creda, osando offrirti

Shed your majesty, which often delays
The course of eloquent truth.
And let the man be, just let the man be. For some
Ten years now I have been drinking the Danube waters;
To your Joseph my name

Was not completely unknown. Despite those
Who tried to damage my reputation. And are now trying to do so with you,
Leopold. But golden honesty

Cannot be stained. I remain triumphant;
The hero within sustained me, the hero shielded
My innocence, not the innocence
Which is innocence only in name,
Which under a deceiving cloak hides
Cabals, envy, treachery, fraud
Lack of talent, calumny, to kings and kingdoms
Equally fatal; but in truth (the innocence)

Not of angels, but of men. With this advice
I come to you, I speak to you, and I have the right
To be listened to and believed, daring to offer

Per fido ostaggio e libertade e vita;	As your hostage my freedom and my life,
Una vita che ancor cara mi sembra,	A life which is still precious to me,
Perché scevra di colpe a perché spero,	Because free from guilt and because I hope
Spendendola per te, ch'ella diventi	That spending it on your behalf, it will become
Utile al giusto, al traditor funesta.	Useful for the just, fatal to the betrayer.

As if this were not enough – and it was said to have profoundly offended the new Emperor – Da Ponte composed and circulated a highly indiscreet satire on Leopold. It does not survive, alas, but reading it led Zaguri to pen the *locus classicus* on Da Ponte's capacity for being his own worst enemy. Writing to their mutual friend Casanova on 11 June 1791, Zaguri said: 'I have read those verses by Da Ponte. He carries within him, and will always carry, a canker which eats away all the roots of his good fortune. I had hardly read the verses when I exclaimed: "It's too bad. It's too much! He deserves one thing only – contempt." II y a des choses qui ne piquent point à force d'être extrêmes.'

Da Ponte makes no mention of this verse in his memoirs, and always emphatically denied writing it. So what had Zaguri read? And why else, on the first day of the new opera season, did its purported author hear news which cannot have been unexpected? As he had been from Venice ten years before, Lorenzo Da Ponte was now formally banished from Vienna.

9

The Married Man

OZART GAVE serious thought to the idea of going to
London with Da Ponte. 'Give me six months,' the composer
asked when his desperate librettist pleaded with him. The
failure of *Così fan tutte* in Vienna had moved Mozart to lose patience
with courtly operagoers and turn towards the bourgeois culture of
suburban theatres such as the Freihaus-Theater auf der Wieden,
run by his Masonic friend, the actor-manager Emanuel Schikaneder.
Together they were working on an idealistic vaudeville piece called *Die
Zauberflöte* (*The Magic Flute*). When he had finished this, Mozart assured
Da Ponte, he might certainly go with him to seek a better welcome in
London.

But Mozart would not live to see that day. Within six months of
writing *Die Zauberflöte*, he was dead, at the age of thirty-five. During the
two years left to him after *Così fan tutte*, he travelled to Berlin, in hope
(again vain) of a post; to Frankfurt in 1790, to play at Leopold's coronation;
and to Prague, in the last year of his life, for the premiere of his opera *La
clemenza di Tito*, to a libretto adapted from Metastasio by Da Ponte's old
friend Mazzola, his successor as theatre poet. Otherwise Mozart stayed
in Vienna, where he enjoyed one last but very different kind of success
with *Die Zauberflöte* – in which the central role of Pamina was sung
by young Nancy Gottlieb, the original Barbarina in *Figaro*, now all of
seventeen.

Already Mozart was dying of the mysterious illness that would kill
him, five minutes after midnight on 5 December 1791, while he lay writing
his Requiem to a commission from a mysterious stranger. The house in
Vienna where Mozart died, Rauensteingasse 8, was later, inexplicably,

torn down; in its place there now stands a plate-glass department store called Steffl, with only a small plaque to mark the site's significance.

The next day, Mozart was buried in suburban Vienna in an unmarked communal grave. Da Ponte, too, would end up in an unmarked grave, five thousand miles to the west in another continent, another world. But he had plenty of living to do yet. Although six years older than Mozart, Da Ponte would outlive him by nearly half a century.

At the time of Mozart's death, in December 1791, Da Ponte was exiled in Trieste – broke, unemployed and wretched. 'Trieste, the usual refuge of those in disgrace' was how Zaguri described the prosperous Adriatic port, technically part of the Austrian empire but close enough to the Venetian border to be thoroughly Italian in its tastes, habits and way of life. The wisecrack certainly applied to Da Ponte at this miserable mid-point of his life; in vain he had spent six months trying to clear his name in Vienna and win the new Emperor's permission to return.

He had lingered in Vienna for six weeks after his banishment; the Emperor had left town, and Da Ponte was engaged in frantic efforts to negotiate a return to Venice, despite the three years still remaining on his sentence of exile. Though living there in conditions of great secrecy – the Viennese press had already announced his departure – he was even writing and rewriting arias and recitatives for Benucci, Calvesi and Tomeoni while awaiting news from his half-brother Agostino, whom he had asked to represent his interests back home.

Alas, he had asked the wrong man. Agostino had a track record almost as chequered as his own; deeply in debt, an absentee father and scandalous womanizer, Agostino was the last person likely to win Da Ponte a reprieve. Sure enough, word came from Venice in mid-April that the Council of Ten had rejected his application. By the end of the month, Da Ponte had finally left Vienna for the nearby mountain village of Brühl-bei-Mödling.

'What torture it was to find myself alone!' he recalled years later. His first day in this second exile had been the worst of his life, precipitating another bout of self-pity:

Sacrificed to the hatred, envy and self-interest of rogues, driven out of a city where I had lived by the honest rewards of my abilities for eleven years, abandoned by friends to whom I had so often shown signal acts of kindness, censured, execrated and reviled by the idle, by

hypocrites and by my victorious enemies, and, finally, driven out of a
theatre which owed its very existence to my efforts – there were times
I was on the verge of taking my own life.

For once, his complaints were not entirely paranoid. There is no doubt
that a cabal had conspired against Da Ponte, and were glad to see the
back of him; while taking solace in the knowledge of his own innocence,
he became obsessed with finding a way to persuade the new Emperor that
the charges against him were false.

In the first few wretched days of his exile, two loyal friends (whom he
does not name) took the risk of coming to visit him, urging him to await
Leopold's return from Italy and seek an audience to clear his name, maybe
even winning a return to Vienna. Soon he was seeking the help of a third
friend named Thaddäus Steiber, a soldier-turned-spy who seemed willing
to help. Through Steiber Da Ponte managed to get two documents to the
Emperor, a fulsome letter protesting his innocence, and a detailed account
of the conspiracy against him. Steiber even came to a secret rendezvous
with Da Ponte, to assure him that he had checked out all his allegations,
found them proven, and told the Emperor so.

Steiber also risked telling Leopold that he had seen Da Ponte. 'I swear
that Your Majesty could not have seen and heard him without being
deeply moved. He looked like a madman, and repeated a hundred times
that no grief could be greater than to know himself forever rejected by
Your Majesty, that his earthly well-being would thereby vanish for the
rest of his life, and that he would drag his father and brothers into
misfortune with him.'

It was very much to Da Ponte's advantage in this crisis that all these
years he had been supporting his father and younger siblings back in
Ceneda, regularly sending them money – as confirmed by Viennese emis-
saries now sent there to check. By this stage, it seems, Da Ponte was more
anxious to clear his name, and restore his reputation, than to cling to any
realistic hopes of getting his job back. But his concern for his dependants
was genuine enough to impress those whose help he sought.

One night in May he was dragged from his bed by two police agents,
who escorted him into Vienna without a word of explanation and left him
alone for two hours 'wondering whether I was to be sent to prison or to
the gallows'. When he asked on whose orders they were acting, the reply
came: 'From him who is all-powerful.' The next thing he knew, Da

Ponte was ordered to leave the capital and all neighbouring towns within twenty-four hours. This command came from 'the chief'.

A desperate Da Ponte was allowed to speak to the court president, Count Sarau, to whom he repeated his protestations of innocence. An honourable man, Sarau told him that he was only acting on orders; no charges had been laid against Da Ponte; no evidence of wrongdoing had been placed before the tribunal of which he was president. But Da Ponte had made powerful enemies in Vienna. They had blackened his name at court, especially with the new Empress, and his case looked hopeless.

At Da Ponte's request, Sarau asked the Emperor's son Francis, regent in his father's absence, for leave for the poet to remain in Vienna one more week. This was granted, along with the advice that Da Ponte should then return to Trieste, and await Leopold's arrival on his way back to Vienna, in the hope of an audience to plead his case. Francis, too, was only acting on orders; this was not the last occasion on which he would show kindness to the increasingly desperate exile.

By the end of June Da Ponte had left Vienna, returning to Trieste with yet another woman in tow. Here he lived in hope of seeing Leopold, who duly arrived ten days later. Many an audience was granted, but not to the exiled poet. On hearing that the Emperor was attending a performance of *Lo studente bizzarro*, Da Ponte went along too, in the hope of catching his eye. This he managed, but not with the result he had hoped for. Leopold was 'astonished and outraged to see him at the theatre', breaking the terms of his banishment from Vienna and all neighbouring towns, their mutual friend Pittoni told Casanova. 'He told me it was not to be tolerated. This man was a rogue, who had been banished from Vienna on his orders.'

Help was at hand in the shape of the Governor of Trieste, Count Pompeo Brigido, whom Da Ponte had shrewdly befriended on his arrival. Brigido told the Emperor that the poet's only reason for being in Trieste was to seek an audience, in the hope of refuting the charges against him. After flatly refusing to grant any such audience, Leopold abruptly changed his mind, sending Prince Lichtenstein to command the Abbé Da Ponte to attend upon him at 11 a.m. the next day.

When an excited Da Ponte entered the Imperial presence, burning to pour out his grievances, he found Leopold with his back towards him, staring out of the window. Sensibly, he bit his tongue and waited for the Emperor to turn his way.

'May one ask', Leopold began frostily, 'why Signor Da Ponte never came to see the Emperor Leopold in Vienna?'

'Because Your Majesty would not receive me.'

'I sent word that you could come to me freely at any time.'

'I was told that Your Majesty had no time to see me.'

'That is so, when you asked for a private audience.'

'My innocence had a right to hope for one from Your Majesty.'

'If you were innocent, you would have found some way of letting me know it. You know where I live.'

After this inauspicious start, Da Ponte was permitted to give his version of the events leading up to his banishment, laying particular blame on the conduct of his 'enemies' Rosenberg, Salieri, Thorwart and the new theatre director, Ugarte. Gradually the ice between Emperor and poet melted; at first indifferent, Leopold was soon listening with an interest that suggested more sympathy. He had reservations of his own, which he expressed with surprising candour, about the names on Da Ponte's blacklist. Eventually he declared: 'I now see that you aren't the man they want me to think you.'

'Oh, I am not, Sire!' replied an impassioned Da Ponte. 'As God is my witness, I am not!'

Leopold was finally persuaded of Da Ponte's innocence of the accusations against him, but not yet ready for him to return to Vienna. It was too soon, he told the dismayed poet, who was still on his knees begging for permission to return as the only way of providing for his family in Ceneda.

'I know how generous you are to your family,' said Leopold with approval. But it was, he repeated, too soon for Da Ponte to return to Vienna. His reputation was still tarnished, but he could rely on Leopold himself to rehabilitate him. For the present, he must stay in Trieste, send news of himself, and await the Emperor's pleasure.

Still Da Ponte remained on his knees, imploring the Emperor to reconsider. Three times Leopold told him to rise, but each time the poet stayed put, desperately repeating his mantra that anything but his return to Vienna would be a victory for his enemies.

At the fourth attempt, when Da Ponte still would not stand, the Emperor offered his hand to help him up, saying, 'I believe you have been wronged, and I promise that amends shall be made.' He then asked if there was anything else Da Ponte wished for.

'No, Sire. It is enough for me that my name is deserving of the remembrance of a monarch busied in matters of so much greater importance, and that Your Majesty should deign to believe that the perhaps excessive ardour I have shown today arises from nothing but consciousness of the outrageous treatment I have received at the hands of my enemies.'

'I believe it, and will forgive everything,' replied Leopold, who was eager to move on. 'Now listen,' he continued. 'I have had letters today from Vienna telling me that affairs at the theatre are going very badly, that there is nothing but trouble and intrigues between the singers. I wish you would suggest how all this can be sorted out.'

Da Ponte replied at length, repeating the very suggestions he had already made in Vienna, while the Emperor meekly took notes. This lasted all of an hour. The audience ended with Leopold asking Da Ponte if he needed money – an offer the impoverished poet was too proud (or, as even he concedes, too foolish) to accept. The various accounts of the meeting – including Da Ponte's, which for once can be largely believed – agree on two facts: that it lasted ninety minutes in all, and resulted in the removal of the Abbé Da Ponte's name from the police blacklist.

On his return to Vienna the following week, Leopold proved as good as his word. Thorwart and Lattanzi were both dismissed from the opera house, swiftly followed by Ugarte, who was also strongly advised to leave Vienna. The Bussanis sank into obscurity, denied leading roles, and eventually moved on in 1794. Even Salieri's fortunes flagged under his old patron Joseph's successor; by the following year, he too had moved on, replaced as court composer by his assistant and sometime pupil, Joseph Weigl.

For several months Da Ponte kicked his heels in Mödling. After ten glittering years in the capital, this dismal spell back in a small, suburban town proved the latest low point in his forty-two-year life. The news of Mozart's death, in December 1791, spelt the end of his plans to team up and go to London, where their friends Kelly and Storace were managing an opera house. Frustrated in his hopes of returning to Venice or Vienna, his thoughts had begun to rove elsewhere.

The Vienna option did not last long, despite his rapprochement with the Emperor, who even asked his advice about Thorwart's replacement. Da Ponte made the mistake of suggesting his close friend Giuseppe

Lucchesi, a Trieste lawyer who had fed and housed him in his hours of need; when he heard nothing back, he declared himself confirmed in his belief that Leopold, though himself a decent and fair-minded man, was 'surrounded by evil advisers, and a horde of sycophants who betray as much as they obey him'. Even Steiber, Da Ponte's loyal intermediary and advocate, soon fell out of favour with the Emperor. The final blow came when Casti passed through Trieste and advised him to seek a position in Russia, England or France.

'But the Emperor has promised to recall me,' protested Da Ponte.

'The Emperor will not keep his word,' replied Casti, confiding that he himself was en route to Vienna to take up the position of Caesarean Poet. After a brief spell with Mazzola as caretaker, Bertati was to be appointed poet to the Imperial Theatres.

And so it proved. As his hopes of a return to Vienna receded, Da Ponte became involved in a last, desperate throw in the direction of Venice. La Ferrarese had clearly failed to represent his interests there, as she had promised. His former mistress, he now learned, had fallen for yet another man; Da Ponte's only consolation, as he wrote to Casanova, was that at last he was freed from 'the shameful passion that for three whole years has enslaved me to this wretched woman'.

But a document seriously damaging to La Ferrarese's husband, Luigi del Bene, had come Da Ponte's way – whether from his faithless wife or elsewhere we do not know. This he now proceeded to exploit in the most shameless way. The son of the Papal vice-consul in Venice, who had never approved of his marriage, del Bene sought to inherit his father's job on his death in early 1791; in a letter to the Pope applying for the position, he offered to act as a spy supplying the Vatican with confidential information about the Venetian government. Through an intermediary in Trieste, Da Ponte now offered to share the contents of this highly incriminating document with the Venetian authorities, in the hope that it might win him a pardon.

Despite some cloak-and-dagger dealings, including secret meetings with shadowy go-betweens, he appeared to be making as little progress as he had in Vienna. Response from Venice came there none. By now reduced to selling his clothes to survive, and to support the mystery woman he had brought with him from Vienna, Da Ponte was reduced to the desperate act of a letter direct to the Venetian Inquisitors, enclosing the document (with which he had hitherto refused to part), while throwing

himself on their mercy, with abject protestations of his love for his homeland and his longing to return.

The ploy worked in one respect; del Bene was not appointed consul.
He and his wife now severed relations with Da Ponte for good. But he
received no acknowledgement, let alone thanks, least of all a pardon, from
the Venetian authorities. Quite the reverse, as they chose to leak the source
of their information. Proof that Da Ponte's double-dealing rebounded with
a vengeance can be found in a letter from Zaguri to Casanova that October:

'If it is true that Da Ponte remains banished, and that he is capable of
acting as an informer, God knows where he will go and cause trouble
next. He was passionately in love with La Ferrarese; he told me he had
sacrificed everything for her sake; she dumped him and is not in touch
with him any more.' This seems to have precipitated a break between Da
Ponte and Zaguri, who writes to Casanova the following January: 'Da
Ponte doesn't write to me any more. La Ferrarese, to whom I have spoken,
says he has gone mad.'

In December 1791, the month Mozart died, a tragedy called *Il menenzio*
was playing in Trieste to packed houses – three thousand people over five
performances. Begun by Girolamo Da Ponte, it had been finished by
his brother Lorenzo, at the insistence of four influential Trieste friends
concerned for his welfare. For a while, at least it would have saved him
from writing the begging letters of which he gives an example in his
memoirs.

To a wealthy banker acquaintance in Naples, whom Da Ponte had
housed and fed (so he says) in his own hour of need:

My dear Signor Piatti,
    I am in need of a hundred piastres. If you will lend me that sum, I
will repay you in two to three months. There is no need for me to say
more, I believe, to obtain this small favour of you. Yours, L. D. P.

My dear Signor Da Ponte,
    The man who lends his money to a friend nearly always loses both
his money and his friend. I do not wish to lose either.
Yours, D. P.

With what relish does Da Ponte remind us that, shortly thereafter,
Domenico Piatti 'died young, and not in his bed'. An adherent of the
short-lived Parthenopean Republic in Naples, set up by the French repub-

lican forces, Piatti was arrested on the return of the Bourbons and executed on 20 August 1799.

No wonder, with his future still so uncertain, Da Ponte was eager to avoid more such humiliations. The following month, January 1792, saw a new version of *L'ape musicale*, an entertainment he had written in Vienna for La Ferrarese, staged in Trieste by a visiting opera company, with Da Ponte co-producing and his brother Paolo singing the second *mezzo carattere*. This, too, was well received.

But such financial relief as its success afforded did not last long; now, at last, Da Ponte decided it was time to move on, well away from Venice and Vienna. After considering St Petersburg, where there was a thriving community of exiled Italian artists and musicians, he sought the advice of Casanova, who suggested Rome or Madrid. His one worldly asset being a letter of introduction from the late Emperor to his sister, Marie-Antoinette – 'Antoinette', Joseph had told him, 'loves your *Cosa rara*' – Da Ponte decided to ignore him and head for Paris.

Remembering the new Emperor's offer of financial assistance, he asked Casti to tell Leopold of his decision to travel west, and seek his help. When no reply came, he appealed direct to the Emperor. Still no reply, so Da Ponte headed back to Vienna one last time in the hope of arguing his case in person.

He arrived in March 1792 to find that Leopold was dead, suddenly and unexpectedly, at the age of forty-four. His successor was Francis, the eldest of his eight sons (and sixteen children), who had already treated Da Ponte with decency. While not retracting his banishment, Francis gave him permission to stay in Vienna long enough to see proofs of his innocence published in the Austrian press. He also granted him enough money not only to travel to Paris, but to pay off all his debts in Vienna. It is with some feeling that Da Ponte writes, within a year of his friend Mozart's last opera *La clemenza di Tito*, of 'the clemency with which the new Emperor consoled and alleviated my misery in Vienna'.

He stayed three weeks, during which he enjoyed snubbing his perceived 'enemies' by refusing to receive them, and revelled as word of his rehabilitation spread. He especially enjoyed a confrontation with Bertati, who seemed out of his depth in the job of theatre poet (and was indeed replaced in three years by Giovanni de Gamerra). He also steered well clear of La Ferrarese and her ruined husband.

Once back in Trieste, Da Ponte's preparations for the journey to Paris were interrupted only by an unexpected development which took him as much by surprise as it did all who had ever known him.

After the humiliations of his entanglement with La Ferrarese, Da Ponte had fretted that he would never fall in love again. But he was, he now discovered, quite wrong. 'My heart was not, and perhaps still is not, capable of existing without love; and for all the deceptions and betrayals I have known at the hands of women in the course of my life, in truth I do not remember having passed six months in all that time without being in love – with, I will boast, a single-hearted devotion.'

An English girl had arrived in Trieste, Ann Celestine Ernestine Grahl, known as 'Nancy', the daughter of a wealthy merchant whom Da Ponte strategically befriended. Nancy's father was born in Dresden, and her mother was French; but the Grahls had spent many years living in England, where Nancy had passed the first sixteen years of her life, converting from Judaism to the Anglican church. Then the family had travelled through France, Germany and Holland, where Nancy had spent some time as tutor to the children of a General van den Butzeler. She was multilingual, and reputed to be a great beauty, known in Trieste as 'la bella Inglesina'.

Da Ponte was anxious to meet this new arrival, who 'was said by all, apart from her beauty, to unite agreeable manners with all the charms of a cultivated mind'. But Nancy was not living with her parents, to whose house he was a frequent visitor; she was staying nearby with English friends. When his chance finally came, 'la bella Inglesina' was wearing a veil, which concealed her face, thus preventing him from checking out reports of her beauty. So he decided to play one of his little tricks.

'Mademoiselle,' he addressed her, 'you are not wearing your veil in the fashionable style.'

'And what is that?' she enquired demurely.

'This way, Signorina,' said Da Ponte, boldly taking the edge of her veil and lifting it up over her head.

Nancy, it seems, was not amused; she stalked out of the room. For several days she did not show her face, to Da Ponte's dismay, though he was assured by her family that her wrath would soon fade. Her father and brother, John Grahl and his son Peter, were expert if itinerant chemists, trading in drugs, spices, liquors and medicines, with a sideline as distillers and moneylenders, speculating in loans, discounts, mortgages and property. They had arrived in Trieste, according to an advert in the *Osservatore Triestino*, to sell goods ranging from English and French jewellery, gold watches and chains to knives, scissors and buckles, even artificial flowers and ostrich feathers. They may have been wealthy at the time, or have seemed it, but the records show that the following year they went bankrupt.

This was of minimal concern at the time to Da Ponte, who could sense a killing for himself in these exotic arrivals. He told Nancy's father that a rich Italian friend of his named Galliano, living in Vienna, had expressed the wish to marry an Englishwoman. Might he act as go-between? After satisfying himself as to Galliano's age, character and means, Grahl consented – as, it seems, did Nancy, for portraits were exchanged to the apparent satisfaction of both parties, and negotiations continued pending a meeting.

As they proceeded, Da Ponte and Nancy spent many an evening together, he perfecting her Italian, she polishing his French with Paris in mind. If she had not forgotten the incident of the veil, she seems to have forgiven it, for both soon found that they were falling in love. Nothing was said, because of the contract with Da Ponte's Viennese friend, but each could read something in the other's eyes.

Da Ponte could not believe his luck. 'I never felt it possible that she could feel even the beginnings of love for me, not only because I was twenty years older than her, but I was poor while she was the daughter of a rich father, with many admirers aspiring to her hand in marriage – all of them younger and wealthier than me.'

He also lived in daily apprehension of Galliano's arrival to claim Nancy as his bride. But Da Ponte's luck, for once, was in. He visited the family one evening to find Nancy's father outraged by a letter from his would-be son-in-law demanding a substantial dowry. And Grahl had no doubt noticed the bond that seemed to be developing between Nancy and the charming Italian poet. With a cry of 'Hah, Signor Galliano would marry my money, not my daughter, would he?', Grahl tore the letter into shreds and hurled it in the fire. Then he turned to the visitor and said, 'Friend Da Ponte, will you take her?'

'Whom?' enquired Da Ponte, feigning innocence with a smile.

'My daughter,' replied Grahl, turning to Nancy as still Da Ponte smiled. 'And you, Nancy, what do you say? Will you have him?'

Now she too smiled, by Da Ponte's account, and 'lowered her eyes, then looked up at me shyly and lovingly. Her father, reading from my smile and her silence what was in our hearts, took our hands and joined them together, saying "Nancy is yours", and to her, "Da Ponte is yours."' Her mother, brother and sister-in-law applauded this unexpected scene. 'But my joy and, I believe, hers too was so great at that moment that neither of us was able to speak for the rest of the evening.'

For once, as he left the house, Da Ponte was lost for words. 'All I had in the world at the time was five piastres. I had no job, nor much prospect of one, and the way her father had torn up the letter because of her suitor's financial demands gave me no hope or encouragement of a fortune from him. But I loved her, and was loved in return – enough to give me the courage to brave anything, to surmount all obstacles.'

On 12 August 1792 Lorenzo Da Ponte and Nancy Grahl were married. Or were they? There exists no documentary evidence of a wedding between the lapsed Catholic priest and the beautiful English girl twenty years his junior, both Jewish-born; Da Ponte himself speaks only of 'social ceremonies and formalities'. But, to universal surprise, the forty-three-year-old roué was at last no longer single.

It would be years yet before he would write the memoirs in which Nicholas Till detects 'a desire for domestic respectability'. Nancy, as it has been well put, was 'given into his care'. Whether or not she mended his ways – and there is no evidence that anything more than his eye strayed over the four decades they would spend together – she was to prove the devoted mainstay of the rest of his life.

That same day, the couple set off for Paris. Da Ponte was in a state of disbelief that he was not alone, that this bright and beautiful young English girl had chosen to throw in her lot with him. That night, in Ljubljana – then an outpost of the Habsburg empire, now capital of the independent state of Slovenia – 'Love and Hymen showed me how to dry the tears of a tender girl who was leaving family and friends, perhaps forever, in order to be mine.'

Unsurprisingly, Da Ponte seems to have hidden much of his past from Nancy and his penniless state from her father – at least for now, pending many adventures during which many old truths would re-emerge. Asked by his father-in-law if he needed money, Da Ponte had 'seen the shreds of Galliano's letter fly blazing up the chimney', and boldly replied that his purse was 'all right', that he was 'perfectly happy with his daughter without demanding an ounce of gold'. He was obliged to conceal his relief at seeing Nancy's mother discreetly slip her a purse containing gold to the value of a hundred florins, 'a trifling sum, yet one which would prove most serviceable'.

Within a few days, however, the purse was lost during a false alarm when Nancy became convinced that two innocent horsemen approaching their carriage were bandits. After an extensive search of their tracks, entailing an overnight stay at a monastery, the couple waited in vain for news from its friendly abbot, who had undertaken to return the purse if it was found. There was consolation in the fact that all three Mozart–Da Ponte operas were playing in Prague during their brief stopover, so that Lorenzo could at least persuade Nancy that some of his stories about his past self were true.

As they were leaving Prague for Dresden, Da Ponte remembered that Casanova owed him money; so he decided to divert via the Castle of Dux, in northern Bohemia, where his old friend was living as librarian to the Count Joseph Karl Emanuel Waldstein. Now in his sixties, Casanova had been in Dux (today Duchcov, in the Czech Republic) since 1785, and would remain there until his death in 1798. Although he missed his homeland as much as his younger self, and suffered delusions (not all, alas, false) that the Count and his staff were mocking him behind his back, he was in truth fortunate to have landed so comfortable a sinecure, enabling him to see out his life with no real money worries, at a safe distance from the scenes of his greater glories – which he recorded at length in his memoirs, written at Dux.

But cash had he none, as Da Ponte soon realized. So the poet bit his tongue about the debt, and passed a few pleasant days with the great raconteur, who was delighted to see a fellow countryman and relive old times. Still quick to appreciate a pretty face, Casanova immediately took to Nancy, who in turn was fascinated by his stories and easy prey to his charms. In future years she would usually add a flirtatious postscript to her husband's letters to his friend.

When, after three days, the Da Pontes set off for Dresden, Casanova escorted them halfway, to the border town of Töplitz. Here he kissed Nancy farewell and gave her husband three pieces of advice: 'Don't go to Paris – go to London. But when you are there, be careful not to go near the Italian Café (Caffè degl'Italiani), and never sign your name to anything.'

These precepts duly lodged, the travellers journeyed on, with Nancy eagerly plying her husband with questions about Casanova, and Da Ponte giving her a censored version of their mutual past among a host of Casanova anecdotes. In Dresden, he tells us, they were 'most kindly' received by Father Hueber and Mazzola, now back from Vienna; but Da Ponte decided against staying on in the hope of a post, still sensing that Mazzola would not welcome a rival poet in town. Was it this, or his want of money, or the need to hide the truth of his relationship with Nancy from Hueber, that haunted a desperate letter he wrote to Casanova from Dresden on 24 September 1792?

> Now I no longer feel my own master. All my movements are ordered by Providence. I am no more than a machine which correctly obeys any given impulse. I force myself to behave blindly, like a man who has fallen into the sea and moves his hands and feet in order not to drown, so as to reach the shore. Really, I am staking all for all. If the risk be great, the reward I have received in advance makes it worthwhile. I can no longer say 'nocet empta dolore voluptas': I am giving myself up completely to the search for happiness, and only misfortune is possible. Misfortune may perhaps come, but I have no intention of making myself miserable by anticipating it.

After ten days he and Nancy left Dresden – still, despite Casanova's advice, heading for Paris – with Da Ponte no doubt patting the letter of introduction to Marie-Antoinette in his pocket. On the road to Cassel, they made an overnight stop in Spires, where Providence intervened right on cue. As they disembarked at the inn, a young nobleman of Da Ponte's acquaintance recognized him, and rushed to greet him with abnormal enthusiasm. 'Heaven must have sent you here today to help me!' he gasped. 'You must write me a sonnet.'

The young man, it transpired, was in desperate but unrequited love with a local beauty, who had rejected even her father's encouragement to take an interest in him, and promised to entertain his advances only if he wrote her a sonnet – a task, she well knew, of which he was incapable. In barely half an hour, Da Ponte knocked off a love sonnet – which swiftly did the trick. The young man soon returned with the news that it had won his beloved's heart, and rewarded Da Ponte with a valuable gold watch for his Cyrano-esque services.

Thus back in funds, Da Ponte was about to leave Spires for Paris when he heard the news of Marie-Antoinette's imprisonment. French forces, meanwhile, were advancing on Mainz. The letter in his pocket now rendered useless, and other directions dangerous, he determined finally to take Casanova's first piece of advice and head for London.

The change of plan delighted Nancy, whose sister Louisa was living in London with her husband Charles Niccolini. After a detour through Holland, and a journey uneventful apart from a close brush with brigands, the Da Pontes arrived safely in the English capital. All Mozart's librettist now possessed was that gold watch, six louis, a ring that he soon pawned for six guineas, and the love of a good woman.

10

The Londoner

A T 20 FRITH STREET in the heart of London's Soho, above the stage door of the old London Casino – now the Prince Edward Theatre, latterly the home of the long-running stage musical *Mary Poppins* – a blue plaque proclaims that in 1764–5 Wolfgang Amadeus Mozart lived here while dazzling high London society with his precocious eight-year-old skills.

There is no such plaque around the corner in Beak Street (then Silver Street), where Da Ponte and his bride lodged at No. 7 (now part of the clothing store Massimo Duti) with her in-laws, the Niccolinis, on their arrival in London in the autumn of 1792. Nor at nearby 16 Sherwood Street (then Sherrard Street), just off Piccadilly Circus, where they soon moved to a small single room in what Da Ponte described as 'a handsome, broad, well-built and inhabited place'. Today it is the goods entrance to the Regent Palace Hotel.

But the eponymous Prince Regent, the future King George IV, had yet to assume power. His father, George III, was midway through the sixty-year reign that had begun with the loss of the American colonies and would end with his descent into madness. It was not long since the Gordon Riots against the prospect of Catholic emancipation had seen the street of London in the grip of an uncontrollable mob for three days. But the English capital was now more apprehensive about events in France; this was the year in which King Louis XVI and the Emperor Joseph's sister, Marie-Antoinette, were guillotined.

So Da Ponte had made the right decision in bypassing Paris; but his first impressions of London were none too bright. This was the age of Sheridan, Kemble and Mrs Siddons, with an opera house the envy of

Europe, and all London at the feet of Italian singers. But no one had even heard of Da Ponte. 'The air of London has qualities similar to those of the Waters of Lethe,' he wrote to Casanova soon after his arrival. He disliked his in-laws, the Niccolinis, who were 'neither rich nor generous'; and, amid his continuing money worries, could find little prospect of work – not least because he possessed none of the requirements for success: money, influential friends or even much of a command of the language.

The only people he knew in London were the Storaces and Michael Kelly. Kelly was one of the principal singers at Drury Lane Theatre and stage manager at the home of Italian opera, the King's Theatre, Haymarket. Stephen Storace was one of the leading opera composers of the day, also involved with the King's Theatre, and his sister Nancy a prominent soprano. Surely they could help him find work? But they were all busy celebrities, with problems of their own, and little to offer a down-on-his-luck Italian librettist. It is from this period, no doubt, that Da Ponte's ill-feeling towards Kelly truly stemmed.

Would they have been more responsive if he had come with Mozart? For months, Da Ponte was obliged to put a brave face on a wretched situation. 'I have sold or pawned all my possessions rather than let people see my plight,' he wrote to Casanova.

His name should have been familiar to London operagoers; *Una cosa rara* had been successfully performed there four years earlier – but all the credit went, as usual, to the composer. The post of opera poet was, as it happened, vacant, following the death of Antonioli; but Da Ponte had a formidable rival in the shape of Carlo Francesco Badini, who had lived in London twenty-five years and written countless libretti for the King's Theatre. With his sharp nose for opera politics, Da Ponte soon adjudged that the theatre's manager, William Taylor, was 'completely under the sway' of Badini and the house conductor Vincenzo Federici, who himself composed the occasional opera. While not even attempting to challenge Badini for the post – for which he privately considered him 'as qualified as Bertati's shoes' – he put forward the idea that he be commissioned to write two libretti a year.

This was rebuffed, thanks to Badini's hold over Taylor, which stemmed from the unlikely fact that the librettist doubled as a critic – and, as Da Ponte noted, 'attention is paid to the opinions of the newspapers in London perhaps more than anywhere else.' Federici endeared himself to his employer by doubling as a fundraiser, shoring up his job security by persuading wealthy opera-lovers to open their wallets for the theatre. 'With these two villains at the head of the establishment,' Da Ponte realized, 'I had not then the slightest hope of ever gaining employment there.'

He began courting aristocratic patrons, among them the Marquess of Salisbury, Prince Lichtenstein and the Duke of Bedford, who took a benign interest in the opera house's finances. But none offered him financial support. Only his happiness with Nancy, he wrote to Casanova, kept him going at this wretched time. Politely rejecting Casanova's suggestion that he set up as a teacher of Italian, he told him it was 'a profession at present pursued by valets, cobblers, bandits and exiles, spies etc. etc. who by way of payment have flung in their faces a few ha'pence, or a shilling, or a glass of beer'. He would later have reason to amend this view.

As always, however, he was somehow managing to keep up appearances:

> If you ask me how I've managed to survive these last six months and more, I would not know how to answer. I know I've got through ninety guineas, but whether they sprang from the earth or dropped out of heaven only an angel could testify. The best thing is that I have few debts; those I do have don't bother me, as I can pay them off when I choose, and because everyone regards me as pretty well-off, since I'm careful to conceal the ugly truth.

But his desperation is evident in his appeals for funds to Casanova himself, and to his patron Count Waldstein, both of whom he knew to be as hard-up as he was. ('When Cicero wrote to his friend,' complained Casanova, 'he never talked of business.') For a while, given his view of the significance of English newspapers, Da Ponte contemplated founding a review called *La bilancia teatrale*, in which he could write what he really thought of the state of opera in London, perhaps even persuading Taylor to hire him; but the potential cost of the project proved prohibitive.

As he cast about with increasing desperation, Da Ponte rashly got involved in an exchange of abusive poems with Badini, which alerted *le tout Londres* to his colourful past – and then some, for Badini had a fertile imagination. He told the world the embarrassing truth Da Ponte had begged Casanova and others to keep secret: that he was a Catholic priest, apparently married. He even accused him of sodomy, but Da Ponte did not have the means to sue. Proud of his own ornate replies, which were in truth less effective than Badini's assaults, he found himself obliged to watch his name dragged through the London mud.

The only Londoner who showed Da Ponte any kindness, and occasionally lent him money, was his fellow exile Carlo Pozzi, whom he describes as 'a composer of charming music, affable, generous and kindly, albeit not wealthy'. In truth, Pozzi was a jobbing composer who earned a meagre living writing arias for insertion into other composers' operas to gratify the egos of singers. In the process, he had endeared himself to one of the leading sopranos of the moment, the German-born diva Gertrude Elisabeth Mara, whom he now introduced to Da Ponte. In her forties, 'Madame' Mara had largely abandoned opera for concerts and oratorios; nevertheless, she now commissioned an opera from Da Ponte, who responded by adapting his own play *Il menenzio*. It was set to music by Giacomo Ferrari, an Italian composer then lodging with Pozzi in Great Pulteney Street.

Although the piece was never performed, according to Badini's memoirs, it earned Da Ponte the handsome sum of thirty guineas, which he now decided to use as an escape route from London, where his prospects seemed so hopeless. The discovery that Nancy was pregnant lent his quest for work an added urgency. In July 1793, leaving Nancy behind in London, he set off for the Low Countries.

Brussels ... Rotterdam ... The Hague ... wherever he went, offering to establish an Italian opera company in towns he deemed in need of it, Da Ponte found only doors slammed in his face. There was some support in high places, notably from the General Butzeler whose daughters had once been tutored by Nancy; but the political situation was not helping his case. The French defeat of the Anglo-Dutch forces at Hoondschoote in early September, in which the Prince of Orange was gravely wounded, made opera seem somewhat irrelevant. 'All thoughts of amusement and festivities', as Da Ponte put it, 'gave place to sorrow, lamentation and prayer.'

He wrote to Nancy Storace in London, to Guardasoni in Prague, to Rovedino and Ferrari (both now in Brussels), even to La Ferrarese in Vienna, but all declined to join forces in his operatic venture. The one piece of good news to reach him was probably the least expected; a letter from Nancy announced that her purse, lost on the road between Trieste and Prague, had been found and returned to her – complete with its hundred florins, twenty of which would enable her to join him.

She enclosed the remaining eighty, and herself arrived a few days later. But eighty florins 'did not last long', as Da Ponte himself acknowledged, 'in the hands of a man who had never learnt economy'. Now they were forced to start selling their clothes to survive:

> We had bread for breakfast, and bread for lunch, and sometimes not even that for dinner, but only tears. It was not, however, my companion who wept. She bore everything with angelic patience, even managing to joke and laugh. She got me to play chess with her, and liked to play for large amounts, the loser to pay the winner in kisses and caresses. These tender little ways of hers, which at any other time would have made me blissfully happy, only deepened my anguish and despair.

They had taken a room in the house of a kindly German, himself on the breadline, who let them live rent-free for a week, then politely asked them to leave if they could come up with no money at all. The very next morning, if Da Ponte is to be believed, the landlord entered their room clutching an envelope, which at first he thought to contain a bill. But no, it was a letter from Nancy's sister in London.

> Dear Da Ponte,
>
> Badini's misdeeds have compelled the impresario (Taylor) to dismiss him. As he needed a poet and had heard of you, he sent for me and commissioned me to write and offer you the post. As Badini has swindled him out of sixty guineas on account of his salary, he would want you to agree to pay it back to him by deducting it from the two hundred he offers you. This I believe you will agree to, because you ought to be attracted not by the money but by the opportunity of making yourself known in London. With this in mind I ventured to assure him that you would come. So he gave me twenty guineas for your travelling expenses. Make haste and come. You are eagerly expected by your friends, and amongst them by Ferrari, Rovedino, Kelly and Storace, and I am dying to embrace my Nancy again.

Such was the impact of this news upon Da Ponte that he burst into tears, jumped out of bed and knelt to pray, choosing the lines spoken by 'my' Atar in *Axur*. 'Oh God, who dost protect the wretched, Thou never failest those who trust and hope in Thee.'

Where then stood the King's Theatre, at the foot of the Haymarket opposite the Theatre Royal, now stands Her Majesty's, home since

1986 to Andrew Lloyd Webber's musical *The Phantom of the Opera*.

The current Her Majesty's (the name changes according to the sex of the monarch) is the fourth theatre to occupy the site. The King's Theatre that now boasted Da Ponte as its house poet was the second, then only two years old, designed by Michael Novosielski to replace Sir John Vanbrugh's Queen's, which had opened in April 1705. After becoming the King's Theatre on the accession of George I in 1714, it was destroyed by fire in 1789.

Its successor (Her Majesty's after the accession of Queen Victoria in 1837) would also burn down in 1867, to be replaced by a short-lived Charles Lee design, demolished in 1892. Since its opening in 1897 the present theatre, designed by C. J. Phipps, has specialized in musicals, often long-running, notably *Chu Chin Chow* in 1916 (2,238 performances), Noel Coward's *Bitter Sweet* in 1929 (697) and, after the Second World War, *Brigadoon* (1949), *Paint Your Wagon* (1953), *West Side Story* (1958) and *Fiddler on the Roof* (1967, 2,030 performances). Lloyd Webber's *Phantom of the Opera* celebrated its eight-thousandth performance on 3 January 2006.

Not until after Da Ponte's departure, for all his efforts over a dozen years, did the King's Theatre first bring any Mozart operas to London: *La clemenza di Tito* in 1806, *Così fan tutte* in 1811 and *Don Giovanni* in 1816. After the success of the latter, alterations were made to the auditorium and facade by George Renton and John Nash, who also added the Royal Opera Arcade which runs along the rear of the theatre to this day. Such was the theatre's reputation for opera that, on Queen Victoria's accession in 1837, its name was changed (if only for ten years) to Her Majesty's Italian Opera House.

The state of the King's Theatre was rather more parlous when Da Ponte joined the staff in November 1793, after settling his debts in Holland and rushing back to London. Taylor's offer, he wrote to Casanova, came 'at a time when I seemed to be on the edge of a precipice, in a state of total desperation, convincing me more than ever that there is a hand in heaven which governs all matters below'.

So darkly had he painted their plight that it seems Casanova suggested making money out of Nancy's charms. 'Anything in the world, but not horns,' replied Da Ponte. 'I believe that God has given me a brain as well as a heart: this will enable me to endure the worst turns of Fortune, to find one way or another of living honourably, without having to reproach myself for any ignoble or dishonest deed. *Aude aliquid* (Dare anything), but not at the expense of virtue.' Nancy's acerbic postscript makes it clear that she, too, took an extremely dim view of Casanova's suggestion.

As for Taylor, Da Ponte's timely benefactor, it would be some time before he had the chance to gauge his true measure. Born in Aberdeen, the son of a tenant farmer, 'Opera Taylor' had started in London as a bank clerk before rising to become manager and part-owner of the King's Theatre via an elaborate subscription scheme. According to the memoirs of a later manager, John Ebers, Taylor was 'one of the most singular of mankind ... His whole life was a continued hoax ... He quarrelled with everybody, ridiculed everybody, and hoaxed everybody.' But Taylor was so charming and affable a figure that his constant requests for money were rarely refused.

Da Ponte had no way of knowing all this when the summons from Taylor came to his rescue. 'Plucked casually by him from the dire straits in which I found myself in Holland, I had, and have always maintained, all the feelings for him that gratitude, pity and friendship inspire in a sympathetic and well-intentioned mind.' But their first encounter did not bode well. 'From the reception he gave me, I perceived that he bore no great affection for the Muses.'

Taylor was writing at a small table when his friend Federici led the new house poet into his room:

> He was facing the window with his back to the door. 'Here is Signor Da Ponte,' said Federici. The impresario went on writing, without taking any notice. 'Mr Taylor, here is the poet,' repeated Federici, a little louder. The impresario turned round, nodded his head slightly, and then continued with his writing. I waited in the room five minutes, until Signor Federici, putting his finger to his lips as a sign of respectful silence, motioned to me to leave.
>
> To speak plainly, this was not a very promising start for one who had for ten years been poet to Joseph II, a prince who was the very model of affability, kindliness and good manners ...

Taylor had been running the King's Theatre a dozen years, since 1781. An ebullient man, whose lofty circle of acquaintances included Nelson's mistress Lady (Emma) Hamilton, he could get drunk to the point where a hostess once emptied a boiling kettle over him. From 1792 to 1843 the King's was the only theatre in London licensed to perform Italian opera;

unlike continental houses, it was privately owned, with no subsidy from the state, financed by aristocratic music-lovers who in fact used the performances as social salons, eating their supper in the boxes or playing cards and pausing their chatter only to applaud favourite singers. 'Whatever we may pretend,' wrote the *Morning Chronicle* in 1795, 'we are too ignorant of musical science as a nation to find pleasure in what produces rapture on an Italian stage.' Although perpetually short of funds, reeling from crisis to crisis, Taylor seems to have relished the perks of the job sufficiently to have fought off all attempts to remove him.

It was to be all of three months before Da Ponte so much as saw Taylor again. In March 1794, when the theatre was presenting Gazzaniga's *Don Giovanni* – which Federici had 'stupidly' chosen over Mozart's, for all Da Ponte's protestations – he was suddenly summoned and asked for his views 'on various matters touching the theatre'. Its finances were in so dire a state that the King's Theatre was in danger of demolition and Taylor himself of ruin. The solution, they appear to have decided, was to commission an opera from the popular Martín y Soler. Taylor asked Da Ponte to persuade his old friend to leave St Petersburg for London at once.

Alas, Martín was engaged in writing operas for no less a librettist than Catherine the Great. He could not come to London for at least twelve months. So, for a menial salary plus royalties, Da Ponte tried to keep Taylor's fragile ship afloat by adapting to English standards – i.e. shortening – Cimarosa's *Il matrimonio segreto*, Paisiello's *I contadini bizzarri* and Cimarosa's *Il capriccio drammatico*, which was presented in a double bill with Gazzaniga's one-act *Don Giovanni*. After complaints summed up by *The Times* – 'So determined an opposition to this kind of entertainment we have never witnessed' – *Don Giovanni* was withdrawn, and replaced by Guglielmi's *La bella pescatrice*, later by *La prova dell'opera*, a confection by Da Ponte fitted to Cimarosa's music. Da Ponte would tighten up the narrative, maybe inserting an aria from elsewhere, and another house hack would translate the results into English. Copies of each libretto, Italian and English, were on sale in the theatre foyer, for operagoers to follow by candlelight during the performance.

While awaiting Martín's arrival, Da Ponte soon found himself caught in a titanic feud between the opera company's two leading ladies, who had both just arrived from Spain: Brigida Banti, who specialized in *opera seria*, and Anna Morichelli, renowned for her *buffa*. Each diva was past her prime. Banti made up for her lack of musicianship with an immensely powerful voice; Morichelli was more of an actress than a singer. It was the wily Banti who won the battle for Taylor's affections, and thus the contest as to who would sing first; she commissioned Da Ponte to adjust Moretti's text to Franceso Bianchi's *Semiramide* to suit her unusual requirements. She was, he wrote, an 'ignorant, silly, insolent woman who . . . could become an asp, a fury, a demon of hell, who could have overturned an empire, let alone a theatre'.

'Woe betide you', Banti told Da Ponte, 'if Morichelli pleases more than I do.' But her debut was a spectacular success. 'No opera has ever had greater success or a longer run,' according to one audience member. 'Indeed, it was one of those of which it is impossible to tire.' Three weeks later Morichelli's debut was well received, but not on the scale of Banti's triumph. With Martín y Soler still in St Petersburg, she chose *Il burbero di buon cuore*, adding arias by Ferrari and Pozzi, even Haydn, to whose duet from *Orlando Paladino* Da Ponte wrote new words ('Quel cor umano e tenero'). Strangely, he makes no mention at all in his memoirs of Haydn, whom he must have known in both Vienna and London.

At the beginning of the 1794 season, Martín y Soler arrived in London and accepted Da Ponte's invitation to lodge at his house. The old friends and colleagues were delighted to be living and working together again; immediately they set to work on a piece for Morichelli, *La scala de' maritati*. The plot is absurd, but the libretto stylish, and it went down well enough with the King's Theatre audience. 'There was not one single scene or song that dragged,' declared the *Morning Post*, reporting 'rapturous applause'. As for Martín y Soler: 'So perfectly has he adapted his airs to the character of a nation where he has been so short a time a resident, that many pieces of his first essay will surely come to the barrel organ.'

The opera became a favourite at the King's Theatre, and was later performed abroad under a variety of titles: *La capricciosa corretta*, *Gli sposi in contrasto* and *La moglie corretta*. But it provoked another fierce public row between Da Ponte and Badini, who accused him of plagiarism and indecency. Da Ponte's reply was, as always, extreme, abusing Badini in venomous, even obscene terms.

Nor was this the last conflict that would dog Da Ponte's time in London: as he himself recognized, he seemed to attract disagreements with his colleagues. 'I am well,' Da Ponte wrote to Casanova. 'I enjoy perfect health, and except for the fact that I have twenty-four or twenty-six teeth missing, . . . no one would think I am forty-six. My Nancy is with me; I love her, and she loves me. I could be perfectly happy if I didn't happen to be one of those men whom fortune and enemies love treating badly.'

Now the enemy was, of all people, Da Ponte's beloved 'Martini', with whom he had a serious falling-out halfway through their next collaboration. The first half of *L'isola del piacere* went fine; then Martìn suddenly upped and went to live with Morichelli, blackening Da Ponte's name as he did so. It seems that Martín had made the Da Pontes' maid pregnant, and tried to lay the blame at her master's door. 'Our long, delightful and enviable friendship grew cold,' Da Ponte told Casanova, 'and the second act of *L'isola del piacere* was written entirely on an island of ice; it seemed to me, as I wrote it, that I was writing for Righini, not for Martini or the composer of *Una cosa rara*.'

Relations were not improved when Morichelli inserted a mad scene from another opera into the piece, which 'fitted as well as Pilate would have done in the Credo'. The work received only four performances, though it proved more popular across Europe, being translated into German, Spanish and Hungarian. Haydn thought it poor stuff: 'The overture from *L'arbore di Diana* and a lot of old material from *Cosa rara*.' His relationship with Morichelli doomed by the work's failure, Martín returned to St Petersburg, and the singer to Venice.

Of the twelve operas staged at the King's Theatre during the 1795–96 season, Da Ponte had a hand in half. The first was *La bella Arsene*, with music by Monsigny and a text by Favart 'improved' by Da Ponte. 'Pleasing, but not great,' was one newspaper's verdict. 'Gay and slight, but not striking.'

Next came Gluck's *Iphigenia in Tauride*, to capitalize on the success during the previous season of his *Alceste*, with Banti in the title role. 'The most splendid opera we ever saw,' declared one paper of this huge success. *Antigona* followed, the first of many collaborations with Bianchi, succeeded by *Il tesoro*, with music by Joseph Mazzinghi. 'The tale is a tolerable one for the Italian stage,' opined *The Times*, with music 'adapted to the season, light and airy'.

Finally came *Zemira e Azor*, an adaptation by Da Ponte of the French text of Marmontel, with music by André Grétry. 'For some mysterious reason,' he recalled, 'the French piece was given to Messrs Bonajuti and Baldonotti with an order to translate it into Italian. But no dialogue was to be curtailed, none of the *dramatis personae* to be dropped, no air to be added, nothing of the plot to be changed ... A decent fee was offered for the work. But who would believe it? Messrs B and B, after labouring hard but fruitlessly for twenty days, returned the book to the prompter, and the opera-house poet was told to make the translation.' Da Ponte completed the work quickly and 'went to see a friend who knew music well, tried out the score with the words, and with a few small changes we found that it matched the composer's notes perfectly'.

Throughout all this, Nancy was running the theatre's coffee-shop with her sister Louisa, and managing to make a handy amount of extra money. 'All the first society are regularly to be seen there,' according to the London press, which also printed adverts for the 'delicious refreshments' offered by 'Madame Daponte'.

But her husband was forgetting Casanova's advice not to sign his name. Suddenly, during the 1796–97 season, Taylor became friendlier, taking Da Ponte for long walks and often calling at his house. One day he asked him if he could help him by getting cash for a bill of exchange from Federici, to the value of £300. 'If you can,' said La Banti, who sat menacingly at Taylor's side, 'your fortune is made.'

'How could I undertake such a thing?' wondered Da Ponte. 'I, a poet by profession, with only a modest salary, and little understanding of the words "acceptance", "endorsement" or "bill of exchange" – where can I find money?' Remembering the magic word 'Money' written over his door, he took it to the pawnbroker where he had sold his diamond ring when first he had arrived in London. Here a young man named Parker said that, if he bought some small item like a ring or a watch, he would give him the change in cash. Da Ponte chose a gun, a repeater – 'which he put at twenty-two guineas, though it was perhaps worth fifteen' – and gave him a Bank of England order for the rest. When he held out his hand to take the order, Parker instead gave him a pen to sign his name below Federico's on the bill of exchange.

Casanova's advice flashed through Da Ponte's mind. 'Happy me, had I religiously followed it! ... I trembled like a leaf, and at that moment a deadly presentiment seemed to say to me: "You are lost!" But he was so desperate that he signed his name and returned with the money to Taylor, who was delighted to receive so high a percentage of the bill's value. 'Bravo, poet!' exclaimed Banti, pocketing the repeater as well as the cash.

As more such transactions followed, a grateful Taylor gave Da Ponte an improved contract and occasionally lent him money. But Da Ponte was getting himself hopelessly snared in Taylor's disastrous finances. Matters grew worse when, after several unsuccessful attempts, the crafty impresario managed to get himself elected MP for Leominster – 'to the surprise', as *The Times* put it, 'of everyone'. Members of Parliament could not be arrested for debt.

'I never wanted to examine too closely or severely his defects and weaknesses, which I tried to defend or excuse as a father does those of his son,' wrote Da Ponte of Taylor. 'And when they wounded me I was silent, or took no revenge except tears. This singular man was a perfect mixture of two contrary natures. Left to himself, he was humane, noble, generous; led by others, he entirely assumed the colour of those who had led him, and particularly of the woman whom he loved and of her favourites, who immediately became his own.'

Gradually, Da Ponte was sucked into a financial hole from which he would never be able to climb out. Over the next few years he signed many bills of exchange for Taylor, often for large amounts, and so was held liable when Taylor was unable to pay. He would dash from money-lender to moneylender, 'until, either to pay what was due, or to satisfy the needs, the caprices and the appetites of the she-wolf of the theatre, the sum that I found in less than a year amounted to six thousand five hundred guineas.'

Henceforth he was a veritable Figaro – 'the treasurer, the disburser, the agent, the paymaster and the favourite of Taylor. Did they have to go to the country while the theatre was closed? Da Ponte would find the money. "There is no wine in the cellar," says Banti. Da Ponte will get it on credit from wine merchants. Signor Taylor needs hose, shirts, handkerchiefs etc. etc. He tells Da Ponte. The theatre ushers, the actors, the ballet-dancers, the singers need money? They go to Da Ponte.'

But Da Ponte's protestations that he became embroiled in Taylor's financial embarrassments through innocence and ignorance 'should be taken with a certain reservation', as Sheila Hodges observes. 'As so often in his life, it is likely that his inability to refuse Taylor was due to a combination of credulity, eternal optimism that everything would come right in the end, the desire to ingratiate himself and to show his rivals that *he* was the impresario's favourite – and surely, also, to a genuine warm-hearted impulse to help Taylor out of a jam.'

Much of Taylor's money went on Banti, who was in the habit of changing her (invariably secret) lovers 'as often as most women change their hats'. During this time she flirted with Da Ponte himself for a while, praising his goodness, his altruism, his talent, 'even my beautiful eyes!' He was forty-nine, with a wife whom he loved, considerably younger and more beautiful than Banti. 'It is no marvel that I played deaf and blind, and feel I deserve no merit for doing so.'

But the more he ignored her advances, the angrier this 'she-wolf' became. When Taylor decided to go to his country house, Banti insisted on inviting Da Ponte, too ('Come, my dear, give your good friend Banti this pleasure'). When he took Nancy with him, Banti was very put out. Able to observe Taylor at close quarters for a few days, however, Da Ponte became convinced that 'left to himself, and with plenty of money, he would have been one of the best men in the world'. As for Banti, once she had got over being spurned, 'she was affable, gentle and positively amiable. The constant attention Taylor paid her, his generosity without show, his simplicity of manner and his hospitality towards all visitors, made even Banti quite different from what she truly was.'

Da Ponte's first professional contribution at the King's that season was another collaboration with Bianchi, *Il consiglio imprudente*, based on a Goldoni play set in The Hague, so perhaps informed by memories of his dismal visit there. In his memoirs he calls it 'an *operetta buffa* in one act which was one of Bianchi's best things in the *buffa* style'. *The Times* hailed the absence of the usual 'ribaldry and buffoonery that in general debase similar productions'. It was followed in a double-bill by a heroic cantata, *Le nozze del Tamigi e Bellona*, to celebrate the naval victory off Cape St Vincent that February.

Two more Da Ponte works followed: *L'albero di Diana*, an Anglicized version of *L'arbore di Diana*, a showcase for Nancy Storace as Amore; and *Merope*, another collaboration with Bianchi, a heroic opera based on a text by Voltaire. One paper talked of his 'most admirable translation', while *The Times* hailed 'the skilful and affecting manner in which it has been introduced on the Italian stage'.

Amid all this, still looking for ways to make money, Da Ponte had the bright idea of setting up his own printing press, to double his profits as librettist by acting as printer as well. Libretti sold well in the theatre foyer, to patrons who wanted to pretend that they were there for the opera. The first work to appear under Da Ponte's imprint was his *Evelina*, a translation from the French of N. F. Guillard, with Sacchini's music adapted by Mazzinghi. Staged in January 1797, it was performed before

Lorenzo Da Ponte in
late middle age, after an
engraving by N. Rogers.

In 1793 Da Ponte arrived in London, where he became theatre poet at the King's Theatre, Haymarket, today Her Majesty's.

By now married to Nancy Grahl (left), Da Ponte received little help in London from friends he had made in Vienna: the English soprano Nancy Storace (below) and the Irish tenor Michael Kelly (below left).

In 1825, twenty years after he emigrated to the US, Da Ponte became the first Professor of Italian at New York's Columbia University, then College (above), which still owns this portrait of him at the time (left), by an unknown artist.

Da Ponte brought to New
York in 1825 an Italian opera
company led by the Spaniard
Manuel Garcia (left), where
the following year they
performed Don Giovanni at
the Park Theatre, starring
Garcia and his daughter
Maria Malibran (above).

Da Ponte's final achievement was to see
the first opera house in the United States
built in New York in 1833 (above). It
later became the National Theatre before
burning down in 1839 (below).

Da Ponte was
painted in extreme
old age by N.
Monachesi, before
his death in 1838 in
his ninetieth year.

Da Ponte's remains were lost
during their removal in 1903
from Manhattan to the Calvary
Cemetery in Queen's, where he is
now remembered on a tombstone
beneath the flight-path into JFK
airport.

'the most crowded and brilliant audience we have witnessed this season', with the librettist singled out for the fidelity of his translation.

By the beginning of the following season, in mid-1797, Taylor was able to find no replacement for Storace, who had left for Europe with a new lover. Da Ponte was working on only two texts that season: *Cinna*, again with music by Bianchi, and *La cifra*, originally seen in Vienna. He would have time on his hands. Perhaps, suggested Taylor, he would like to go to Italy to find two first-class singers, one of each gender, for the King's Theatre?

Da Ponte accepted with great excitement. The trip would give him the chance he had longed for to visit his family in Ceneda, whom he hadn't seen since his banishment from Venice. After five years spent largely reworking other men's operas, he was also anxious for a break and thoughts of pastures new.

Between them, largely thanks to Nancy's prudence, the Da Pontes had managed to save £1,000 – more than enough for a modest carriage. Taylor also gave them travelling expenses of a hundred guineas. Leaving four-year-old Louisa with her namesake aunt Niccolini, the couple set off for Italy in a state of excited anticipation.

11

The Bankrupt

I T WAS more than twenty years since Da Ponte had seen his father.
So for once he does not linger over the details of the month-long
journey in October–November 1798: from London to Hamburg, and
Hamburg to Castelfranco, thirty miles north of Venice. Here he left Nancy,
asking her to meet him in Treviso two nights later. By evening he was at
Conegliano, just eight miles from Ceneda, and within an hour at his
father's door – now, since he had left the ghetto, on Ceneda's main square.
Today the house is a tobacconist's, next to the corner café.

Da Ponte's emotions at his homecoming were intense:

> When my feet again trod the ground of my infancy, and I breathed
> the air of that sky which had nourished me and given me life for so
> many years, I trembled in every limb and there ran through my veins
> such feelings of gratitude and reverence that for some time I stood
> quite still, unable to move. I don't know how long I might have
> remained like this, had I not heard at the window a voice which I
> seemed to know, and which went straight to my heart.

He had disembarked from the post-wagon some distance away, to avoid
the noise of the wheels giving any notice of his arrival, and put his kerchief
around his head so that he should not be recognized from the windows
by the light of the lanterns:

> When I knocked at the door, and heard a voice cry from a window
> 'Who is there?', I disguised my voice and replied simply 'Open!' But
> this was enough for one of my sisters to recognize my voice, and cry
> to her sisters 'It is Lorenzo!' They all rushed down the stairs, threw
> their arms around me and almost suffocated me with their embraces

and kisses. Then they led me in to my father, who, when he heard my name and saw me, remained motionless for several minutes.

Gaspare Da Ponte was now seventy-six, and had been a widower for almost a decade. It was All Souls' Day, so all the family was gathered at home around the patriarch; soon, as the news of Da Ponte's arrival spread, friends and other villagers crowded into the Da Ponte house. His brothers Girolamo and Luigi were gone, but Paolo was still there, as were his friends from childhood, Antonio Michelini and Girolamo Perucchini. For the first time he met his stepsister Faustina, almost twenty, born after his escape from Venice to Gorizia.

Da Ponte speaks of Faustina with such tenderness, even of taking her back to London with him, that Sheila Hodges has wondered if she might have been his natural daughter. Early in 1779, as Hodges recalls, he had spent some weeks with his younger brother Luigi and his stepmother Orsola, first in Venice and then in Ceneda. Da Ponte's stepmother, it should be remembered, was only two years older than him. 'Is it possible that he and his stepmother became lovers and that he thought Faustina was his daughter? There is no proof of this hypothesis, and the relevant dates are not known with sufficient exactness to advance it with confidence, but in his letters and memoirs his references are so tender as to imply a feeling deeper than that of a brother for a stepsister whom he saw for only a few days.'

That night, after they had prayed together for half an hour, Da Ponte's father told him: 'My son, now I have seen you again, I can die content.' Next morning the old man was up at dawn, fetching flowers and fruit to scatter on his prodigal son's bed. The entire family crowded into Lorenzo's bedroom, while a 'very pretty' maid brought coffee, and the whole assembly sat down to breakfast around his bed. 'I truly think, I never saw before or since that day a sight so merry. It felt more like being in the centre of a band of angels than of mortal beings.'

Among many reminiscences, his father told of the occupation of Ceneda, and his fears for his daughters' honour as French troops were billeted in private houses. Napoleon Bonaparte himself, general of this division, marched his troops to the centre of the town and sat himself down in the café beside the central piazza, next door to the Da Ponte home. After locking his front door, Lorenzo's father leaned out of the window and addressed Napoleon directly: 'General, the old man who is speaking to you is the father of seven honest daughters who lost their mother many years ago. Only two are married, the others are with me. Their older brothers are not here to protect them, and I, their father, must occasionally leave the house to fetch them bread. I respectfully ask exemption from your order that your brave troops should be billeted in our houses. I beg that you will protect my white hair, the innocence of these young girls and the honour of my sons. If you will grant me this, I will pray to God for the prosperity of you and your armies. If you will not grant this wish, I will not open the door of my house, but, at the first sign of any soldiers or officers attempting to open it, I will save the virtue of my daughters with a barrel of gunpowder.' Napoleon looked up, and granted the old man his wish; the Da Ponte house was the only one in Ceneda spared French troops.

After this recollection the conversation with Lorenzo naturally turned to his dead brothers, at the mention of whose names he saw his ancient father's eyes well with tears. So he changed the subject, to tell them that he had brought with him from London a beautiful dancer, whom they would all meet in the next day or two.

'Is she really beautiful?' asked Faustina.

'Yes, even lovelier than you.'

'Then we must see this treasure of yours!'

Da Ponte spent that day visiting old friends around Ceneda – including some former sweethearts, who were 'as glad to see me as I to see them' – before telling his family over dinner that he must leave for Treviso the next morning. He would take Paolo and Faustina with him, and be back within a few days.

The next morning, as he prepared to set off, a crowd of young men surrounded the door of the family house. 'I thought it was to see me off and wish me a pleasant journey. Not at all! It was to ask me with one accord not to take Faustina with me, and as their requests had almost the air of threats, I had to promise and swear I would bring her back to Ceneda within three days.'

It was evening before they reached Treviso – only to find that Nancy was not there. That evening Paolo teased his brother about his anxiety that this 'dancer' had failed to keep their rendezvous. But early next morning he was at the window of his room as her carriage approached the inn. Nancy was wearing a veil, which Paolo lifted in the same way his brother first had to see her face. He was overjoyed to find that it was the

Nancy he had grown so fond of in Trieste, now his brother's wife. 'Yes, it is true,' said the beautiful Faustina (who 'had pride enough to know she was'), 'she is handsomer than I am.'

As word of Da Ponte's arrival in Treviso spread, old friends again began to gather: Giulio Trento, and a host of middle-aged men, now holding important offices in the town, who had been his pupils and still (to his delight) called him 'Master'. Who else should be there, too, but Bernardo Memmo, still with his Teresa: 'grown old and fat, she was still his idol and mistress of his will.'

On hearing that two *prime donne* of some merit were singing in Venice, Da Ponte suddenly remembered the real reason for his trip. Sending Nancy back to Ceneda with Paolo and Faustina, he himself went on to the city he had not seen for more than two decades. And how it had changed. 'I had heard tell a good deal about the piteous state the city was in, but all that I had heard was a joke compared with what I saw in one day and one night.'

It was eighteen months since the French had taken possession of Venice; the Doge had abdicated, and Napoleon had handed over control to the Austrians. Entering the Piazza San Marco, 'where in happy times there is nothing but a great concourse of noisy, laughing people', Da Ponte saw 'on every side only melancholy, silence, solitude and desolation'. Even the cafés were empty. Reaching the last of them, he spotted a nose 'of extraordinary size', which had attracted his attention from a distance. It was the man who had denounced him, and precipitated his banishment, by dropping his name into the lion's mouth in San Moisé: Gabriele Doria, brother-in-law of his lost love, Angioletta.

The city was full of spies; and Doria was one of them, an agent of the Inquisitors of State. He told Da Ponte that Angioletta and her husband were still together, still in Venice. Only now, in his memoirs, does Da Ponte feel obliged to give a censored version of his entanglement with Angioletta, who becomes a wronged woman he had rescued from her murderous husband. When he reaches the point where he must spell out the precise nature of their relationship, he suddenly breaks off:

> By an odd mishap, a page of this story is missing. I had already written it, and was about to dry the ink with sand, when I mistakenly took up the inkwell instead of the sandbox and poured ink all over the page. As I have not the time to copy it out again, I will leave my reader to write what he pleases in its place . . .

This curiously charming blunt instrument is used by the elderly husband on two other occasions to gloss over his youthful indiscretions.

After visiting his friends Perucchini and Lucchesi – Zaguri was away, and Pisani at Ferrara – he paid a call on La Ferrarese, who greeted him with 'an exclamation of joy', redoubled when she heard that he was recruiting for the London theatre. But he knew she had already sung in London with little success. 'However much I should like to have taken one of my usual revenges, returning good to her for the evil she had done me, I did not think it honest or right to give her the smallest hope before I had heard what her voice was like.'

Ferrarese sang a few ariette, and Da Ponte changed the subject. On hearing she had no *cavaliere servente*, he agreed to take her to the opera that evening, and stopped at a café for some ices en route. Here his old lover took his hand, gazed deep into his eyes and told him: 'You know, Da Ponte, you are handsomer than ever.'

'I am extremely sorry', he replied, 'not to be able to say the same of you.'

Adriana blushed; her eyes filled with tears; and Da Ponte regretted this cheap revenge. So he told her he was pledged to another for life, which prevented him from talking of love, particularly to her. This 'particularly' seemed to mollify her, and they passed a pleasant evening at a performance of Casti's *Il re Teodoro in Venezia*.

The soprano was 'very good'; but she was already engaged for the next carnival, so Da Ponte did not trouble to speak to her. He and La Ferrarese went to dinner with two other very beautiful singers, 'but I wanted voices, not beauty'. After seeing Ferrarese home, Da Ponte returned to his hotel.

The next day, 8 November, he was to declare 'memorable'. It began in the cafés around San Marco, where he listened to the complaints of the locals about the occupying forces, and the rise in the prices of everything, especially food, until the proprietor shushed them, telling them how such talk could earn him a beating. Leaving the café 'more sorrowfully than a loving son turns away from a mother's grave', Da Ponte wandered on to the fish market, to see if the 'gifts of the sea' had also increased in price. On asking an old man, with a pale, dirty face and the air of a beggar, he found him exclaiming, 'By heaven! Lorenzo Da Ponte!' It was Girolamo, brother of Angiola Tiepolo, the woman for whom he had renounced Matilda and suffered three years of tribulation. Da Ponte took him back to his inn, clothed and fed him, and spent a few hours righting past wrongs, as Girolamo told him how the new rulers had deprived ancient families such as his of their income, reducing them to destitution. 'Alas,' he added, 'my sister is dead. Would that she were here to see and know what she has lost!'

After over-tipping a barber, and hearing yet more stories of suffering under the new regime, Da Ponte had decided that he could bear this new Venice no longer – when who should arrive at his hotel, briefed by Doria, but Angioletta Bellaudi and her husband Carlo. Their reunion was predictably emotional, followed by a dinner at which they told him much about Doria, now Angioletta's *cavaliere servente*, and desperately jealous since seeing Da Ponte back in Venice. As they parted, Angioletta slipped a note into his hand, warning him that he was in great danger and should leave the city with all speed.

That night he went again to the opera, but could not concentrate on the music, let alone the singers. Meeting another friend as he left, the Abbé Artusi, he took him back to his hotel, where they found Doria waiting with an Imperial messenger from the chief of police. He kept the Abbé in his room as a witness while the messenger took a document from his pocket and read: 'By the orders of His Imperial and Royal Majesty, Signor Lorenzo Da Ponte will be pleased to leave Venice before tomorrow morning.'

After assuring him that he would be gone by dawn, Da Ponte laughed so much that the innkeeper advised him to quieten down; the Imperial messenger was still on the premises, and this could get him into even deeper trouble. So Da Ponte took Artusi for a walk, during which he heard things that 'vastly increased my wish to depart'.

Before daybreak he had left for Padua. By his own account, he learned there that clashes between the French and Austrian armies would make his journey back to Ceneda dangerous; if he returned, he might not get out again for some time. So he sent word to Nancy to join him in Padua.

But history records that there were no militant troops, French or Austrian, in the area at the time. This is not just another inaccuracy on Da Ponte's part; it conceals some reason for not wishing to return to Ceneda, to his father and the rest of his family, for one last emotional farewell. Perhaps he simply could not face it. Whatever the truth behind this puzzling moment, Da Ponte would never see them again.

*

Heading south, Da Ponte and Nancy were soon in Bologna, after a nasty moment when the German authorities suspected the polyglot Nancy of being a spy, and a meeting in Ferrara with the young poet Ugo Foscolo, whom Da Ponte much admired. Well-known in Bologna, where his operas were popular, Da Ponte enjoyed being lionized so much that he again almost forgot the true purpose of his trip – until the arrival of a letter informing him that La Banti had settled her differences with Federici. His position in London, in other words, was now endangered by his absence. Bologna was renowned as a cradle of singers; but Da Ponte found none to suit his purpose. So he moved swiftly on to Florence, not least because it was a city he had never visited, leaving Nancy behind in Bologna because winter was closing in, and she was again pregnant.

La Firenze lived up to her billing. Da Ponte thrilled to the beauties of the city's ancient buildings and art galleries, and adored being surrounded by beautiful women at the literary soirées, where he played the part of Aristodemus in a tragedy by Monti, and recited his own early poem 'Sugli odori'. Here, too, he thrilled to Alfieri's *Saul*. But again there were no singers worth his attention, so he headed back to Bologna through treacherous snows that nearly saw him killed when thrown out of his carriage, which landed on top of him. Taken to a nearby house 'more dead than alive', he was soon revived with Chianti and Alkermes, a Florentine liqueur. He arrived back in Bologna on a donkey.

With rumours of war getting louder, and armies mustering all around, Da Ponte decided it was time to head back to London. Next day he went to see an agent named Tamburini, through whom he hired two singers. They were not 'of the first rank', as he describes them, and unlikely to have been 'the only ones unemployed in Italy'. The soprano Maddalena Allegranti and the tenor Vitale Damiani were serviceable, second-rank singers – far from the prizes Da Ponte had been sent to Italy to find. Allegranti's main claim to fame was that, in her youth, she had seduced Casanova. 'Her appearance, her grace, the sound of her voice', the old rogue declared in his memoirs, 'were more than I could resist.'

With Banti's eleven-year-old son, whom he had also been commissioned to bring back, and Allegranti's husband and son, the Da Pontes set off for London at once. There was the usual run of adventures – failing to sleep in rat-infested barns, stopping Banti's son running off with their valuables, travelling down the iced-over Elbe, past the wreckage of carriages that had not made it – before they reached Hamburg, where they had to wait a month for the ice in the harbour to melt. The stay used up what little was left of Da Ponte's thousand guineas. In March 1799 he arrived back in London with only fifty, but no regrets: 'I experienced such pleasure and enjoyment from the journey that I would not have missed it for all the money in the world.'

Taylor's reception was less than warm – as was that given to the singers Da Ponte had brought him. Damiani, in fact, never once appeared on the stage of the King's Theatre. Da Ponte had allowed him contractual choice of the opera in which he appeared; there ensued a heated debate with Taylor, and Damiani left London soon thereafter. Allegranti appeared in Cimarosa's *Il matrimonio segreto* in April 1799. But, in the words of a former admirer, 'Never was there a more pitiable attempt; she had scarcely a thread of a voice remaining, nor the power to sing a note in tune; her figure and acting were equally altered for the worse, and after a few nights she was obliged to retire, and quit the stage altogether.' Soon she, too, went home.

Taylor was furious. That autumn he dismissed Da Ponte, replacing him with Serafino Buonaiuti – whose verses, to Da Ponte, were 'even rougher and harder than his head, with which he could very well have butted a goat'. That autumn he bombarded Taylor with letters demanding his job back; all went unanswered, some thrown in the fire unopened. In the early morning of 10 March 1800 Da Ponte was lying in bed, con-tentedly receiving Nancy's greetings on his fifty-first birthday, when suddenly a stranger was in the room, throwing open the shutters and demanding that he rise, get dressed and go with him. Da Ponte seized a revolver he kept beside the bed, and 'with a terrific shout' ordered him out of the room. The stranger left, but stationed himself outside the door, sending in word that he had a warrant for Da Ponte's arrest. He had endorsed a bill of £300 for Taylor, which remained unpaid.

Again cursing himself for ignoring Casanova's advice, Da Ponte was escorted to the King's Bench, where it took him twenty-four hours to find a friend willing to stand bail. But he was rearrested twice in the next twenty-four hours, and jailed some thirty times over the next three months.

As MP for Leominster, Taylor was immune from arrest for debt; all his forfeits now fell on Da Ponte, whose life became insufferable. 'After spending my last penny in paying the costs of the courts, the officers, my lodgings, the lawyers on both sides, coaches, messengers, etc., after having given the greater part of my furniture to that merciless man's creditors, I was obliged to declare myself bankrupt – the first poor wretch in England, I believe, to do so without owing a man in the world a farthing.'

He was thus freed from the danger of house arrest. But what was he to live on? Federici and Gallerini also found themselves in jail, having endorsed Taylor's bills, and had the nerve to appeal for Da Ponte's help. Reduced to 'a state of affliction difficult to describe', Da Ponte was out walking in the Strand, near Temple Bar, when a bull that had escaped from the nearby slaughterhouse came rampaging towards him. Forced to seek shelter in the nearest shop, as the tumult went by, he found himself in a bookseller's, where his eye fell on a copy of Virgil. Leafing through it, he was reminded of his perennial motto: 'No need to despair.' He would open a bookshop.

Since 1797 he had been printing opera libretti; now he would sell them as well, plus the Italian literature to which he had always been so devoted. For thirty guineas, which he obtained by endorsing yet another of Taylor's bills, he bought the bookseller's entire stock of Italian literature – some six or seven hundred volumes, which he guessed to be worth some four hundred guineas. After scouring London bookshops for more, and thanking God for the booksellers' ignorance while bemoaning the low repute into which Italian literature had fallen, he soon had a collection of more than a thousand volumes. In 1800 he published an annotated catalogue of his collection and opened his own shop at 5 Pall Mall (today Farlow's Country Girl, an outfitters specializing in outdoor clothing for tweedy women).

So successful did his new business prove that Da Ponte had soon paid off the mortgage on his printing office, and published several books of his own, including a volume of his poems under the title *Saggi poetici*. His customers included nobility and an Italian scholar who became a close friend, Thomas James Mathias, later librarian at Buckingham Palace. Having paid a visit to Da Ponte's shop, and especially admired his ode to Joseph II, Mathias became an evangelist for Da Ponte's *Saggi poetici*, sending a copy to his poet friend Samuel Henley with a commendation of Da Ponte as 'a man of genius, learning and taste'. His ode to Joseph was 'one of the finest lyrical compositions in the language ... I believe that if Petrarch had heard it, he would have given the author a place quite close to his own, without asking for any other proof of his lively, fertile, cultured and sublime mind.'

The lofty-minded Mathias took a dim view of *opera buffa*, and was dismayed by Da Ponte's continuing freelance work as poet to the King's Theatre, which had recently resulted in his first new opera for some years, *Armida*, with music by Bianchi. That autumn gave Da Ponte a chance to change Mathias's mind. Banti had given her last performance, and was finally heading home to Italy; having escorted her as far as Paris, Taylor stayed there to avoid arrest for debt during the dissolution of parliament. He lost control of the King's Theatre, whose debtors recalled Da Ponte to his post on 'very handsome' terms. In short order he wrote two new libretti, both of which proved popular successes, and gave Mathias 'a less unfavourable view of theatre poets'.

With money, for once, less of a problem, Da Ponte persuaded his brother Paolo to come to London, to work in a piano business to which he had taken a fancy. 'If it doesn't ruin me,' he wrote, 'perhaps it will make my fortune. Who knows?' Paolo duly came, and joined Mathias as the only two men in London on whom Da Ponte could rely. All others, by his account, were treacherous villains. Many of them, nonetheless, even Taylor, he helped out as his own benevolent form of revenge. These perverse acts of charity were to prove his London undoing.

In 1803 the Irish impresario Francis Gould bought out Taylor's interest in the King's Theatre, whose fortunes soon improved dramatically. Banti's replacement, Elizabeth Billington, proved very popular with audiences if less so with critics; her stage charms, wrote one, had been impaired by 'a degree of embonpoint which deprived her actions of the elegance and grace which had formerly distinguished them'. Within the year she had been joined by the Italian contralto Giuseppina Grassini, accounted a fine actress by no less a judge than Mrs Siddons. An accomplished new composer was also imported: Peter von Winter, born in Mannheim in 1754, appointed Kapellmeister to Karl Theodor, Elector of Bavaria, at the age of only twenty-four.

It was for Winter that Da Ponte wrote his last three libretti. On 31 May 1803 *La grotta di Calipso* was very well received, apparently inaugurating a promising new partnership. On 22 March 1804 Mrs Billington took the leading role in *Il trionfo dell'amor fraterno*, again to great acclaim, with *The Times* of the opinion that 'the invention of the poet has embellished the ground-work with several incidents which, although not strictly classical, may be fairly allowed'. And 31 May was the first night of *Il ratto di Proserpina*, an especial triumph for Grassini, who sang Proserpina to Billington's Ceres (the only time they ever appeared together). This was one of those first nights that become legendary, making Grassini's name in London and winning Da Ponte as much praise as Winter. 'It is a grand and sublime production,' wrote the *Morning Post*, 'and in every point – in the composition both of music and poetry ... is altogether without a parallel.' This was also to prove, after some fifty operas over twenty-two years, the last libretto Lorenzo Da Ponte would write.

If he had stuck solely to writing libretti, all might have been well. But Da Ponte would insist on dabbling in business, never his forte. His bookshop thrived; in 1803 he moved to larger premises on the Haymarket, near the Caffè degl'Italiani which Casanova had told him to avoid – advice he again, no doubt, ignored. But he was soon forced to start offloading stock to pay the bills he had underwritten for Taylor and others. A partnership with the music publishers Corn and Dussek foundered, to the point where one fled abroad and the other was jailed, leaving Da Ponte liable for their debts. Another collaboration, with the printers and publishers Dulau and Nardini, at first prospered, despite a titanic row with Casti over an expurgated edition of his *Gli animali parlanti*. But in time these two also went bankrupt.

The beginning of the end for Da Ponte was the return of Taylor to London – in secret, for fear of arrest. But he was betrayed by his debtors, and thrown into jail. Inexplicably, Da Ponte went out of his way to help his old tormentor. Perhaps it was his pride, perhaps his innocent good nature, most likely his paradoxical belief that a good turn is the best form of revenge. But he undertook a complex series of transactions to get a surprised and grateful Taylor released from jail – for a while.

Soon Taylor was back in prison again, to spend most of the rest of his life under King's Bench rules – an acceptable fate, for a man of his disposition, as a small payment on account meant the debtor was released from jail but confined to a certain area, crowded with like-minded, convivial souls with whom the time could be passed pleasantly enough. Occasionally Taylor even managed to escape to the country and indulge in his favourite pastime, fishing. But soon he would be hauled back to the jurisdiction of the King's Bench and 'a coterie ... which, in point of vivacity and zest of enjoyment, could not be excelled by the freest of the free'.

Da Ponte remained inextricably involved in Taylor's financial dis-
asters, which gradually rendered his life unmanageable. It wasn't
enough to sell off precious stock from his bookshop at a fraction of its
true value, as recorded in a catalogue of sale in the British Museum:
'One of the finest Collections of Books which has been offered to the
Public in this country for many years, being the first and scarce part
of the genuine property of Mr. L. Daponte, Bookseller (Retiring from
the Bookselling business) ...'

Soon he was also forced to move his family to a smaller house; now
there was a new son, Lorenzo, as well as four-year-old Joseph, five-year-
old Frances (known as Fanny) and eleven-year-old Louisa. By the summer
of 1804 his situation was so desperate that he was forced to confront
perhaps the most difficult decision of his life. In 1794 Nancy's parents had
moved to America, with her brother and his wife; now they had put down
roots there, they wrote begging Nancy to visit. In those days, a voyage
to America could last several months, and was not lightly undertaken,
especially with four small children.

If Nancy went, she would have to go for at least six months, perhaps
a year; and it would be months before Da Ponte even knew whether she
had made it safely across the Atlantic. By deciding to let her go to America,
with their four children, he seems to have begun to contemplate the idea
of moving there himself. He would stay in London for now; there were
too many business enterprises in hand, one of which might just come
good. And Nancy could take her savings with her, which would keep them
out of reach of his creditors. But he could not bear the thought of life
without his wife and children.

A devoted family man, the sometime libertine was utterly bereft as he
watched the *Pigou* sail off from Gravesend to Philadelphia in early August
1804 with his wife and children aboard. 'When it first began to move, my
feelings as a loving father and husband who had pronounced his own hard
sentence by permitting his loved ones to set off on a long voyage were
not to be described.'

In a wretched state he hurried back to London to keep his promise to
rescue the opera's principal bass, Rovedino, from his creditors. But life
without Nancy and the children soon became insupportable. Occasionally
he would tell Mathias that he was going to follow Nancy to America,
urging him to come along, only to be asked: 'But what would you do in

America, Lorenzo?' It was a good question. There was no opera in America, and scant interest in Italian literature.

Mathias and his brother Paolo, 'whom I loved as dearly as myself', were the only people who made life in London tolerable. Even they, however, were unable to assuage the torrent of debt that soon overwhelmed him. Da Ponte's life became 'hell on earth'.

Promissory notes on behalf of Taylor, Corri, Rovedino and many others soon outbalanced the value of Da Ponte's remaining books, and his financial problems were compounded by the cost of running a barely stocked bookshop. Seeing no way out, he decided to call all his creditors together, explain his situation, and put his affairs in the hands of 'two honest men' who, when all his accounts had been balanced, would have enough left 'to pay everyone to the last farthing'. Taylor thought his plan ridiculous. 'You've lived in London all these years,' he told Da Ponte, 'and still you haven't worked out the kind of men you're dealing with.' All his creditors, or those of the men whose promissory notes he had signed, were lawyers or usurers. 'You can try,' Taylor continued, 'and if it doesn't work, go to America, stay there until my affairs are settled ... and then don't be afraid to return to London.' He even promised Da Ponte he would ensure that he was still sent his salary as theatre poet, in return for 'the occasional opera'.

On 1 April 1805, towards six in the evening, the meeting was duly convened. Da Ponte's lawyer showed his creditors the accounts, offering to collect what was owed him and to pay what he owed. 'They heard him out patiently, drank twelve bottles of wine (which they graciously allowed me to pay for), and after many murmurings of "We shall see", "Let us calculate" and "We'll talk it over", and other such meaningless phrases, bade me goodnight and left at around nine o'clock. I began to feel that Taylor had spoken the truth, went home to bed, and after some time fell asleep.'

The next thing he knew, someone was banging on the door. Outside he found a friendly policeman, come to warn him that he was to be arrested in the morning. Da Ponte thanked him and tried to tip him; instead he found himself gratefully accepting a parting gift of a few guineas. The constable went on his way, and Da Ponte realized he had only one choice.

Quickly he dressed and took himself to Gould's house to explain his dilemma. It was nearly midnight, but the good-hearted impresario listened carefully, and gave him an advance on his salary of one hundred guineas. Then it was back home for a few hours' sleep before going into town to enquire about ships sailing for America. In the first shop he tried, he found Captain Abishai Hayden of Nantucket, master of the *Columbia*, posting a notice that he would be sailing for Philadelphia on 7 April.

Da Ponte paid Hayden forty-four guineas for his passage, and rushed to the Aliens' Office, where the director heard him out with surprising sympathy (or, as Da Ponte saw it, 'a kindness and dignity befitting him'). He gave orders that Da Ponte should be issued with a passport, in conditions of the utmost discretion. He then took a post-chaise to Gravesend with his brother Paolo.

When Da Ponte told Paolo that he was going to America, 'I thought he would die.' But he promised either to send for him, or to return within six months. Neither, in fact, would come to pass; Paolo would be declared bankrupt later that month, and would be hounded to death by his creditors within a couple of years. Lorenzo Da Ponte, for his part, would never see Europe again.

PART THREE

—

America

12

The Grocer

I T IS typical of his tendency to exaggerate that, in his memoirs, Da Ponte recalls his 'long, unfortunate, tedious and uncomfortable' voyage to Philadelphia as lasting eighty-six days, or almost three months. In truth, it was quite long and arduous enough at fifty-seven, or slightly less than two months.

The captain turned out to be a 'swindler' more accustomed to whale-fishing, who 'treated his passengers as if they were the lowest of his sailors, and his sailors like the sea-monsters he hunted'. All Da Ponte got for his forty-four guineas was a hard wooden bunk – he was obliged to improvise a mattress from his clothes – and barely edible food. In the centre of his bowl of gruel sat something looking less like a chicken than 'a plucked crow which had been mauled by a cat'.

Miserable and bored, Da Ponte killed the time by lapsing back into one of his old Venetian habits, gambling – losing what little money he had playing cards with the only other passenger of any interest, a Pennsylvania merchant named Richard Edwards, known to him as 'Odoardo'. When the *Columbia* reached Philadelphia on 4 June 1805, 'Odoardo' had to lend Da Ponte $32.31 to rescue his few remaining worldly goods – a violin, tea urn, carpet, some books and 'one box of fiddle strings and suspenders' – from the United States Customs.

After landing in a New World barely thirty years old, Da Ponte's first challenge was to find Nancy and their children. It may seem strange that he did not know where his family was living; but he testifies that he was obliged to seek out the captain who had brought them over, to be given only the name of a street in New York. By sunrise the next day, after borrowing the four-dollar stagecoach fare from 'Odoardo', Da Ponte was knocking on a random door, which turned out to be the right one. Fearing that he might have been shipwrecked, so long had his journey taken, Nancy welcomed her feckless husband with 'every mark of tenderness', despite the fact that he had brought so little from London beyond the clothes he stood up in. By what means we do not know, this resourceful woman had herself managed to accumulate almost seven thousand dollars, which she now placed at her husband's disposal.

Wary of wasting it by sitting idle, Da Ponte ruefully contemplated the unwelcome truth that, with Italian opera yet to arrive in America, there was no chance of work as a poet or librettist. Whatever the 'Old World' now represented to him – Venice and Casanova, Vienna and Mozart, London and Taylor – this New World, exemplified by the mere village that was New York, had very little to offer a man of his gifts and qualities. So he had little choice but to accept the unlikely, misguided advice of his mercantile father-in-law, John Grahl, that he espouse capitalism and set up shop as a grocer. This was not a calling for which Mozart's librettist was ideally suited. 'Anyone with the least imagination will understand how I laughed at myself every time my poetic hand was obliged to weigh out two ounces of tea or measure half a yard of "pigtail" (tobacco) for a cobbler or carter, or pour him out a morning dram for three cents.'

At first he prospered. After only three months, however, an outbreak of yellow fever in New York obliged him to move his family out to New Jersey, where Nancy's family had settled. In Elizabethtown he bought a small plot of land boasting a 'shack' from which he continued to ply his new trade. Here their fifth child was born, and christened Charles Grahl (though always known to his father as 'Carlo').

Soon, not for the first (or last) time, Da Ponte fell among dishonest business partners. While obliged to let customers pay him in kind, to keep the business afloat – 'lame horses, broken carts, disjointed chairs, old shoes, rancid butter, watery cider, rotten eggs, apples, brooms, turnips, potatoes' – he was meanwhile being swindled by unscrupulous money-lenders. Those who owed him money followed his own London example by performing midnight flits – one, who owed him a thousand dollars, to Jamaica – while those who lent him money inflated the amounts and threatened him with legal action. Within a year Da Ponte was obliged to sell up – land, house, business, all – to avoid jail by paying off debts of some four thousand dollars.

At the beginning of 1807, broke and with no prospect of work, he led his family back to New York. Nearly sixty, with no talents beyond the literary, his only hope was to become a teacher of Italian – the job he had so despised in London. But he soon discovered that in New York there was as much interest in Italian language and literature as in 'Turkish or Chinese'.

On enquiring about his chances of teaching Latin, he was told that 'the American gentleman thinks he knows it well enough not to need instruction from an Italian Latinist'. At this seemingly hopeless moment came the chance encounter which would launch Da Ponte upon the latest of his many lives.

Riley's bookstore on lower Broadway then stood much where today you will find the world-famous Strand, that vast honeycomb of second-hand books two blocks below Union Square. Wandering into Riley's one day in mid-December 1807, intent on assessing the local interest in Italian literature, Da Ponte fell into conversation with the proprietor. He had few Italian volumes in stock, Riley told him, because 'no one ever asks for them'.

The conversation was overheard by another customer, an elegantly dressed American who strolled over and joined in. At once Da Ponte could tell that this was a cultured man, sympathetic to his cause. So he asked him why Italian literature was so little studied in the enlightened country he believed America to be.

'Ah, sir,' replied the stranger, 'modern Italy is not, unfortunately, the Italy of ancient times. It is not she who has given to the world for all time the emulators or rather the rivals of the greatest of the Ancient Greeks.' With which he proceeded to tell the outraged Italian that his country could boast only five great writers, six at most, over the preceding six centuries. Asked by Da Ponte to name them, he came up with Dante, Petrarch, Boccaccio, Ariosto and Tasso before pausing, and saying, 'I really can't remember the sixth.'

Seizing the stranger's hand, on which he had been counting off his shortlist of great Italian writers, Da Ponte declared: 'You won't get your fingers free for a month, if you will let me keep hold of them until I have finished naming, one by one, the great Italian writers of the last six centuries.' Amused and intrigued, the customer replied: 'But we don't know them.' To which Da Ponte wistfully ventured: 'So I see. But if only you thought a teacher of Italian might be met with favour and encouragement ...'

'You can be sure of that,' smiled Riley, to the customer's enthusiastic agreement. It was Da Ponte's great good fortune that he had chanced to meet Clement Clarke Moore, then twenty-eight (less than half Da Ponte's age), later to achieve eminence as a theologian and lexicographer, and a lasting place in American folklore as the author of the poem 'A Visit from St Nicholas', which famously begins: "Twas the night before Christmas, / when all through the house, / Not a creature was stirring, / not even a mouse . . .'

Moore's father was Bishop Benjamin Moore, New York's second Protestant Episcopal Bishop, Rector of Trinity Church and then President of Columbia College. Knowing that his erudite parent would be intrigued by Da Ponte – a poet who had not merely read Metastasio, but known him – Moore invited him to dinner at his father's official residence at Columbia, then situated at the foot of Park Place, near Broadway. The Bishop had a smattering of Hebrew, but here was an Italian poet who could 'quote and even make apothegms in that sacred tongue'. The Vulgate and the Roman ritual Da Ponte also had 'at his fingers' tips', as his American admirer Arthur Livingston put it.

> Everyone had read six books of Virgil, and the more venturesome had gone on to nine or twelve. This person knew Virgil, Horace and other Latin poets by heart. He could turn a perfect Latin distich *ex tempore*. With Homer, too, and others of the Greeks, his knowledge, while not so vast, was precise and alive . . .

This was the man who had written the words for Mozart's operas! 'A man who had *heard* an opera – and was actually author of the words for two score librettos, knowing the ins and outs of immortal rhythms and melodies so that he could talk about music with a precision that dazzled and an authority that brooked no argument!'

And so it came to pass that just three days after their chance meeting in Riley's bookstore, thanks to the kindly enthusiasm of the aspiring young poet and his civilized father, Da Ponte found himself conducting his first Italian class in the Bishop's residence, with twelve pupils including both Riley and Moore *fils*. Among the others were the Bishop's nephew, Nathaniel Moore, later to become Professor of Greek and Latin at Columbia, eventually its President, and John MacVikar, its future Professor of Philosophy.

This momentous meeting, on 15 December 1807, was to prove the launch of the last, and in some ways the most glorious, of Da Ponte's many careers. Within a month, the class had doubled in size; soon, by his own account, he had more pupils than he could handle. This was the beginning of Da Ponte's passionate mission to bring the literature and culture of his motherland to his new, adopted home.

'Others came and looked Mr Da Ponte over,' as one historian puts it, the Livingstons, the Hamiltons, the Schuylers, the Duers, the Duanes, the Beekmans, the Ogilbies, the Onderdoncks. 'The ladies thought they might call on his wife. She too was a nice person – sweet, hard-working, stern with her children, intelligent.' Nancy's cooking was a revelation: *spaghetti alla napoletana, cappelletti alla bolognese, bisi col riso alla veneziana*. But this English-born woman could also speak French, German, Italian, Spanish and Dutch, and discuss literature and music 'quite as learnedly, and even less disconcertingly, than her husband'. The exotic Da Pontes were swiftly pronounced 'the find of the social season of 1807 in New York'.

Advertisements in the New York press soon announced the establishment of the Manhattan Academy for Young Gentlemen, proprietor Lorenzo Da Ponte, who would himself be teaching French, Latin and Italian while a 'very able' assistant would take classes in writing and ciphering, English grammar, geography and other 'juvenile rudiments'. The reformed libertine also vowed that 'every attention will be paid to the morals of those entrusted to his care' – which suggests that some were taken into the Da Ponte home as paying boarders. Under the name of 'Madame Duponte', Nancy would meanwhile head up the Manhattan Academy for Young Ladies, offering lessons in French, Italian and 'the art of making of artificial flowers', along with expert coaching in drawing, dancing and music.

Unable to obtain the Italian classics anywhere in New York, Da Ponte got his brother Paolo to send a consignment from London (despite his own lack of funds, shortly to see him die in abject poverty). Soon the business was thriving as a reborn Da Ponte threw himself into what had always been his forte: teaching. Whatever his other failings, there is no doubt that throughout his life, from ancient Treviso to emergent Manhattan, he had real gifts as an inspirational teacher, able to fire the young with such enthusiasm for literature that they remembered his lessons for the rest of their lives.

'The sweetest moments of existence were those passed in literary conversation and sympathetic study of the leading authors of Italy with the *caro maestro,*' according to one of his pupils, quoted in an 1868 edition of *Putnam's* magazine. 'There is no doubt at all that this was an important moment for the American mind,' in the judgement of Arthur Livingston. 'Da Ponte made Europe, poetry, painting, music, the artistic spirit, classical lore, a creative classical education, live for many important Americans as no one, I venture, had done before.'

For Livingston, Da Ponte's 'real self' was less librettist than teacher. 'A flare of real genius as a teacher Da Ponte had shown at Portogruaro and Treviso.' Now his years as a teacher in New York were bringing out the best in Da Ponte. In Livingston's estimation, 'it is a greater moment than his casual attachment to Mozart's fame.'

By 1811, when Alfieri's *Mirra* was performed (in Italian, of course) in a small theatre Da Ponte had built in his house, he was able to boast that 'our audience consisted of one hundred and fifty people whom, in the space of just three years, I had initiated into the Italian tongue'. He had achieved this in part by establishing 'day-time and evening assemblies where nothing but Italian was spoken'. The play may have shocked some of his audience's parents – Americans were still very puritanical about the theatre, especially if their daughters were taking part – but it says much for Da Ponte's evangelical skills as a teacher that so many former students turned out to hear a play in Italian.

Da Ponte's classical scholarship, testifies Livingston, 'his competence as a creative Latinist, dazzled quite as much as his fame as an Italian poet ... It was not so much Da Ponte as Da Ponte and his setting – the cultural atmosphere of his home that survived in his children and thereafter.' Almost a century after Da Ponte's death, Livingston had thrice heard 'some New Yorker boast, not quite knowing the significance of his words, that his grandmother, or his mother, "studied with Da Ponte"'.

By 1811, prospering at last, Da Ponte had become a thoroughgoing American. His native country no longer being an independent state, he had been an Austrian national since the fall of the Venetian Republic; but he had never really felt comfortable as a subject of the Habsburgs. With the common zeal of the immigrant exile, Da Ponte became 'far more patriotic than he had ever been before – a true American, not only according to the letter of the law, but in spirit as well'.

As April FitzLyon has aptly pointed out, Da Ponte had shown distinctively American qualities long before setting foot in the New World:

'his tremendous energy, his freshness of approach to every problem, his capacity for making friends, his adaptability, his strong enthusiasms, his love of novelty.' The radicalism of his Venetian youth, moreover, put him in the vanguard of Europeans looking to the new, democratic world order symbolized by the fledgling United States.

Now he would make it his personal mission to infuse this young country with a love and knowledge of European, especially Italian, culture, particularly music and literature. But just when things were, for once, going so well, Da Ponte made yet another wrong choice, allowing himself to be persuaded by his father-in-law to pursue his mission outside New York, in Pennsylvania. Here his attempts to establish another Academy failed, and he was forced to return to life as a grocer.

By his own account, it was more 'venomous bloodsuckers', or un-scrupulous business partners, who forced his reluctant retreat from New York. Just as the finances of the Manhattan Academies took a turn for the worse, apparently due as much to 'another enriching himself at my expense' as to a sudden decline in enrolment, the Da Pontes received a letter from Nancy's sister Louisa singing the praises of Sunbury, the small Pennsylvanian town where she and the Grahls had now settled. Given their altered circumstances, and her fondness for her family, Nancy and her husband decided they might as well join them.

As is so often the way in America, the Da Pontes went to Sunbury for seven days and wound up staying seven years. At first, the newly natu-ralized American loved the place, waxing lyrical about its idyllic setting, its hills and forests, flora and fauna, game and wildlife – and mountain lakes, whose waters were 'as clear, fresh and sweet as those in which Petrarch's Laura "bathed her fair limbs"', and whose trout were 'as tasty as those which the Lakes of Como or Garda produce for the Lombard gourmand'. (This is significant as the only moment in all Da Ponte's prose writings when he chooses to describe his natural surroundings.)

Spread out along the east bank of the Susquehanna River, the town itself was unexceptional – 'the streets are not neat, nor the buildings handsome' – but the view across its 'fine, navigable' river was 'truly wonderful, showing the windings of the river, the woods and hills and hamlets with which the opposite bank is adorned'.

The small town of Sunbury, population just over ten thousand, is still largely white today, a suburb of nowhere – the nearest city, Baltimore, is more than a hundred miles away – with a population of predominantly

German ancestry, proud of its historic town centre, complete with eighteenth-century fort and covered bridge. Already settled there in 1811 were Nancy's father John Grahl, her brother Peter and her sister Louisa (from London) and their families.

Like most husbands, Da Ponte was marginally less enthusiastic about his wife's family than she was. So what was it about Sunbury that beguiled him, a city-dweller all his life, to the point where he could feel at home in a provincial backwater peopled by uncultured, strait-laced Puritans? It has been suggested that 'he was tempted by the idea of an idyllic, peaceful old age in the country, a mirage which sometimes appears to essentially urban men in late middle-age'. More likely, as an opportunist younger than his sixty-two years, he nourished hopes of being close to the Grahls as the time approached for the reading of their wills.

So Da Ponte put down roots in Sunbury. Soon he and Nancy were joined there by their eldest daughter Louisa, and her husband of two years, Miles Franklin Clossey. The family patriarch took a house in Sunbury's most fashionable neighbourhood, among the 'best' families – the Grants, the Halls, the Bujers, the Smiths – with whom he soon forged warm friendships. Or so he says; there is a note of desperation in his account of their 'evening parties, country dances, jolly feasts and the usual games'. Could the revels of bourgeois Sunbury really survive comparison with those of Venice and Vienna, Casanova and Mozart?

Still, he insists, his first eighteen months there passed 'very agreeably', as he made an adequate living by more than mere grocery; as well as provisions, he procured medical supplies from Philadelphia to sell to his doctor brother-in-law, Peter Grahl, and other customers. Once a few of the 'best' families also took advantage of his presence by hiring him to educate their offspring, he managed to avoid making inroads into the savings of 'three or four' thousand dollars he had managed to bring from New York.

The rot set in when his brother-in-law Grahl persuaded him that, pleasant though it was to make a decent living on a cash turnover, there were far greater profits to be had from allowing his customers to trade on credit. The ever gullible Da Ponte went along with the scheme, with the good doctor himself vouching for the debtors in question. By the autumn the shelves of his store were empty, as indeed was his till – apart from 'phantoms of real money' such as bills of exchange and IOUs, which turned out, when the sums came due, to have 'about as much value as the leaves on the trees in the middle of November'. Never again would he trust his brother-in-law – 'no longer the man I had known at Trieste'.

At this point in his memoirs Da Ponte again embarks on long, tedious tirades against sundry merchants who had duped and deceived him, including one Philadelphian who avoided paying him back by stealing one of his London promissory notes to Taylor and handing it over to the constabulary, thus getting him arrested. Whatever the rights and wrongs of his dealings – though never much of a businessman, he was by no means as innocent as he portrays himself – it is hard to believe that Da Ponte was anything other than thoroughly miserable during these long years shuffling between Philadelphia and Sunbury in the hope of eking out a modest living. 'Instead of writing odes to the crowned heads of Europe,' as it has been succinctly put, 'he was now writing out bills for sausages and dried prunes to the citizens of a Pennsylvania village.'

On one occasion, having been sold a dud chaise and horses in Philadelphia, he was pitched out of the carriage when its shafts broke, suffering a broken rib, fractured collar-bone and 'more than a dozen' other injuries. After three weeks' convalescence in the village of Orvisburg, he was carried back to Sunbury on a pile of straw – and then presented with a bill for fifty-six dollars for his twenty-two-day stay.

Despite such low points, and a general sense that he was making the best of a very bad patch, Da Ponte had as many ups as downs during those Sunbury years. At one point he owned at least two houses and as many as six horses. His enforced travels back and forth turned into a flourishing courier service for other businesses as well as his own; 'L. de Ponty's Wagon', as it was called, became a familiar sight on the road between Sunbury and Philadelphia. By 1814 he was diversifying into other business ventures; in Philadelphia, at 29 North Street, he opened a millinery store, in Sunbury a distillery. This may seem as incongruous a fate for Mozart's librettist as making hats or selling sausages, but it was in his blood; to this day, in the Treviso area of the Veneto, Northern Italy, distillers are to be found by the name of Conegliano-Da Ponte. The descendants of his half-brothers, it seems, retained their adopted name while reverting to their original one.

The Sunbury records show that, by the end of 1814, Lorenzo Da Ponte was the town's second largest taxpayer, prosperous enough to build himself a brick house, the only three-storey home in the county. But his hopes of inheriting his in-laws' wealth proved vain. He had not been mentioned in the wills of either his father-in-law John Grahl or his brother-in-law Charles Niccolini, both of whom had died during his time in Sunbury. When his sister-in-law Louisa, Niccolo's widow, died in 1815, she left $5,000 to her sister Nancy, in a trust fund to be administered by one of the town worthies (and, gallingly, Da Ponte family friends), Charles Hall. The interest would go to Nancy during her lifetime; upon her death, the capital was to be divided among her children. In other words, Louisa Grahl knew her brother-in-law well enough to be determined to keep his hands off her money.

Da Ponte's bitter complaints sound like special pleading, if not sour grapes:

> This woman had been a widow for some years, and was absolute mistress of a considerable fortune which she had acquired almost entirely through my charity and through the industry and talents of her sister; she had no children, and although I knew that she did not particularly like me, nevertheless I hoped that on her deathbed she would not dare to be so unjust as to deprive me entirely and for ever of property which her sister, through exaggerated caution and too much sisterly confidence, placed in her hands.

When his nemesis Peter Grahl died a year later, in 1816, Da Ponte breathed a sigh of relief about the $500 he owed his brother-in-law, only to find it called in by his estate. 'The unhealthy side of this town corrupted his good nature and hardened his heart,' he wrote of the man he had first known in Trieste. By way of petulant retaliation, he sued Peter's widow, Nancy's sister-in-law Elizabeth, for the return of jewellery due his wife (as he saw it) from their mother's estate.

When this gambit, too, failed, Da Ponte decided that Sunbury had nothing more to offer him. In later years, in his memoirs, he referred to it as 'the fatal town of Sunbury'. Then still a frontier town, full of con-men and opportunists, it had ruined him. 'When I left New York, I took with me merchandise worth more than three thousand dollars,' he testified. 'When I left Sunbury, an old carriage, a broken-down horse and twelve thalers contained everything I possessed.' During his seven years there, he told Nathaniel Moore, he had lost more than twelve thousand dollars.

But he had gained his first grandchild, Matilda, born to his daughter Louisa and her husband Clossey in 1815. (They chose the name, presumably, without knowing of her grandfather's adventure in Venice with that Neapolitan Matilda more than forty years earlier.) Da Ponte had seen another daughter, Fanny, marry a local boy, but less happily. His new son-in-law turned out to be a wastrel, a 'parasite' in Da Ponte's word; within four years Fanny had divorced him and moved back in with her parents. Da Ponte may have lost money, but he had made friends and won admirers. His Sunbury physician, Dr Samuel Jackson, remembered him as 'a perfectly honest man, a delightful companion, unsuspicious and often led into trouble by rogues'.

The disappointment of Da Ponte's expectations from the Grahl family left him nothing more to hope for in this provincial backwater, whereas his frequent visits to the great city of Philadelphia had persuaded him that it was promise-crammed. Starved, above all, of anything approaching a life of the intellect – in his seven years in Sunbury he had written but one short poem, a *canzone* dedicated in 1816 to his London friend Mathias – he determined to uproot his family again, and move to the state capital in hope of a return to teaching. On 24 August 1818 Da Ponte left Sunbury for Philadelphia with his son Joseph, leaving Nancy behind to settle their affairs before joining him.

This latest life was to last less than a year. The first month saw Nancy stranded back in Sunbury, desperately appealing to Charles Hall for an advance on future interest to pay off their debts, while Da Ponte found only two pupils in Philadelphia and had soon run out of money.

Chance again intervened in the shape of a letter from his sometime pupil, Nathaniel Moore, Clement's cousin, now Professor of Greek at Columbia (though his letter, charmingly enough, was written in Italian). Da Ponte wrote back with details of his many creditors, the paucity of Nancy's income, and the 'dreadful' crisis in which he found himself. Might it be possible, he asked Moore, for a New York publisher to advance him some money on a manuscript he was writing? It was a fuller version of his *Storia Compendia della vita di Lorenzo Da Ponte*, published twelve years before, entitled (in translation) *An extract from the Life of Lorenzo Da Ponte, with the History of several dramas by him, and among others, il Figaro, il Don Giovanni and La Scuola degli amanti, set to music by Mozart.*

This was to prove an early version, if not a first draft, of Da Ponte's memoirs. Moore seems to have pulled off a deal; for the following month Da Ponte was writing him an effusive letter of thanks, and his short book was indeed published the following year. After expressing his 'boundless' gratitude, Da Ponte congratulates his sometime pupil on becoming a Columbia professor: 'How I should love in my old age to find a similar post in Italian literature! This dream often haunts me; but I am very much afraid that in America it will never be anything more than a dream . . .'

There were not enough pupils in Philadelphia, he told Moore, and insufficient interest in Italian literature, to sustain any sort of life as a teacher or poet. Life in the Philadelphia suburbs, moreover, was little more stimulating than the dead hand of Sunbury. Despite a happy domestic life, now that Nancy had finally joined him, Da Ponte was desperately bored, an intellectual and a music-lover stranded in a thoroughly philistine community. He was bereft of like-minded companionship, as he complained in a letter to Clement Moore in New York, lamenting how much he missed him and his other erudite, metropolitan friends.

When Moore replied that the feeling was mutual, with an offer to line up more Italian pupils in New York, Da Ponte seized the chance to return. 'Benedetta sia il giorno!': it was a blessed day, after seven years in Sunbury, and eight months in Philadelphia, on which he headed back to New York in April 1819 – leaving Nancy behind again for now, in case this last, desperate throw of the dice also proved futile.

Da Ponte's get-rich-quick American dream was over. Now it was time to return to teaching, with equanimity, as what turned out to be just the latest of the last few of his many lives.

13

The Professor

NOW SEVENTY, Da Ponte still cut a dashing figure. He was 'tall, well-built, very beautiful, and of highly polished manners', in the words of his Sunbury physician, Dr Jackson. The sometime libertine was also 'very temperate and regular in all his ways'. His cheeks may now have become hollow, and his gums toothless, but his eyes were as sharp and glistening as ever, lending him a resemblance to Voltaire.

Marriage and the years had mellowed Da Ponte, who was now anxious that his own children observe due propriety. A much better father than his own, he took his son Joseph with him to New York because 'the dissipations of the young men of that city frightened me so much that I thought it dangerous to leave him there for long without a father to keep an eye on him'.

Da Ponte's new-found respectability – or plausibility, as and when required – also explains his unlikely appeal to Clement Moore, not the most obvious candidate to become his close friend and admirer. Three years before their first meeting in Riley's bookstore, when only twenty-five, Moore had written of his regret that 'more of the well-disposed among (his) young countrymen do not devote their leisure hours to the attainment of useful learning, rather than to frivolous amusements or political wrangling'.

This strait-laced, God-fearing, high-minded man, founder of New York's General Theological Seminary, had much in common with Father Hueber, Da Ponte's Jesuit friend in Dresden. So, these days, did Da Ponte himself. It was therefore vital, with Joseph successfully installed at Columbia College (despite his father's inability to pay the fees), and Moore helping him rebuild his teaching career, that his past did not return to haunt him – as now it threatened to.

New York had changed as much as it had grown during Da Ponte's decade away; shedding its self-conscious provincialism, the city was waking up to culture as defined by everything European. It was not just that the offspring of the new American fortunes were embarking on the European Grand Tour and bringing back with them some fancy goods and notions. While Da Ponte's back had been turned, New York had been invaded by a 'whole stream' of Italian exiles, 'who, without careers, means, or – alas for them – talent, had exchanged guns and bayonets for dictionaries and grammars and begun to teach language'.

As desperate as Da Ponte to find pupils, these *arrivistes* resented the return to town of this popular, well-connected teacher, whose connection with Mozart lent him such glamour; and one in particular set out to destroy him. Marco Antonio Casati, a defrocked priest, anonymously published a pamphlet – which he sent to the parents of all Da Ponte's pupils, among many others – accusing him of a dozen heinous crimes ranging from embezzlement and adultery to murder.

Amid the wild accusations were some which hit home, as in: 'He was obliged in his early life to quit Venice for his misbehaviour.' Luckily for Da Ponte, his accuser had no more detail; in fact Casati got more of his facts wrong than right, even suggesting that Da Ponte's 'impudent' claim to have been Joseph II's court poet in Vienna was 'a ridiculous falsehood'. There was nothing about his Jewish origins, which were not unknown in New York, or even that he had been a Catholic priest. The accusation of adultery was invented, when so many true cases were available, and that of murder plain absurd: 'A young Miss Williams was sent to his house to finish her education. She soon became corrupted, and one day ... (Da Ponte) in his rage so ill-treated this unfortunate girl that she soon took to her bed, from which she never arose.'

In fact this young woman was still alive, by now the mother of five children; and Da Ponte needed only to produce testimonials from her parents to see off this gravest charge against him. The rest were so scurrilous, and tainted by association, that he probably need not have bothered to refute them to preserve his place in decent New York society. But such reticence was never in his nature. He wheeled out various friends and patrons to defend his good name, among them a former pupil named Samuel Jarvis, now a Professor at Yale, and the doctor whom Casati had named as blaming Miss Williams's illness on Da Ponte. Each paid tribute to him as 'firstly, a man of letters; second, a good husband, blessed with a loving wife, and a good father; and, thirdly, a complete gentleman'.

The truth of Da Ponte's early life was, of course, at least as bad, if not worse, than Casati's charges. Had his accuser been more competent, would he have been ruined? 'There is no doubt at all,' by one account, that in Puritan New York 'he would not have had a single pupil.' In an introduction to the first English translation of Da Ponte's memoirs, however, Arthur Livingston takes a more convincing (and characteristically generous) New World line. There had been 'unpleasant rumours' from time to time, from London, from Italy, from Austria – banishments, immoralities, bankruptcies. But America was 'a free country and no questions asked! Didn't Joseph Priestley leave England in a barrel? Between the past in Europe and the future in America the Atlantic Ocean rolled. It took republican institutions to bring out the man in a man!'

For all his faults, moreover, Da Ponte was turning out to be a model immigrant. 'Among the millions of immigrants that America has received from Europe, Lorenzo Da Ponte stands almost in a class by himself,' in Livingston's view:

> We had religious believers cast off by the religious wars of Europe. We had patriots hurled upon our shores by political convulsions abroad. We had the hopeful and laborious poor of every nation attracted by the economic prospects of a new country. But in him we had an individual pressed forth by a chain of circumstances from the rotting core of the collapsing intellectual aristocracy of the Old *Régime*.
>
> Why so much astonishment that in Europe he should have had the defects and blemishes of that dying *Régime*? When, on the morning of June 4, in the year of 1805, he passed the Custom House in Philadelphia, a new life began for him – the life of Lorenzo Da Ponte, the American, an American who lived an interesting and useful life in the country of his adoption, left abiding traces upon the trend of American culture, and imparted a high-minded conception of the spiritual life to his children and his children's children, whereby our country, both North and South, has profited not a little.

That was written more than a century later, in 1929. Seven years earlier Da Ponte's first English-language biographer, Professor Joseph Russo of Columbia University's Italian department, had expressed the view that 'seldom if ever, indeed, has a more interesting personality come to these shores from Europe'.

Even in his eighth decade, Da Ponte had yet to achieve much that would prompt Livingston's encomium. But the seeds of his contribution to American life, via his championship of Italian literature and music, were now sown in the shape of his donation of Italian books to various libraries, forming the nucleus of their world-class collections today.

'Anyone perusing the mid-nineteenth-century book catalogues of New York City's two oldest libraries would be struck by the amazing number of Italian books listed,' observes the literary historian Paul Cohen. The 1839 catalogue of the Columbia College library lists as many Italian works of fiction as there are works in all other literatures combined, including English; in this manuscript catalogue, 'Romaic, Latin, Spanish, French and English' fiction make up a single group, while there are so many entries for Italian fiction that it merits a separate category of its own.

Likewise, the 1838 printed catalogue of the New York Society Library includes a disproportionate number of Italian books among its entries. 'Did Italian studies really rate so high among Columbia College students and members of the New York Society Library in the 1830s?' asks Cohen in a 1987 edition of *American Book Collector*. 'The surge of interest in Italian culture was the result of a single-handed effort by Lorenzo Da Ponte to promote Italian studies in America.' Cohen approvingly quotes the Professor of Columbia University's Italian department as calling Da Ponte nothing less than 'the founder of Italian culture in America'.

What began out of necessity became quintessentially American philanthropy. While in Philadelphia, though he could ill afford it, Da Ponte had not been able to resist acquiring from an itinerant fellow countryman a complete set of the Italian classics in the (then recent) Milan edition – 'a veritable treasure-house of literature'; amid his financial crisis, he had then offered to sell it to Philadelphia's Public Library. After some months of deliberation, the city elders declined his offer, leaving him with a large debt. He presented them with half a dozen volumes, anyway, to demonstrate the error of their ways, and sent Joseph to New York to raise money by selling half the rest.

Now he was back there again, with a decent-sized class of twenty-four (twelve of each gender), he sold some eighty volumes to his pupils as textbooks, with the proviso that on graduation they donate them to the New York Public Library – which, 'though rich in Greek and Latin works, had not yet given a place on its shelves to Italian, their eldest successor'. Da Ponte himself initiated the bequest with sixty volumes from his own collection.

In time, he would perform the same signal service for Columbia College, though he would never realize his dream of founding an Italian library in New York. The city was rich in wines and grapes from Sicily, he reflected, oil, olives and silk from Venice, cheese from Parma, straw hats from Livorno, rope from Rome and Padua, rosolio from Trieste, sausages from Bologna, macaroni from Naples and statuettes from Lucca. But Italian books still remained conspicuous by their absence.

By now, the autumn of 1820, Nancy and the other children had joined Da Ponte in a rented house on Jay Street, the first of at least twelve New York addresses over the next two decades. Just as young Lorenzo was duly installed at Columbia, his older brother Joseph was desperately persuading his reluctant father to let him leave, after only twelve months, to return to Philadelphia, where he would graduate as a lawyer in one more year rather than two. After six months Joseph returned home unexpectedly – 'so thin, wasted and pale, that the moment I saw him I knew there was no hope'. Six more months, and Joseph was dead of consumption in his twenty-first year.

As Da Ponte grieved, one of his pupils attempted to console him with a volume of Byron, his *Prophecy of Dante*, written two years earlier when the poet was living in Ravenna, near Dante's tomb. It proved a shrewd choice. In an open letter to Byron Da Ponte wrote that 'the gentle melancholy pervading it from the first pages did not so much console my sadness as minister to it'. Sensing a kinship between Dante's travails and his own – both old, exiled, unsung and homesick – he resolved to translate the work into Italian *terza rima*.

To do so, he felt he must get away for a while from New York and its attendant sadness. So he persuaded a dozen of his pupils to accompany him and his family to the upstate country estate of some wealthy friends, the John R. Livingstons, who had offered him an open invitation. Here at Staatsburg on the Hudson he spent a restorative summer writing and teaching. 'I got up at dawn, spent an hour with my pupils or my sons reading some Italian writer of prose or poetry. I then had a country breakfast with them, and half an hour later I lay beneath a peach or apple tree, and translated a passage of the poem, which eased my grief.'

When tired of writing, he would give Italian lessons to three local ladies whose 'warm welcome' and 'peerless beauty' also helped him forget his sorrows. Two months of this, and he returned to New York with his wounds 'not altogether healed', but with 'the strength and the courage to endure them'.

Soon after the publication of his translation, word reached Da Ponte from Florence that Byron himself had read *Le profezia di Dante* 'with much satisfaction'. The news came in a letter from the American vice-consul, Giacomo Ombrosi, who also warmly approved his pamphlet *Discorso apologetico*. This defence of his homeland was written in white heat the previous year, after a New York City councillor, an Irish-born lawyer named Charles Phillips, had used the scandal surrounding Caroline of Brunswick, estranged wife of King George IV, to 'blacken, slander and vilify the name and character of the Italian nation'.

Even republican New York was agog at the wayward Caroline's lurid trial for adultery after a trip through Europe during which she had supposedly taken her Italian courier, Bartolomeo Pergami, as her lover. In an open letter to the King, Phillips deplored the Queen's conduct while arguing that Pergami's was typical of all Italian men. Considering himself the senior Italian then living in New York, if not the entire United States, an enraged Da Ponte felt obliged to defend his fellow countrymen by springing to the Queen's defence, arguing that Pergami had been 'her counsellor, companion, guest, confidant, friend ... Here let it rest.' There followed an impassioned defence of his homeland, which, 'though an ungrateful and cruel stepmother towards me, I have loved and shall always love with the most tender filial affection, until the last moment of my life'.

Although an accomplished linguist, who had by now lived in English-speaking countries for twenty-five years, Da Ponte wrote the article in Italian, then translated it into English – which he always spoke with a heavy Italian accent – for public consumption. At a public lecture-room on Barclay Street he declaimed it aloud one evening to an audience of more than two hundred – 'one of the most numerous assemblages, of wit and fashion, which ever graced a lecture room in this city', according to the *Columbian*, a daily newspaper which reported them as listening 'with delighted attention'. One of those present, a Dr Francis, testified that Da Ponte delivered his tirade 'with all the earnestness and animation of a great speaker'. His *Discorso apologetico* was published, in English, that same day.

As so often in Da Ponte's life, this one spontaneous, almost arbitrary act had momentous consequences – involving yet more sacrifice on the part of his wife and family. Before writing to thank the vice-consul in Florence for his letter, he 'did not hesitate to deprive my family of many necessities' in order to scrape together one hundred dollars, which he sent to Ombrosi in Florence with a request that he dispatch him as many Italian classics as possible. At the same time, after many vain attempts to negotiate discounts with European publishers, he reached arrangements with two prominent firms – Bossange of Paris and Fusi & Stella of Milan – to send him books at wholesale prices. Soon he was the proud possessor of more than a thousand volumes of Italian literature. If he could not start an Italian library, he would open an Italian bookshop.

Thus did seventy-five-year-old Lorenzo Da Ponte – priest and poet, librettist and libertine, grocer and teacher – renew his other career as a bookseller. At the same time, he took in pupils as paying boarders, who were able to lend their landlord and his son Carlo a hand in this latest enterprise. Another paying boarder at his new home, 343 Greenwich Street (today, appropriately enough, a pricey Italian deli named Bazzini) was a leading member of New York's new literary set, Gulian Verplanck – a well-meaning but over-excitable essayist, richer than he was gifted, with an indiscriminate enthusiasm for all things European. 'One of his unfortunate discoveries,' according to the *New Yorker*, was 'a dwarf called Billy the Fiddler, who passed himself off as a protégé of Mozart in Vienna, and as the actual author of one of Mozart's violin sonatas (the opus varied with the telling)'. Once Da Ponte had persuaded him of Billy's mendacity, Verplanck took to his new friend and landlord 'with all the relief and gratitude of a man who has at last found the real thing'.

Through Verplanck, Da Ponte found another pupil in a young poet named Fitz-Greene Halleck, who would become part of the small literary group who gathered in Windust's basement café on Park Row: Washington Irving, James Fenimore Cooper, Samuel F. B. Morse, Richard Henry Dana, William Cullen Bryant, Nathaniel Parker Willis. If Bryant would later have the distinction of lending his name to the small park in which the New York Public Library would eventually stand, at the junction of Fifth Avenue and Forty-Second Street, Halleck would become the first native New World poet to whom a statue was erected, in the mall of

Central Park. Another Greenwich Street lodger at this time was Henry James Anderson, who later became Professor of Mathematics at Columbia and a distinguished astronomer – and, in 1831, the second husband of the Da Pontes' daughter Fanny.

With Carlo's assistance, Da Ponte compiled an annotated catalogue of all the books in his inventory, its dates and critiques largely drawn from memory; published in 1823, Da Ponte's *catalogo ragionato* proved an invaluable guide to American libraries and other collectors when they finally started acquiring Italian literature. His motives may have run psychologically deep. In his 'dedicated affectation' of the role of man of letters, to the English musicologist Nicholas Till, 'Da Ponte reveals a longing to lay claim to the great inheritance of Italian literature, the only church which would accept the prodigal son, and also confirm that he had indeed escaped the ghetto of Ceneda.'

Another of Da Ponte's few remaining dreams, the importation of Italian opera to America, was realized in 1825 with the arrival in New York of the celebrated company led by Manuel Vicente ('del Populo') Garcia.

A Spaniard, born in Seville in 1775, Garcia had begun his musical life as a six-year-old chorister; by his teens he had become famous throughout Spain as a bravura tenor and composer of church music and comic operas. His Paris debut in 1808 was the beginning of a wholesale conquest of Europe, which saw him play the original Count Almaviva in the first performance of Rossini's *The Barber of Seville* in Rome in 1816. Garcia's triumphant progress had recently climaxed in London, where his seventeen-year-old daughter Maria had made a triumphant debut of her own at Covent Garden. Later she would become a world-renowned contralto under her married name of Maria Malibran; after Maria's early, accidental death, Garcia's younger daughter would also find fame under the name of Pauline Viardot, remembered as much as George Sand's friend and Turgenev's muse as for her peerless singing in mezzo-soprano and soprano roles, and frequently in her own compositions.

After his family's London triumph, Garcia's one remaining ambition was to export Italian opera to the New World. It was no small under-taking. Beyond the long and arduous journey, and the unknown reception awaiting them from audiences who had never heard any opera at all, there would be none of the sophisticated support system opera stars could already expect throughout Europe. At the time, reported the *New Yorker* in 1944, the 'most important' musical events in New York were the 'occasional' appearances of 'such performers as Madame de Seze and her seven-year-old daughter, who played the pianoforte to her mother's harp accompaniment'. There was a nascent Philharmonic Society, whose 'infrequent musicales' at the City Tavern amounted to members of a private club performing 'programs of anonymous instrumental music for one another's pleasure'. The musical, literary and intellectual life of the city, which was 'to come into its own in the next twenty years', was then 'practically dormant'.

There was not yet one professional orchestra in New York; indeed, there was said to be only one competent oboist in the whole of North America. Bassoons, trumpets and kettle-drums were also in short supply. When orchestras were needed, scratch outfits were cobbled together from the nearest available pool of amateurs as well as professionals. 'In spite of their incompleteness,' reported one visiting German musician of a New York concert, 'they play symphonies by Haydn, and grand overtures; if a gap occurs, they think "this is only of passing importance", provided it continues to rattle on afterwards.'

Undaunted, Garcia led his company west, recruited as many local musicians as he could find – including a chorus comprised of English mechanics and factory workers who sang in church choirs – and prepared to open the first season of Italian opera in America. Da Ponte rushed to see him. As the Spaniard rehearsed his ramshackle forces in Rossini, here was Mozart's own friend and librettist offering him the most enthusiastically Italian of welcomes. A delighted Garcia embraced Da Ponte warmly, and burst into 'Fin ch'han dal vino', Don Giovanni's so-called 'champagne' aria. They became firm friends, and Da Ponte spread the word about the Garcia company's forthcoming season with evangelical zeal, taking his students to rehearsals to persuade the doubtful of the treat in store for them.

On 29 November 1825, at New York's Park Theatre, Da Ponte was among the excited audience at the first performance of any opera anywhere in North America, Rossini's *The Barber of Seville*. To him, this was a momentous milestone in his mission to enthuse Americans about Italian culture; this was their chance to join 'all the cultured nations of the world' in regarding Italian opera as 'the noblest and most delightful of spectacles which human genius has invented'.

At what is now 21 to 25 Park Row – today, fittingly, the music department of the huge computer and electronics store J&R – the Park was then New York's only theatre, specializing in musical soirées often involving butchered scenes stolen from such works as Gay's *Beggar's Opera*. The highlight of the Park summer of Da Ponte's arrival in New York had been an Italian season led by Manfredi and his Company of Rope Dancers – 'lately arrived from Paris', according to the handbills. They climaxed their show with a 'Venetian masquerade' involving thirteen dancers who would 'place themselves in several surprising attitudes in the Roman style'. It is not known whether Da Ponte took himself to witness this New World version of his motherland's culture; 'if he did,' as one commentator has mused, 'it might explain his decision to go into the grocery business.'

Now, thanks to Garcia, he was setting things aright. That first night has been described as 'one of the most brilliant social occasions that New York had witnessed for many years'. Among the audience was none other than Joseph Bonaparte, half-brother of Napoleon, and himself the former King of Spain. 'An assemblage of ladies so fashionable, so numerous and so elegantly attired was probably never witnessed in our theatre,' declared the *New York Post* the next day. Unsure of the correct dress, audience members had been writing to newspapers seeking advice about the etiquette of opera attendance 'in the European style'; unsure, in turn, how to respond to this strange new art-form, some papers postponed their review pending advice from 'scientific experts'. Apart from one critic, who dismissed the music as 'monstrous', Rossini was as well received as Garcia and his company, in spite of the odd spectacle they must have presented.

Conducting when he was not onstage, Garcia himself reprised the tenor role of Count Almaviva, opposite his daughter Maria Felicia as Rosina and his son Manuel Jr as Figaro. The orchestra, one of the largest New York had then seen, was comprised of seven violins, two violas, three cellos, two double-basses, two flutes, two clarinets, one bassoon, two horns, two trumpets and a kettle-drum, with one Monsieur Etienne 'presiding at the pianoforte'.

'Until it is seen,' the *Post* nonetheless adjudged of the first time New York had seen an opera, 'it will never be believed that a play can be conducted in recitative or singing, and yet appear as natural as the ordinary drama … There were no less than six (singers) whom we would esteem, in the ordinary comedy, performers of the first order.'

'At the time,' in the words of the contemporary observer Henry T. Tuckerman, who soon became a friend of the Da Pontes, 'society in New York . . . was limited, but cordial and united, and, therefore, there was more unanimity and mutual interest in every social experiment. Da Ponte's fair pupils were in a state of sympathetic expectancy, and their husbands and fathers embarked generously in the attempt to establish the most recherché amusement of Europe in their thriving city.'

Emboldened by a sell-out success, Garcia proceeded to present productions of two operas he had written himself, as well as five more by Rossini: *Tancredi*, *Otello*, *La Cenerentola*, *Il Turco in Italia* and *Semiramide*. There was particular interest in the *Otello* as it coincided with a New York performance of Shakespeare's original with the great English actor Edmund Kean in the title role.

Throughout it all, an ecstatic Da Ponte did all he could to make the company welcome and assure its success. 'Not only did the popular Italian professor encourage the artists, win over the wealthy patrons, and glory in the whole phenomena,' writes Tuckerman, 'but he came gallantly to the rescue where ignorant critics, or perverse objectors, found fault and breathed encouragement . . . Some of our elder citizens yet describe his tall figure and handsome face at the opera, "monarch of all he surveyed", infecting others with his enthusiasm, and serving as a vital bond between the musical strangers and the fascinated public.'

As well as proselytizing all over town, Da Ponte laid on lavish entertainment for Garcia, his family and colleagues. Mindful of the 'delicate' treatment required by the soloists, according to one of his pupils, he had taught a 'worthy' American woman, a boarding-house keeper known to her clients as 'Sallie', the finer points of Italian cuisine. In the Broome Street boarding-house Aunt Sallie's, 'soprano, contralto, basso and baritone were agreeably surprised to find the viands and cookery to which they had been accustomed at home'.

The establishment retained its prestige long after the opera company had moved on. According to Tuckerman:

> no Italian or old habitué of that classic land, who had ever dined at Aunt Sallie's, was likely to forget the soup, macaroni, or red wine, to say nothing of the bread and vegetables – so like what he associated with the *trattorias* of Florence and Rome; indeed, to dine there, as was my fortune occasionally, and hear *la lingua Toscana in bocca Romana*, on all sides, with furious discussion of Italian politics and delectable

praise of composers and vocalists or pictorial critiques, transported one by magic from Broome Street to the Piazza Vecchia or the Via Condotta ... The death of Aunt Sallie a few years ago dispersed the few survivors of the circle that succeeded Da Ponte's singing-birds and the alimentive associations of his active and magnetic sojourn have no more a local habitation.

Corned beef versus macaroni was the problem Da Ponte himself most loved 'to state and to solve' at Aunt Sallie's, after a night at the opera. 'The success which attended his efforts to make the Italian element, literary, musical and prandial, familiar, and appreciated in the commercial metropolis of the New World,' testifies Tuckerman, 'was certainly a rare triumph of personal zeal and social attraction.'

As Da Ponte revelled in his honorary membership of Garcia's enterprising company, and worked tirelessly to ensure its artistic and commercial success, there was but one obvious bonus which would ensure he could die happy: a performance of one of his 'own' operas, the most popular of the three he had written with Mozart, *Don Giovanni*. Otherwise only too happy to oblige, Garcia pointed out that his company contained no singer up to the part of Don Ottavio. Da Ponte himself undertook to locate one. Having done so, only to find the theatre manager objecting to the extra expense, he organized a whip-round among his friends and pupils to raise the singer's fee.

Thus it came to pass, on the evening of 23 May 1826, that seventy-seven-year-old Lorenzo Da Ponte relived one of the high points of his youth. He was exactly twice the age he had been when collaborating with Mozart on *Don Giovanni*. Did the young Garcia's Leporello compare with Benucci's, Maria's Zerlina with Mombelli's? What did it matter when Garcia in the title role and even Monsieur Etienne at the pianoforte could fill him with such memories – and bring him such rewards, as the theatre director allowed him the royalties from an English translation of the libretto by his son, Lorenzo Jr?

'Everything pleased, everything was praised and admired, words, music, actors and production,' recalled Da Ponte of that memorable evening. With *Don Giovanni* given three more performances during Garcia's New York season, to universal acclaim, Da Ponte was as pleased by his enhanced standing in social and cultural circles as he was by this unexpected financial bonus. It was one of the rare times in his life when he could do no wrong. While in a bookshop one day, delighted to hear that his libretti had sold out, he settled for a lottery ticket in lieu of the six dollars he was owed – and proceeded to win one hundred and fifty.

He spent it on importing more rare books from Italy, restocking his bookshop and gradually ensuring that the Italian library at Columbia College grew from one 'old, loose-leaved, moth-eaten Boccaccio' to more than seven hundred 'choice' volumes. After six months in New York, meanwhile, Garcia and his company had gross takings of $56,685 to show for seventy-nine performances. Garcia moved on to Mexico, and a year of continued success with Italian opera, before being attacked by brigands while leaving the country and robbed of everything he had to show for his two-year adventure. By his death in Paris only five years later, at the age of fifty-seven, Garcia had composed more than forty operas and maintained his singing career while establishing himself as a highly successful teacher.

Garcia's daughter Maria stayed on in New York, where she made a rash and unhappy marriage to a man older than her father, Monsieur Malibran, who eventually went bankrupt and wound up in jail. Obliged to support herself by singing in dire English operettas with titles like *The Devil's Bridge* and *Love in a Village*, Maria finally returned to Europe to find fame under her married name as the 'divine' Maria Malibran, one of the great singers of her age. Her brother Manuel Jr enjoyed less success as a singer, but considerable renown as a teacher; the 'Swedish nightingale' Jenny Lind, Johanna Wagner and Marie Tempest were among his many pupils before his death in 1906 at the age of 101.

A quarter of a century older than his new friend Garcia, who was twelve years old when *Don Giovanni* was first performed, Da Ponte would outlive him by six years. As if these performances of 'his' opera were not enough to make 1825 an *annus mirabilis* for a man who had already lived so many lives, that September also brought an invitation from the faculty of Columbia College to become its Professor of Italian.

For his latest trick, Da Ponte would become not just the first holder of that post at what was to be one of the foremost universities of America's Ivy League; he was indeed the first Professor of Italian to be appointed at any college in the United States. Later that same year his compatriot Pietro Bachi was named Professor of Italian at Harvard; but, as Russo points out, Bachi was 'a relatively obscure man who had only recently arrived in the United States', while Lorenzo Da Ponte's appointment at Columbia 'crowned a teaching career of nearly twenty years, during which no less than two thousand American students had learned from him the beauties of the Italian language and acquired a first-hand appreciation of its world famous authors, from Dante and Petrarch down to that young legion of writers and poets with whom the movement of the Risorgimento had its inception'.

Da Ponte was, of course, grateful for the recognition offered by the post of his efforts to disseminate Italian language and literature in his adopted land. But it was not to change his life as materially as he must have hoped. Extracts from the minutes of the meetings of the Trustees of Columbia College show what a miserly offer it was:

> September 5, 1825. *Resolved*, that a Professorship of Italian Literature be established in this College, but that the Professor be not considered one of the Board of the College, nor subject to the provisions of the second chapter of the statutes.
>
> *Resolved*, That the attendance of the students upon the said Professor be voluntary, and that the hours of attendance be appointed by the Professor, under the direction of the President.
>
> *Resolved*, That Signore Da Ponte be and is hereby appointed to the said Professorship, and that he shall be allowed to receive from the students who shall attend his lectures a reasonable compensation; but that no salary be allowed him from the College.

Da Ponte was to be, as he put it, a Professor *'sine exemplo, cioè senza scolari e senza stipendio'*, uniquely without pupils or salary. This remained the case until the end of 1829, when the death of Columbia's president precipitated a debate as to its conversion into a university. Again Da Ponte was confirmed in the post of Professor of Italian; but again he was to be 'Professor *sine exemplo'*, paid only by students he could himself enlist.

While other Professors received a stipend of $2,200 a year, and a guaranteed pool of pupils, Da Ponte was forced to improvise, working around the fact that students were paying the 'not inconsiderable' sum of ninety dollars per language, and were thus (in his view) much more likely to choose that of Voltaire or Don Quixote, 'which they will think useful in business', than the language of his beloved Dante or Petrarch. At the end of the University's first year, his worst fears were confirmed when

In his own handwriting, the terms Da Ponte proposed to Columbia College for becoming its Professor of Italian.

the Professors of French and Spanish boasted fourteen students between them, while Da Ponte ('Weep, O Tuscans, and with you let the Hudson weep') had precisely none.

So he came up with a plan whereby he would give two lessons a week for forty weeks to a hundred students, each of whom would pay a maximum of fifteen dollars for the eighty lessons, while Da Ponte himself presented to the university up to a thousand volumes of 'selected' works, equal in value to whatever sum he received. When he put his proposition in writing to Clement Moore, he received a bittersweet reply.

'My dear Sir,' it began. 'I advise you not to insist too much on this matter because, to be frank with you, I do not think there is the slightest probability that the Trustees will undertake to alter the present system of the College and oblige the students to learn Italian. You are now a Professor of the College and have the opportunity of teaching it to as many as want to learn of you. The Trustees can do nothing without altering the actual Statutes, and I know well that whatever offers may be made to them by admirers of the Italian language, this they can never consent to do.'

Dismayed as he was by this first paragraph, Da Ponte could not but be cheered by Moore's second:

'It seems to me that you are a little too anxious about the memory you desire to leave behind you. For what you have already done out of love of the Italian language and literature, as long as any taste for polite letters exists in this country, the name of Da Ponte, *clarum et venerabile nomen*, will be held in grateful honour, and young men and women will in declining age look back to the hours spent in pleasant and instructive conversation with their learned and distinguished teacher, as to some of the brightest moments of their lives.'

Moore urged Da Ponte to 'let this suffice you, and do not try, like Bonaparte, to win for yourself alone all the glory of the universe', before signing himself 'Your true friend'. For all this sting in the tail, Da Ponte declared himself as pleased by Moore's 'kind, affectionate and consoling' second paragraph as he had been 'disheartened and depressed' by the first.

The octogenarian Da Ponte reflected that even Moore, 'dear protector and friend' as he was, did not know that 'all I have done seems and will seem to me little enough if, before I die, I do not leave to this famous city all the treasures of Italian letters'. In the teeth of stubborn opposition, he retained a fervent wish to show that, 'in my sad old age, more than riches or comfort, I have at heart the fame of my little-known native land'.

To which end, despite the financial rebuffs from Columbia, he began contributing books to its library which form the nucleus of its collection to this day. On his appointment as Professor, Da Ponte discovered that the college's library possessed only that one Italian book, that bedraggled copy of Boccaccio. In early 1826, with his own needs in mind as much as Columbia's, Da Ponte offered the college 263 volumes of Italian literature for $354.05; on the recommendation of Clement Moore, 161 were purchased for $243.17½. Alfieri, Beccaria, Castiglione, Galileo, Macchiavelli – these volumes were supplemented in 1829 by the purchase from Da Ponte of thirty-three more books for $140.

'What has become of these books?' asked Paul Cohen, who set out to find the answer in 1987. The modern Columbia University still has a Lorenzo Da Ponte Professorship of Italian, and possesses several of his manuscripts and letters. In the sixth-floor conference room of its Casa Italiana hangs the portrait of the elderly Da Ponte (see plate section). 'But there is no expressly designated collection of the books which came from him,' concluded Cohen. Yet 'many are still at Columbia and can still be identified'.

In 1827–28 Da Ponte compiled a catalogue of the books in the Columbia College library – at the request of the librarian, who just happened to be his lodger and future son-in-law, Henry James Anderson. In a report announcing the completion of his work to the College President, Dr Harris, Anderson wrote: 'I cannot refrain from doing justice to the diligent ability and patience of the gentleman employed, under my superintendence, to perform the services required in the arrangement of the Library.' For more than six months he had devoted at least four hours a day to the task, for the princely sum of $100, of which $77 had already been advanced or paid by him to assistants (probably his son Carlo). 'The bargain has certainly been a losing one for Mr Da Ponte,' sympathized Anderson, 'for I make no sort of question that he would have obtained ten times the amount in the way of his profession for the same amount of time and trouble.'

Can we hear, in this last sentence, the pleading of Anderson's landlord over an evening plate of Nancy's macaroni at Greenwich Street? 'As he voluntarily undertook the labor,' his report continues, 'he is sensible that he cannot *claim* a remuneration for the additional work arising from the error of his original estimate. Still, I would respectfully suggest through you to the Trustees whether, in equity, some addition, say $50, to the amount now due to him, ought not to be allowed.' And so it was.

Da Ponte's friend Nathaniel Moore, a later College librarian who subsequently became its President, updated this catalogue of the library's holdings in 1839, the year after Da Ponte's death. Almost a hundred and fifty years later, Cohen reached the conclusion that, despite the lack of inscriptions or 'Ex Libris' bookplates, 'it can be safely assumed that most if not all of the Italian works listed in the 1839 Columbia College catalogue are there because of Da Ponte.'

Just one book listed in the 1839 catalogue and still there today, Ippelito Pindemonte's *Su i giardini inglesi* (Verona, 1817), carries a nineteenth-century Columbia College bookplate reading 'The Gift of Lorenzo Da Ponte'. Despite the College's refusal in 1829 of Da Ponte's offer 'to add a number of Italian books to the college library upon the condition of his having a certain number of pupils provided him to instruct in the Italian language', Cohen concludes that 'this was not the only book Da Ponte had presented as a gift to the library'.

A comparison of Da Ponte's 1823 *catalogo ragionato* and the 1839 College catalogue finds many volumes common to both: Angelo di Costanzo's three-volume *Istoria del Regno di Napoli* (Milan, 1805), for instance, Lorenzo Pignotti's *Storia della Toscana* (Pisa, 1815) and Bernardo Segni's three-volume *Storia Fiorentina* (Milan, 1805). Da Ponte would be dismayed to know that the Pignotti, still on the Columbia shelves in its green marbled boards, has not once been checked out, over almost two centuries; the Segni has been borrowed just once, by the eminent historian Lynn Thorndike (1882–1965), who taught at Columbia from 1924 to his retirement in 1950.

Adumbrations on the endpapers of another two-volume set in both the 1839 Columbia catalogue and Da Ponte's *catalogo ragionato*, Jacopo Passavanti's *Lo Specchio* (Milan, 1808), show that it once had a 'Gift of Lorenzo Da Ponte' bookplate, with the donor's name written in his own hand, only for some Columbia librarian to remove and replace it with a university bookplate.

Another book still in the stacks of the Butler Library, one of the thirty-three purchased from Da Ponte in 1829, Lorenzo Lippi's two-volume *Il Malmantile* (Florence, 1731), has extensive handwritten notes in the margins of both volumes. It is identifiably Da Ponte's hand – but not, as the intrepid Cohen notes, the 'crabbed, almost printed hand of his American years'. These notes resemble the 'flowing script of the librettist's middle years in Europe' – so this may well be one of the books he brought with him from London, as in his customs declaration on his arrival in Philadelphia in 1805. Lippi's book, adds Cohen, is 'a burlesque romance full of racy Florentine idioms'; considered a *testo di lingua* by Italians, its suggestive language 'would have appealed to someone with Da Ponte's love of Italian poetry'.

At this time Da Ponte was importing more Italian books than he could sell, whether to his students, Columbia or other clients, from the Library Company of Philadelphia to the Library of Congress in Washington. The rest filled the shelves of his bookshop, which now became a full-time job, given his lack of pupils. Da Ponte would arrive there 'at cock-crow', never leaving it 'for more than a few moments at a time, staying on late into the night'.

Five months into the venture, he had to concede that 'I do not in truth have many occasions to leave my seat in the course of a day – purchasers are few and rare'. His sole consolation was the sight of carriages driving up to his door and 'some of the prettiest faces in the world' looking out, mistaking his bookstore for the cake and sweet shop next door.

A forlorn old man sitting alone in a folly of a bookshop, his adopted country still apparently unable to share his love of his native language and literature, seventy-five-year-old Da Ponte was still able to raise a wan smile: 'In order that people shall think I have a great many customers, I am thinking of putting a notice in the window saying "Italian sweets and cakes sold here", and if that should attract people into my shop, I will show them Petrarch or some other of our poets, and maintain that ours are the tastiest sweets, for those who have teeth to bite them.'

This was the penultimate paragraph of the first volume of his memoirs, published in 1823. 'The month of October is approaching,' he concluded. 'My scholars and friends will soon be leaving the pleasures of the country-side, recalled by cold and frost to business and study. I hope my classes will flourish, and that when my aim becomes known, the number of my customers will increase. The previous kindness and generosity of those of whom I speak assures me of so much.'

The tone of voice is that of a man who believes his days numbered, somewhat surprised that he is still alive, after so many and various incarnations. Yet Lorenzo Da Ponte still had fifteen years to live. And his last significant contribution to American cultural life still lay ahead of him.

14

The Showman

IN 1828, IN HIS eightieth year, Da Ponte became an American citizen. He had been in the country twenty-three years, and absent from his homeland for thirty. 'When a man becomes a certain age,' he wrote that year, 'he becomes a baby again. I am a baby in my gums because I have no teeth; I am a baby in my legs because of an obstinate rheumatism which makes them weak.'

But contemporary accounts suggest that he still cut a striking, if not quite so dashing figure. By the account of one acquaintance, Henry Tuckerman, 'Lorenzo Da Ponte was still a fine-looking man; he had the head of a Roman; his countenance beamed with intelligence and vivacity; his hair was abundant, and fell luxuriously round his neck, and his manners combined dignity and urbanity to a rare degree.'

Tuckerman paints an engaging portrait of his friend Da Ponte in the last decade of his life:

> Alternating from his *piccolo Eden di campagna*, as he calls it, to his winter-classes in town; carrying on the war with malignant compatriots and rivals; struggling with debts; presiding at private theatricals; making Alfieri and the modern Italian writers known to cultivated New Yorkers; enjoying congenial intercourse with his friends; revelling in the nascent enthusiasm for Italian opera and growing taste for Italian literature, his bon-mots, his greetings, his verses, his friendships, his scholars, protégés, and domestic amenities made up a varied, exceptional and complacent life.

At a party to mark his seventy-ninth birthday, on 10 March 1828, Da Ponte seized the moment to deliver a speech with the express intention of wooing subscribers to the Italian Library he still longed to found in New York. But even an appeal to his pupils and friends, who applauded the idea wholeheartedly, could come up with only one paying subscriber: the estimable Gulian C. Verplanck, Da Ponte's former lodger, now a Congressman. Dismayed but undeterred, Da Ponte was obliged to persist with the other method he had found, the previous year, of performing much the same service for all New Yorkers as he had for the Columbia library.

His name can still be found alongside those of other Columbia Professors, such as Clement Moore, among the forty-six 'Subscribers to the permanent library' listed in the original 1827 subscription book preserved in the New York Society Library, today at 53 East 79th Street. Shares were sold for five dollars, most subscribers buying one or two (though Verplanck bought five). Da Ponte is listed as purchasing a single share, which would have entitled him to such privileges of membership as checking out books. But it was thanks to him that many of those books were there – as most still are.

Founded in 1754 by the New York Society, a group of six 'civic-minded individuals', the Library opened in a room in the old City Hall, on Wall Street facing Broad Street. Through Da Ponte's lifetime and beyond, until the founding of the public library system at the turn of the twentieth century, it was known as 'the city library'. The charter it received from George III in 1772 was confirmed after the revolution by the New York state legislature.

Looted by British troops during the War of Independence, the Library reopened in the old City Hall in 1789–90; with New York then the nation's capital, and the building renamed Federal Hall while occupied by Congress, it served as the first Library of Congress – and was used by, among many others, John Jay and George Washington.

Through his friend Verplanck, Da Ponte succeeded in selling some four hundred dollars' worth of Italian classics to the Library of Congress after its move to Washington, including magnificent editions of Dante's *Divina Commedia*, of Ariosto and Alfieri, the first copy in the United States of Muratori's *Rerum Italicarum Scriptores*, and works by Visconti and Girolamo Tiraboschi. Like so much of his literary business, this was done not just to make money, but to refute certain friends who 'stubbornly maintained that, in the more serious and austere branches, Italy was not to be compared with Germany, forgetting or pretending to forget that "c'est de Italie que nous tenons les sciences" (as an ingenious French writer admits in the preface to the *Encyclopédie*)'.

By Da Ponte's time, meanwhile, the New York Society Library had moved to its own building at 33 Nassau Street, where Washington Irving and James Fenimore Cooper were among those consulting its five thousand volumes. In May 1827 Da Ponte announced that he had placed some six hundred books in the Society Library, and planned to add another four hundred when they arrived from Europe. A list of these volumes, 'the flower of all our literature in all the useful arts and sciences', can be found in that year's printed *Catalogue of Italian Books Deposited in the N. Y. Society Library, for the permanent use of L. Da Ponte's pupils and subscribers.*

In April 1830 the Society librarian, Philip Jones Forbes, noted that 'Mr Da Ponte has taken away all of the books he has deposited in the Library from time to time – excepting those sold to the Italian Library Society'. This coincides with another period of financial difficulty for Da Ponte and his bookshop; but those six hundred volumes, plus almost as many more purchased at Da Ponte's suggestion by Clement Moore, Gulian Verplanck and John I. Morgan, are listed in the Society's holdings to this day. As one of the Library's heaviest borrowers, Da Ponte was also responsible for the disappearance of at least two. On 15 May 1830 he is listed as borrowing Volumes Two and Three of Messer Benedetto Varchi's five-volume *Storia Fiorentina*; when he failed to return them, a librarian pencilled 'still out' beside the entry. A note in the current catalogue of the New York Society Library records that these two volumes still remain missing.

Two years after Da Ponte's death the New York Society Library moved to Leonard Street and Broadway, where Henry David Thoreau and John James Audubon were browsers; in 1856 to 109 University Place, the haunt of Herman Melville and Willa Cather; and in 1937 to its present quarters, where W. H. Auden, Clarence Day, Lillian Hellman, Barbara Tuchman and other illustrious literati are among the thousands to have benefited from Da Ponte's legacy.

While still as cantankerous as ever, seeing potential enemies in every setback, the elderly Da Ponte's last decade saw him increasingly nostalgic about his homeland, whose cultural glories he had striven so hard to import into his adopted country.

In 1829 he moved from Greenwich Street to the grander setting of

342 Broadway – today a bank and UPS store in a faceless, fifteen-storey red-brick building, just one block north of the fifty-storey headquarters of the Immigration and Naturalization Service, a plate-glass reminder to every New Yorker of the city's immigrant roots. And this model immigrant was no exception to the verities of life in exile. His next adventure derived partly from a natural wish 'to see some of my own kin after so many years', and partly from his continuing determination that 'the charm of music … might encourage the study of Italian and the establishment of a library'. It might also help him overcome his sense of disappointment, whatever others might say about his accomplishments, that he had achieved little in America 'in comparison to my hopes and desires'.

Da Ponte had heard that his niece Giulia (or 'Giulietta'), daughter of his half-brother Agostino, was a singer of great promise, possessing 'a very fine voice and many charming personal qualities, along with the rare merit of singing with feeling and expression and entirely naturally'. Her teacher, moreover, was the celebrated Antonio Baglioni, the first Don Ottavio in the Prague premiere of *Don Giovanni*, whom Da Ponte fondly remembered as 'a man of great musical ability and knowledge'.

For some time he had been trying to persuade his brother to bring his daughter to New York, since the success of the Garcia company had created an apparent public appetite for Italian opera. Agostino was willing, but bureaucracy was getting in the way; for reasons best known to themselves, the Austrian authorities proved stubbornly obstructive, continually denying them passports and visas. The stalemate continued for almost two years, to the point where Da Ponte had all but abandoned hope, when he composed an ode in praise of the Emperor Francis which seemed to perform the requisite miracle.

In the autumn of 1829, to her uncle's great delight, Giulietta wrote that she and her father were finally en route to America. The $420 bill for their journey, which Da Ponte had rashly promised to pay, only briefly dashed his high spirits as he finally welcomed them to New York on 18 February 1830. 'We spent the rest of the day and a great part of the night *en famille*, hugging and embracing and questioning one another amidst laughter and tears.'

Agostino had brought with him Italian chestnuts and salami, rosolio and garlic – delights, as Da Ponte put it, 'even to an octogenarian with precious little appetite'. But he also brought trouble. A cameo of Napoleon, which he had imported in the hope of selling it to the ex-Emperor's half-brother Joseph, was stolen from Da Ponte's bookshop, landing him with a large fee in compensation. But even that was as nothing to the debts accrued by the feckless Agostino, whose wife was living in penury in Venice with their elder daughter, Pasquetta, surrounded by her husband's predatory creditors.

Da Ponte's other worry was that Giulietta might not quite live up to her billing as a singer. A few recitals in private houses went well enough; but he was not convinced that she had a big enough voice for a successful stage career. With the management of the Park Theatre trusting his judgement, however, he took the risk of offsetting his debts, and the considerable costs of housing and maintaining Agostino and his daughter, by negotiating her a contract for the decidedly handsome sum of $1,200 for her first two operatic appearances, and half the gross box-office for a third.

Giulietta Da Ponte duly made her New York debut at the Park Theatre on 31 March 1830, in a 'Grand Concert' of vocal and instrumental music. Inevitably, it might be thought, she was suffering from a cold; apart from one rave review, from a critic fond of Da Ponte, she was given an indifferent reception.

Her uncle tried to make the best of it, but harboured private fears about her operatic debut a month later, for which he prepared a special edition of his pasticcio *L'ape musicale*, adding new arias to those he had written for La Ferrarese in Vienna more than forty years earlier. Giulietta was duly paid her fat fees; but she did not really earn them. The piece was too rarefied for American ears, and her uncle could no longer disguise the fact that her voice was distinctly mediocre. 'She was not made for the stage,' as he diplomatically put it, 'nor the stage for her.'

Giulietta made one more New York appearance, at a City Hall concert hosted by the Musical Fund Society on 10 May 1830, in which she sang arias from Mozart, Rossini and Weber, only to find that the audience much preferred a virtuoso trumpeter named Norton, in a concerto which cannily incorporated 'The Star-Spangled Banner' and 'The British Grenadiers'. Emergent American musical taste was especially partial to the 'noisy' section of the orchestra. Much more of this, complained one critic, and New York would be 'blown away'.

Thus ended Giulia Da Ponte's career and her uncle's dreams of his family name further enhancing the standing of Italian culture in high American society. Beyond being a grave disappointment to him, and bringing him close to bankruptcy, Da Ponte's niece also proved as ungrateful as her father for all his efforts on their behalf. As relations between the two brothers deteriorated, Giulietta gave up her stage career to marry a visiting Italian merchant named Stafler. Within two years she had disappeared back to Trieste, taking her father with her, neither of them even bothering to bid Da Ponte farewell.

In 1830, while coping with his recalcitrant relatives, Da Ponte also published the final volume of his revised memoirs, which had been gestating since the earlier versions of 1807, 1819 and 1823. He offered the world an edited and embroidered version of his life primarily to make money, but also in an unabashed bid for the immortality he felt to be his due.

Posterity has differed as to the book's merits. 'Here are the most original and anecdotal artistic Italian memoirs ever to be offered to a curious public,' read an enthusiastic preface to the 1860 French edition. 'The memoirs of Benvenuto Cellini are neither more naïf nor more amusing. In his memoirs, D'Aponte (*sic*) is as much of a writer as his compatriot Goldoni, as frivolously amusing as the Count de Grammont, as adventurous as Gil Blas, as droll and as hapless as Gilbert.'

Thirty years after Da Ponte's death, his friend and admirer Henry Tuckerman averred that 'these and similar adventures remind the reader of those memorable Italian autobiographies written by Cellini, Alfieri and Goldoni – vivid and curious pictures of domestic and social life in Southern Europe before the days of steam, cheap journals and policemen'. But Da Ponte's memoirs have failed to earn even the anecdotal status of those of his friend Casanova, not least because they are plainly mendacious in places, and tediously vengeful in others.

In 1898, a generation after Tuckerman's praise, the musicologist H. E. Krehbiel commented that many of the mysteries lingering about Da Ponte's life, sixty years after his death, were 'doubtless due to the want of definiteness which characterizes the autobiography which Da Ponte published in New York seventy-five years ago. In this work, which has been translated into German and French, but not (then) into English, Da Ponte is garrulous enough about many insignificant things, but silent about many others of vastly more importance, and his biographers in the handbooks on music and literature have been pretty generally evinced by an unwillingness to be guided in all things by Da Ponte's own utterances.'

Another generation on, the New York critic Theodore Koch was musing: 'We would gladly exchange some of his disquisitions upon the worthlessness of seeming friends and the repeated narration of business difficulties for a fuller account of his career as a librettist before coming to America or of his pedagogical experience after finally settling into our metropolis.'

But the late twentieth century saw a revisionist school rallying to the support of Da Ponte, whose memoirs were republished by the *New York Review of Books* (in Elisabeth Abbott's 1929 translation) in 2000. 'All autobiographers lie, by commission as well as omission,' noted the musicologist Charles Rosen in his introduction. 'We do not read them for their accuracy but for their vivacity, and Lorenzo Da Ponte is among the most vivacious ... His memoirs are not an intimate exploration of his own identity and character but rather a picaresque adventure story. What we learn about his personality is revealed inadvertently; he had no intention of giving himself away.'

The memoirs had been 'favourably compared' by some critics, noted the Harvard historian Aram Bakshian Jr in 1978, with those of Da Ponte's 'old friend and occasional fellow swindler Giacomo Casanova'. His autobiography alone, in Bakshian's judgement, entitled Da Ponte to 'more lasting fame than has fallen to his lot; but, even if he had died on the voyage to Philadelphia, his work as the most inspired collaborator of Mozart would have guaranteed him his permanent niche in the history of opera'.

In December 1831, four months after their daughter Fanny's marriage to their lodger Henry Anderson, Da Ponte's beloved wife of forty years died at the age of sixty-two. Twenty years younger than her husband, Nancy contracted a fierce bout of pneumonia and succumbed after only six days.

Da Ponte poured out his grief in an elegant, touching collection of eighteen sonnets and a longer poem collectively entitled *Versi composti da Lorenzo Da Ponte per la morte d'Anna Celestia Ernestina, sua virtuosissima e adorata consorte*. 'Weep with me, for she is dead!' he wrote of his 'wife, friend, companion, consort – a loving mother to her children, and to her everyone in distress was a child'. In the sonnets, according to one of his pupils, 'the heathen mythology was singularly blended with the Roman creed, although at the close St Peter was made to acknowledge that the virtues of the excellent *sposa* entitled her to heaven, independent of all ecclesiastical dogmas – she being an angel even while on earth.'

Da Ponte sent copies of the sonnets to his friends and family in Italy, including his schoolmate Colombo, to whom he wrote: 'The death of this angelic woman has robbed me not only of peace of heart, but also of the means of supporting myself.' If this was a reference to Nancy's inheritance from her sister Louisa, now divided between her children, he was again hiding more palatable truths.

After Nancy's death Da Ponte was given an allowance of $200 a year by his son-in-law Henry Anderson, and a room in their home by his son Lorenzo and daughter-in-law Cornelia. After his early flirtation with the theatre, Lorenzo had followed his father into teaching, first at Maryland and now at New York University.

In the wake of Nancy's death, and the loss of her sister's legacy, 1831 otherwise saw Da Ponte's financial fortunes so low that he was forced to put up for sale two thirds of the three thousand books on his shelves. 'Alas, fate takes from me my only treasure!' he lamented. 'Death would have been less bitter than this last farewell' to 'the most beautiful pages of our literature'.

And there were other ways to make money. Since the success of Garcia's visit and the failure of Giulietta's, Da Ponte had continued his efforts to make Italian opera a permanent fixture on the New York scene, at first by continuing to attempt to woo major companies over from Europe. When Domenico Barbaja, director of the San Carlo Theatre in Naples, proved immune to his advances, he turned his attention to Jacques Montrésor, a French-born tenor who had also become a successful impresario in Bologna.

Sensing more interest, Da Ponte rather overstated the American appetite for Italian opera as he dangled dollar signs before Montrésor during a long correspondence. New Yorkers especially loved Mozart and Rossini, he wrote, omitting to add that they had heard no other composers. He suggested sixteen suitable works, no fewer than six of which were to libretti by himself.

Only when it came to orchestral players and backstage staff did he paint a more realistic picture. Montrésor should bring his own first-rank violinist, oboist, horn player, 'maestro de cembalo' and prompter, as none were available in New York. He should also import his own set-painters; those in America were talented enough, but prohibitively expensive. As for chorus: well, those available were better teachers than singers; Montrésor should bring as many as possible.

For almost two years Da Ponte nagged the Frenchman, assuring him there was a fortune to be made in the New World. 'The Americans are almost all businessmen,' he wrote, 'and they turn everything into business, even their amusements. Come, do your best to please them, and inspire in some of them the prospect of enjoyment, in others the hope of money.'

Finally, he succeeded, and again turned impresario. In 1832 Montrésor led a large and talented company across the Atlantic, headed by such then big names as Pedrotti, Fornasari and Corsetti. There was also a promising young soprano named Mombelli, daughter of the Mombellis who were members of the Vienna company in Da Ponte's day; her mother had been the original Zerlina in *Don Giovanni*. Nothing could seem a more promising harbinger of success.

On 6 October 1832 the Montrésor company opened at the Richmond Hill Theatre – which changed its name to the Italian Opera House for the duration – with Rossini's *La Cenerentola*. The maestro had taken some of Da Ponte's advice – the orchestra, for instance, was declared 'the finest that has yet been heard in New York' and 'the best that ever played dramatic music in America' – but made his own careful choice of repertoire, which included nothing by Da Ponte.

That, of course, could be remedied, as it had been with Garcia. For now, Da Ponte was content enough to preside over a season of thirty-five performances, with works including Rossini's *L'Italiana in Algeri*, Bellini's *Il pirata* and Mercadante's *Elisa e Claudio*. He then escorted the company to Philadelphia, and the Chestnut Theatre, where it gave a further twenty-four performances of opera and several concerts. At one of these they performed 'A Hymn to America', a setting by Bagioli of Da Ponte's words – which has not, alas, survived.

Despite his age, now eighty-three, Da Ponte worked as hard as ever to ensure the company's commercial success. In Philadelphia alone, his efforts ensured advance box-office of more than $8,000 by way of subscriptions to the season. But both he and Montrésor wound up losing money, to the point of a bitter falling-out which moved Da Ponte to publish yet another defensive, rancorous pamphlet entitled *Una storia incredibile ma vera*. While acknowledging Montrésor's musical abilities, he deplored his inadequacies as an administrator and businessman. The truth of the case seems to be that there was a limited appetite for Italian opera in the country which would soon invent jazz, the blues and the musical; the visit of Garcia's company had benefited from a certain novelty value, but the audiences for Montrésor's company were already growing impatient for less highly wrought, elaborate music, set to words in their own language.

In Europe, furthermore, the rise of opera as an art-form had depended on state patronage and the enthusiasm of a wealthy, cultured elite – as remains the case, to a large extent, to this day. There was no court or aristocracy in this young, democratic republic, still only fifty years old, instinctively feeling its way towards cultural innovations of its own, reluctant to be caught in a cultural cringe towards its mother-countries.

Morality was also an issue. Even the spoken theatre had not yet developed a strong following in the United States, where innate Puritanism took a dim view of stage fictions. Typical of the mood of the moment were the meditations of Thomas Hastings, a teacher and writer on church music, who spoke for the majority in his 1822 *Dissertation on Musical Taste*:

> If the question be asked as to the influence of operas, we answer that, as splendid pieces of composition, they cannot fail, in some limited circles, to promote the increase of musical learning and refinement. As to their moral influence, we class them, of course, where they belong – among other dramatic works. In our country this species of composition is unknown. It appears among us only as an exotic from other climes, which is a circumstance on the whole not much to be regretted.

The first music school in America would not be founded until the following year, 1833. But Da Ponte was not to be deterred. Bloodied but unbowed, he remained determined to rise above this latest setback, despite another bout of self-pity, blended with bitter experience. 'I believe', he concluded, 'that my heart is made of a different stuff from that of other men. A noble act, generous, benevolent, blinds me. I am like a soldier who, spurred by the longing for glory, rushes against the mouth of the cannon; like a passionate lover who hurls himself into the arms of a woman who torments him.'

In similar vein, as self-deceiving as self-glorifying, he goes on to list in one very long sentence the reasons he had embarked on this ill-fated adventure:

> The hope of giving, *post funera*, immortality to my name, and of leaving to a nation which I revere a memory of me which will not be ignoble; the sweet allurement of arousing feelings of gratitude and goodwill

in those who follow an art that was not disgraced by my pen; the desire to awaken love for the beautiful language which I brought to America, and love also for our ravishing music; the longing to see once again on the American stage some of the children of my youthful inspiration, which are still remembered in the theatres of the Thames, the Danube and the Elbe; and, finally, a sweet presentiment of joy, reliability of my promises and the happy success of a well-organised spectacle – these were the final spurs which goaded me into this delightful undertaking, and from which nothing, so far, has succeeded in deterring me. I dreamt of roses and laurels; but from roses I had only thorns, and from the laurels bitterness! So goes the world . . .

'No one is grateful, either the Italians or the Americans,' Da Ponte complained elsewhere. 'What can I do? Weep, or laugh. And so that you may laugh, too, I will tell you that in spite of my losses, I believe I can say with Petrarch, "I shall be what I was, and I shall live as I have lived," and continue to write poetry, to love music (and) to bring good artists to America.'

The real reason for Montrésor's failure, he decided as he returned to his bookshop, was the lack of a proper opera house. That was what New York now needed.

And he found enough wealthy New York opera patrons to agree with him, including a former mayor, Philip Hone, and his influential friend Dominick Lynch, a wealthy wine importer, music enthusiast and all-round Europhile. Those performances of *Don Giovanni* had lent the old Professor a reflected glamour from his association with Mozart; after Garcia's success, the failure of Montrésor's company had been less evident in New York than Philadelphia. Within weeks Da Ponte had rounded up enough supporters to raise the substantial sum of $150,000. Soon he found himself heading an association in charge of building the first opera house in New York, and indeed in Northern America, on the north-west corner of Church and Leonard Streets, in the heart of the district now known as TriBeCa.

Here arose one of the grandest buildings New York had yet seen, a sumptuous opera house on the European plan, with tiers comprised solely of boxes, and lit by gas 'in a manner entirely new'. The lavish white, blue and gold interior was carpeted and decorated with paintings imported especially from Europe, beneath a mighty chandelier hanging from an imposing dome. Backstage conditions were excellent, the dressing-rooms spacious and comfortable. The stage was 'vast' and the acoustic said to be excellent. 'The whole of this new and superb edifice,' in the verdict of one newspaper, was 'a credit to the taste and liberality of its founders'. In his diary, Hone called it 'the neatest and most beautiful theatre in the United States, and unsurpassed in Europe'.

Under eighty-four-year-old Da Ponte's management, alongside a grandee called the Chevalier Riva-Finoli, the Opera House opened on 18 November 1833 with a performance of Rossini's *La gazza ladra*. So excited by the building were the audience members that they scarcely listened to the music; there was 'a straining of necks away from, rather than towards, the stage'. There was a universally positive response from the press, with the sole exception of a paper called the *Albion*, which complained that it had not been sent press seats, and could not afford the high prices, so would not be reviewing the operas.

The first season, which lasted until 21 July 1834, continued with Cimarosa's *Il matrimonio segreto*, Pacini's *Gli Arabi nelle Gallie* and five works by Rossini, *Il barbiere di Siviglia*, *La donna del lago*, *Il Turco in Italia*, *La Cenerentola* and *Matilda di Shabran*. There was also an opera by the company's music director, one Salvioni, who had recruited a much-admired orchestra and an almost exclusively Italian company.

But opera has always been an expensive business. The books for some sixty performances that first season showed a deficit of $29,275. The second season fared no better. There was no third season for Da Ponte, who, in April FitzLyon's shrewd judgement, had 'put the cart before the horse; what was needed was not an opera house, but people to fill it'. In 1835 the theatre remained dark; and the following year it was sold to James Wallack, who renamed it the National Theatre and installed a dramatic company. Three years later, it burned down after a brief existence which, in the words of one opera historian, 'brought misfortune upon all who had any connection with it'.

On the site today stands the City of New York Human Resources Administration General Support Services, a dour, fifteen-storey beige brick-and-cement building dating from the 1960s, offering New Yorkers welfare, Medicaid and food stamps. On the opposite corner is a diner called Isobel's Kitchen, across from the library of the New York Law School. One block north is a glitzy, triangular new hotel called the Tribeca Grand. There is no plaque to commemorate Da Ponte's bold venture, or even mourn his folly. Commuters stream by, blissfully unaware that this was where the last of his many American dreams died.

The man himself was granted a few more years yet. He continued to publish a stream of pamphlets and poems, some of which he translated into English, most lamenting that he had not received the recognition he deserved for his contributions to American life.

'Eighteen months have passed since I had a single pupil,' he complained in 1835. 'I, the creator of the Italian language in America, the teacher of more than two thousand persons whose progress astounded Italy! I, the poet of Joseph II, the author of thirty-six dramas, the inspiration of Salieri, of Weigl, of Martín, of Winter, and Mozart! After twenty-seven years of hard labour, I have no longer a pupil! Nearly ninety years old, I have no more bread in America!'

His age did not seem an issue to Da Ponte; he appeared to think he could proceed as normal in his late eighties, while taking the trouble to draft notes towards his own obituary.

In these last few years, the old man grew increasingly homesick. His letters to Italy anxiously ask for news of his family. 'I am overwhelmed by the wretched state of the Da Pontes both in Venice and in Ceneda,' he wrote to the Venetian composer Giovanni Perucchini in January 1837. Enclosed were the proceeds of the sale of some books, which he begged Perucchini to divide between his brother Agostino's widow Caterina, his eldest sister Angioletta, 'if she is still living, as I hope', and Faustina, 'who is not happily married, as I am told the others are'. Da Ponte's last known letter, to Stafler in April 1838, still asks for news of his 'poor and beloved' sisters. 'Perhaps they think that I've forgotten them, but that isn't so ...'

91 Spring Street, the address at which Da Ponte spent the last year of his life, lies in the heart of the fashionable district now called SoHo, between Broadway and Mercer Streets. Today it is a nameless boutique, one in a row of shops at the ground level of a modern black building, full of loud 'house music' and ill-tempered salespersons selling absurdly expensive leather handbags.

It was here, in August 1838, that Da Ponte began to feel unwell. His doctor told him there was nothing specifically wrong; old age was taking its toll, and he should ready himself for the next world. This he had already done some years since, with a conscious effort to make his peace with the church in a long correspondence with the Patriarch of Venice,

Monsignor Jacopo Monico, a former Bishop of Ceneda who had succeeded him as Professor of Literature in Treviso. After thanking Da Ponte for sending him some poems, this 'foremost pillar of the portals of the Church of Christ' expressed the hope that the 'distinguished poet' would 'put his affairs in order in such a way that his last moments would not be embittered by remorse'. Da Ponte – who had never lost his faith, however much he had broken its rules – replied that the Patriarch's 'holy counsels and Christian wishes had the effect which his charitable heart wished to evoke in my soul'.

Even during his last illness, Da Ponte continued to write poetry, including a translation of a section of Hillhouse's *Hadad* described by his physician, Dr John W. Francis, as 'beautiful', rendered with 'scholastic fidelity'. On the day before Da Ponte's death, Dr Francis received a further series of 'verses in his native tongue, partly in tone of gratitude, and partly to evince to his friends that, though speech had nigh left him, his mind was still entire'.

It was not widely known in New York that Da Ponte had been a Catholic priest, but one such was discreetly summoned to hear his confession, and administer the last rites, ensuring the lapsed Abbé as smooth a passage into the next world as his track record might allow. On 16 August, as Dr Francis spread word that the old poet was growing weaker, his son Lorenzo Jr and son-in-law Anderson were walking in the Adirondacks; but a group of his friends and admirers joined the rest of his family at his bedside. 'It was one of those afternoons of waning summer,' wrote one of those present, a former pupil, 'when the mellow sunset foretells approaching autumn':

> The old poet's magnificent head lay upon a sea of pillows, and the conscious eye still shed its beam of regard upon all around him. Besides several of his countrymen were assembled some remnants of the old Italian (opera) troupe, who knelt for a farewell blessing around the pallet of their expiring bard; among them might be seen the fine head of (Luciano) Fornasari, and Bagioli's benevolent countenance. All wept as the patriarch bade them farewell and implored a blessing on their common country.
>
> The doctor watching the flickerings of the life-torch, stood at the head of the couch, and a group of tearful women at the foot completed the scene not unlike the portraiture we have all seen of the last hours of Napoleon.

At nine o'clock the following evening, seven months short of his ninetieth birthday, Da Ponte was finally reunited, as he firmly believed, with his beloved Nancy and his young friend Mozart.

Three days later an 'impressive' Requiem mass was held in New York's old Catholic cathedral, in what is now Little Italy. There was a moving rendition of Allegri's 'Miserere', before a large procession followed Da Ponte's coffin to the Roman Catholic cemetery of St John's in the Bowery, on 11th Street between Avenue A and First Avenue.

The pallbearers included Clement Moore, by then President of Columbia University, and other old friends such as Gulian Verplanck, the Venerable Dr Macneven and Pietro Maroncelli, whose wife had been a leading member of Rivafinoli's company. At the head of the procession was a black banner with gold letters proclaiming:

LAURENTIUS DA PONTE

Italia Natus.
Litterarum Reipublicae et Musis
Dilectissimus.
Patriae et Convicium Justorum
XVII die Augusti MDCCCXXXVIII
XC Anno Aetatis Suae
Amplexu Domini
Ascendit.

According to one mourner, 'the funeral procession testified by its length to the general emotion of regret created by an event so melancholy ... It is the intention of his countrymen to erect a monument (in the Roman cemetery) in memory of their poet.'

No such monument was ever erected. Half a century later, in the summer of 1887, the musical historian Henry E. Krehbiel made a 'laborious' but vain search for Da Ponte's grave:

The place is overgrown with rank grass and weeds. There are no paths. Those who wish to read the inscriptions on the headstones must stumble along as best they can; now over irregular hillocks, now into deep depressions half-filled with old boots, rusty tin cans, and other refuse. Many of the inscriptions have been obliterated by the action of the elements; some of the stones lie prone upon the ground (the bones which once they guarded having been removed, as the bright-eyed, fresh-faced, silver-haired old wife of the decrepit keeper explains), and in one place a large Ailanthus tree in growing has taken up a stone half-way into itself.

For hours Krehbiel 'crossed and re-crossed the decaying cemetery scrutinizing carefully every inscription; but in vain. No headstone was found bearing the name of Da Ponte, and there are no records to identify the spot where, on August 20, 1838, his grave was dug.'

Despite this pioneer work, Da Ponte's first American biographer, Joseph Luigi Russo, felt obliged to look again for himself in the early 1920s. 'The passing years', Russo reported, 'have brought many changes in that neighbourhood, and the block where the cemetery was, is now – except for a little Catholic church and a garage – a dreary open space which strangely contrasts with the bustling life of the thickly settled surroundings.

'Having inquired how it was that, despite the congested conditions of the district, no buildings have been erected in that block, the author received the curious information that a strong prejudice existed in that neighbourhood, notwithstanding the many differences in race and creed, against building on land which had formerly been consecrated ground. The man who built the garage, it was pointed out, had gone into bankruptcy.'

Similar enquiries today, at the Catholic bakeries along 11th Street, reveal no memories at all of a cemetery in the area. Where once New York's leading Catholics were buried stands a school and a dreary series of decaying tenements. Nearby is St Mark's in the Bowery, an Episcopal church founded in 1799, with a longstanding link to New York's arts community. Poetry readings are still held in the church, which bears a plaque to the late poet Allen Ginsberg.

Not far away, at the junction of 2nd Avenue and 2nd Street, is the New York City Marble Cemetery, a non-sectarian burial ground founded in 1831 and now closed to the public. Enquiries at St Stanislaus, a new Roman Catholic church a couple of blocks away from St Mark's, elicit no memories at all of a Catholic cemetery nearby.

The probable reason for the confusion over Da Ponte's original resting-place lies in a letter from his grandson, Edward Ellery Anderson, quoted by Russo in 1922: 'My judgment is that his remains were placed temporarily in some friend's vault, with the intention of erecting a formal monument at a later period, and that this matter has been overlooked or forgotten ... until all remains have been lost.'

Da Ponte would no doubt consider this just his luck. His mortal remains vanished as swiftly as his earthly renown, any chance of finding them finally removed by the mass transportation of coffins from Manhattan's Catholic burial grounds to the Calvary Cemetery, Queens, in 1903. Even in 1868, when the municipality of Ceneda made enquiries in New York as to the date of the poet's death, with a view to erecting a monument to their most famous son, they were given the wrong answer – and anyway never got around to erecting any such memorial. One of Da Ponte's New York friends involved in this episode, Henry Tuckerman, erected a literary monument of his own: 'Not a few elder Knickerbockers associate his name and image with their first acquaintance with and love for Italian literature and music ... He was the first Italian of culture who brought these claims and triumphs of his country into genial relationship with our people.'

Whatever the contributions of Italian immigrants to the United States in the ensuing two centuries, some of them less savoury than others, it took 'Italian heritage and culture month' in October 1987 for culturally minded Italian-Americans finally to remember their founding father, and erect a headstone in his honour, with an inscription written by the Da Ponte Professor Emeritus at Columbia University, Olga Ragusa.

Like those of Mozart, on whom his fame depends, the remains of Lorenzo Da Ponte rest we know not where.

Lorenzo Jr died only two years after his father, in 1840, at the age of just thirty-six; an accomplished Greek scholar, he had written several books, including an admired history of the Florentine Republic. Three more years, and Fanny too was gone, dying in Paris on her way home with her husband from a trip to Europe. She is buried in the city's celebrated Père Lachaise cemetery.

Of Fanny's six children by Anderson, four died in infancy; one of her two surviving sons, Ellery, was reported in the 1920s to be a prominent New York lawyer and active Democrat politician. Of Lorenzo Jr's four with Cornelia, only one survived infancy: John Durant Da Ponte, who went on to make a name in New Orleans. Da Ponte's line in America descends through John Durant, and through Fanny; little is known about the fate of his youngest son, Charles.

Such Da Pontes as remain in the United States are likely to descend from the man remembered by history as Mozart's librettist. One wonders how much else they know about the ancestor buried beneath the JFK flightpath, with the jets roaring overhead.

Describing Da Ponte as 'the last of those literary adventurers who were so characteristic a feature of the eighteenth century', his first biographer, Russo, concluded in 1922 that 'his connection with Mozart … is now generally considered to be his greatest claim to lasting remembrance; yet perhaps of equal, if not even greater, importance, at least in America and Italy, should be deemed his having been one of the foremost pioneers of Italian culture in the United States'.

Six years after Russo's pioneering work, his fellow New Yorker Morris Bishop included Da Ponte alongside Sir Thomas Urquhart, Sir Jeffery Hudson and Edward Wortley Montagu Jr among 'A Gallery of Eccentrics, or, A Set of Twelve *Originals & Extravagants* from Elagabalus, the *Waggish Emperor* to Mr Professor (Richard) Porson, the *Tippling Philosopher*, Designed to Serve, by Example, For the *Correction of Manners* & For the *Edification* of the *Ingenious*'. Bishop's summary of Da Ponte's life was unsparing:

> His was a crowding and aspiring genius, ever unsatisfied. His life was a brilliant series of triumphs of the self leading naturally to failures by every worldly reckoning, for the world esteems continuity, which Lorenzo Da Ponte esteemed not at all. Unstable as water, he excelled too diversely. Having once achieved, he would turn and trample his achievement beneath angry feet. A life of being, a life of doing, it was yet a life of having nothing, a life of losing.

Of the confusion over his burial place, and the loss of his bones, Bishop concludes: 'In death, at any rate, the mistakes from which he suffered were not his own.'

Towards the end of the twentieth century, American writers were still ahead of any Europeans in claiming Da Ponte as one of their own, flaws and all, a classic New Yorker to some degree anticipating the characters of Damon Runyon. In 1987 the New York novelist Paul Auster summarized Da Ponte's extraordinary life story in 'The Locked Room', the third instalment of his *New York Trilogy*, concluding:

> Little by little, everything had changed for him. From the dapper,

unctuous ladies' man of his youth, an opportunist steeped in the political intrigues of both Church and court, he became a perfectly ordinary citizen of New York, which in 1805 must have seemed like the end of the world to him. From all that to this: a hard-working professor, a dutiful husband, the father of four ...

Auster uses Da Ponte's story to reinforce his central point that 'each life is irreducible to anything other than itself. Which is as much as to say: lives make no sense ... The circumstances under which lives shift course are so various that it would seem impossible to say anything about a man until he is dead. Not only is death the one true arbiter of happiness (Solon's remark), it is the only measurement by which we can judge life itself.'

If this won't quite do as an epitaph, no more than Olga Ragusa's misspelt musings on that random tombstone in Queens, perhaps our most fitting curtain-line is Da Ponte's own at the end of his last opera with Mozart, *Così fan tutte*:

> Fortunato l'uom che prende
> Ogni cosa pel buon verso
> E tra i casi e le vicende
> Da ragion guidar si fà.
>
> Quel che suole altrui far piangere
> Fia per lui calgion di riso
> E del mondo in mezzo i turbini
> Bella calma troverà.
>
> (Happy is the man who looks
> At everything on the right side
> And through trials and tribulations
> Makes reason his guide.
>
> What always makes another weep
> Will for him be a cause of mirth
> And in the midst of this world's tempests
> He will find sweet peace.)

The United States owes Da Ponte a greater debt than it realizes, or probably ever will. For all the furious energy he expended over his decades in Venice, Vienna and London, there can be little doubt that his flamboyant contribution to American life, in the last thirty years of his own, is what he himself probably saw as his central achievement. Whether his shade likes it or not, however, the name of Lorenzo Da Ponte will live on as that of Mozart's librettist – and his poetry will be heard in opera houses all over the world every night of every year, for as long as the world turns.

A Note on Sources

(The most recent editions cited are those consulted by the author.)

The memoirs of Lorenzo Da Ponte were first published in Italian by John Gray & Co. of New York, between 1823 and 1827, in four small volumes entitled *Memorie di Lorenzo Da Ponte da Ceneda scritte da esso*. A revised and enlarged edition followed in three volumes in 1829–30, under the title *Memorie di Lorenzo Da Ponte da Ceneda scritte da esso. Seconda edizione corretta e ampliata con note dell'autore e l'aggiunta d'un volume*. Each volume was divided into two parts; the first two were printed in 1829 by Gray & Bunce, the third in 1830 by John Burney.

Not until the early twentieth century were Da Ponte's memoirs republished in Italy, in two editions. The first came in one volume, edited with an introduction by Serafino Poggi, in the Classici Italiani series (Milan, 1916); the second in two volumes, edited by G. Gambarin and F. Nicolini, with notes by the latter, in the Scrittori d'Italia series (Ban, 1918).

The memoirs were translated into German and French before the first English translations appeared on both sides of the Atlantic a decade later, in 1929, in the US by Elisabeth Abbott with an introduction by Arthur Livingston (Lippincott, Philadelphia), and in London (via Houghton of New York) by L. A. Sheppard with his own introduction (Routledge). The Abbott translation was reissued in the US in 2000 by the *New York Review of Books* (distributed in the UK by *Granta*), with an introduction by Charles Rosen. These are the English versions I have used, which have made useful comparisons with my own translations from the 1976 Italian paperback edition of the *Memorie*, published by Garzanti with an introduction by

Giuseppe Armani. My views on the reliability or otherwise of these memoirs are, I hope, made clear in the text.

There have been three previous biographies of Da Ponte in English: by Joseph Louis Russo (New York: Columbia University Press, 1922), April FitzLyon (New York: Abelard Schumann, 1955) and Sheila Hodges, with a foreword by Professor H. C. Robbins Landon (London: Granada, 1985). Each of them impresses; and, as the sadly neglected state of Da Ponte studies ambles forward, has led me in profitable directions, beyond the quotations cited in the text.

Useful studies in Italian include Angelo Marchesan's *Della vita e delle opere di Lorenzo Da Ponte* (Treviso: Turazza, 1900) and Aleramo Lanapoppi's *Da Ponte: Realta e leggenda nella vita del librettista di Mozart* (Bologna: Mulion, 1992). In German there is *Lorenzo Da Ponte als Theaterdichter* by H. Boa (Leipzig: Sammelbaende der Internationale Musikgesellschaft, Heft 2, 1914).

Da Ponte's poems were recently published in two volumes, *Saggi poetici di Lorenzo Da Ponte*, ristampa anastatica dell'edizione Viennese del 1788, by Zoppelli of Treviso in 1988.

On Da Ponte himself I have drawn on a number of useful articles or chapters. In alphabetical order, by the author's surname: 'Lorenzo Da Ponte, Mozart's Librettist' by Aram Bakshian Jr, *History Today*, vol. XXVIII, no. 3, March 1978; 'Lorenzo Da Ponte' by Morris Bishop in *A Gallery of Eccentrics* by Morris Bishop (New York: Minton, Balch, 1928); 'Lorenzo Da Ponte in New York' by Paul Cohen, *American Book Collector*, vol. VIII, no. 5, May 1987; 'Un ignorata episodio della vita dell'abate Lorenzo Da Ponte' by Franco Gaeta, *Giornale storico della Letteratura Italiana*, vol. CXXXI, Turin, 1954; 'Lorenzo Da Ponte' by Theodore W. Koch, from *Dante in America* (Boston, 1896); 'Da Ponte in New York' by Henry E. Krehbiel, first published in the *New York Tribune* on 28 August 1887, later included in the same author's *Review of the New York Musical Season 1889–90* and as Chapter IV of *Music and Manners in the Classical Period* (New York: Scribner, 1898); 'That Was New York: Da Ponte, The Bearer of Culture' by Christopher Lazare, *The New Yorker*, 25 March 1944; 'Lorenzo Da Ponte in London: A Bibliographical Account of His Literary Activity, 1793–1804' by Alfred Loewenberg, *Music Review*, vol. IV, no. 3, 1943; 'Documents on Da Ponte's Italian Library' by Howard R. Marraro, *PMLA*, vol. LVIII, no. 1, Part 3, pp. 1057–72, New York, 1943; 'La vera ragione della fuga di Lorenzo Da Ponte da Venezia' by Fausto

Nicolini, *Archivo storico italiano*, anno LXXVIII, serie VII, vol. XIV, Firenze, 1930; 'Lorenzo Da Ponte' by Luigi Russo, in *Italy and the Italians in Washington's Time* (New York: Arno Press, 1975); 'Il ritorno di Lorenzo Da Ponte a Ceneda nel 1798', *Il Flaminio*, no. 1, December 1979; 'Lorenzo Da Ponte' by H. T. Tuckerman, *Putnam's* magazine, vol. XII, pp. 527–36, November 1868 (later republished in the *Dublin University Magazine*, vol. LXXX, pp. 215–24, August 1872); 'Sketch on the Life of Lorenzo Da Ponte of Ceneda' by Samuel Ward, *The New York Mirror*, 29 September 1838, reprinted in pamphlet form in 1842.

Of the countless books on Mozart the best biographies, in my view, are those by Otto Erich Deutsch (London: A. & C. Black, 1965, reprinted in paperback, Simon & Schuster, 1990); Alfred Einstein (London: Cassell, 1946; Grafton paperback, 1971), Wolfgang Hildesheimer (first published in English by Farrar, Strauss & Giroux, New York, 1982; London: Dent, paperback, 1985); Maynard Solomon (Hutchinson, London, 1995), and the succinct but scholarly Penguin Life by Peter Gay (New York: Viking, 1999). Other books of value to this study of Da Ponte have been, in alphabetical order of their authors: *Mozart The Dramatist* by Brigid Brophy (London: Faber & Faber, 1964); *Opera Buffa in Mozart's Vienna* edited by Mary Hunter and James Webster (Cambridge: Cambridge University Press, 1997); *Three Mozart Operas* by R. B. Moberly (London: Gollancz, 1967); *The Mozart–Da Ponte Operas: An Annotated Bibliography* by Mary Du Mont (Connecticut: Greenwood Press, 2000); *The Complete Operas of Mozart* by Charles Osborne (London: Gollancz, 1978, paperback 1986); *The Mozart–Da Ponte Operas* by Patrick Steptoe (Oxford: Clarendon Press, 1988; paperback, 2001) and *Mozart and the Enlightenment* by Nicholas Till (London: Faber & Faber, 1992).

The standard English edition of Mozart's letters remains the 1938 translation by Emily Anderson (London: Macmillan, 1985). This seminal edition has recently gained a worthy companion in Robert Spaethling's *Mozart's Letters, Mozart's Life* (London: Faber & Faber, 2000). The translations of Mozart's letters in these pages are, with the help of German-speaking friends, my own.

Other informative Mozart books I have consulted include: *Mozart on the Stage* by Christopher Benn (London: Ernest Benn, 1946); *Mozart in Vienna 1781–1791* by Volkmar Braunbehrens (London: André Deutsch, 1986); *Haydn, Mozart and the Viennese School 1740–1789* by Daniel Heartz (New York: Norton, 1995); *Osmin's Rage* by Peter Kivy (Princeton:

Princeton University Press, 1988); *Mozart: The Golden Years, 1781–1791*, by H. C. Robbins Landon (London: Thames & Hudson, 1989); and the same author's *1791: Mozart's Last Year* (London: Thames & Hudson, 1988). My copy of the latter is signed by its author after a pleasant weekend I spent with him at his handsome home in France.

I have also found useful material in *Mozart and the English Connection* by John Jenkins (London: Cygnus Arts, 1998), *Music and Musicians in Vienna* by Richard Rickett (New York: Kinderhook, 1973) and *Mozart in Revolt* by David Schroeder (Yale: Yale University Press, 1999). There is a concise, helpful article entitled 'Mozart in Vienna' by Dorothea Link as Chapter 2 of *The Cambridge Companion to Mozart* edited by Simon P. Keefe (Cambridge: Cambridge University Press, 2003). While correcting proofs of this book, I also enjoyed Jane Glover's *Mozart's Women* (London: Macmillan, 2005), quoted on page 72.

Other useful handbooks include: *The Mozart Compendium, A Guide to Mozart's Life and Music*, edited by H. C. Robbins Landon (London: Thames & Hudson, 1990); The *Cambridge Opera Handbook* on *Don Giovanni* edited by Julian Rushton (Cambridge: Cambridge University Press, 1981) and *The Don Giovanni Book, Myths of Seduction and Betrayal* edited by Jonathan Miller (London: Faber & Faber, 1990). English National Opera's series of guidebooks, edited by the late Nicholas John and published by John Calder, also offers useful detail on *Le Nozze di Figaro* (No. 17), *Don Giovanni* (No. 18) and *Così fan tutte* (No. 22), all published in 1983.

The late John Wells translated the Beaumarchais trilogy as *The Figaro Plays* for productions at the National Theatre, London, published by J. M. Dent, London, 1997. John Wood translated *The Barber of Seville* and *The Marriage of Figaro* for Penguin Classics, London, 1964; and David Coward *The Figaro Trilogy* for Oxford World's Classics in 2003. The French edition I have used is that published in Paris by A. Quantin in 1884.

Other relevant memoirs include those of Giacomo Casanova (1894, translated by Arthur Machen with additions by Arthur Symons; 12-volume English translation by Willard R. Trask published by Harcourt, Brace, New York, 1967) and the tenor Michael Kelly (1826); republished (and now available only) as *Solo Recital* by the Folio Society (London, 1972). Casanova's correspondence was published as *Carteggi Casanova* edited by P. Molmenti (Milan: Sandron, 1930).

Earl Mount Edgcumbe published his *Musical Reminiscences* in London in 1834 and Karl von Dittersdorf his memoirs in 1896. Tobias Smollett published his *Travels through France and Italy* in 1766; and Charles Burney *The Present State of Music in France and Italy* in 1771, and *The Present State of Music in Germany, the Netherlands and the United Provinces* in 1773.

Other volumes consulted include John Ebers's *Seven Years of the King's Theatre* (London, 1828) and Daniel Nalbach's *The King's Theatre 1704–1867* (London, 1972); two volumes of Michele Colombo's letters edited by Angelo Pezzana, published in Parma in 1838 and 1856; three volumes of Patrizio Zaguri's letters edited by Pompeo Molmenti and published in Venice, 1910–11, and Milan, 1916 and 1918; and *Venice in the Eighteenth Century* by Philippe Monnier (Boston: Richard G. Badger, 1910).

The one novel I managed to read while working on this book was *Imagining Don Giovanni* by Anthony Rudel (New York: Atlantic Monthly Press, 2001), an erudite fantasy in which the Marquis de Sade breaks the deadlocked disagreements between Da Ponte, Mozart and Casanova in the run-up to the Prague premiere of the opera in 1787.

My publishers endorsed my wish that this be a 'user-friendly' book, with no superior numbers in the text leading to source notes or bibliography in the back. So I hope this potted guide to my research will also prove valuable to those in search of further reading.

Acknowledgements

My ambition to write a life of Lorenzo Da Ponte dates back to 1985, when Amanda Holden gave me a copy of his memoirs (L. A. Sheppard's translation) while we were translating *Don Giovanni* into English for a Jonathan Miller production at English National Opera (commissioned by the company's then 'Powerhouse' directorate of David Pountney and Mark Elder, who conducted, and subsequently published by Tom Rosenthal of André Deutsch). Twenty years later, with the 250th anniversary of Mozart's birth looming, Alan Samson of Weidenfeld & Nicolson finally gave me the chance.

Throughout those twenty years, I have lived in semi-confident expectation of one day realizing that ambition. I first visited Da Ponte's grave near New York's John F. Kennedy Airport, as an act of homage, during a trip to New York in the late 1980s. I visited it again when I lived in New York, between 1999 and 2002, and made enquiries about him at the New York Historical Society while working on another book as a Fellow of the Center for Scholars and Writers at the New York Public Library.

Since the mid-1980s *Don Giovanni* has ranked alongside *Hamlet* as a work of art I would travel anywhere, any time, to see, with (almost) anyone. I have heard it countless times all over the world – most memorably, perhaps, on 29 October 2003, when I visited Prague with my friend Christian Digby-Firth to celebrate his birthday, which happens to coincide with the first performance of *Don Giovanni* in that city in 1787. On the previous day we visited the Mozart House, or Villa Bertramka, where Mozart is said to have written the overture the night before the premiere; the following evening, we attended the performance given annually on that date in the very theatre, the Estates, where Mozart himself first conducted the first performance.

Through my friend and former neighbour Robert Tear, who has sung Don Basilio in innumerable productions of *Le nozze di Figaro*, I gained an acquaintance with that work as detailed and affectionate as my intimacy with *Don Giovanni*. Through my friend Frank Kermode, far from alone in rating *Così Fan Tutte* as, musically, the finest of the three Mozart–Da Ponte operas, I came to share that view – most of the time, as no opinion on the impossible debate between their respective merits can be authentic unless it is constantly in an agonized state of flux. With Frank, in 2005, while working on this book, I visited Vienna for the first time; we took in *Le nozze* at the Staatsoper, and visited all the Mozart–Da Ponte addresses, as well as paying due homage to the latest version of the ferris-wheel immortalized by Orson Welles and Joseph Cotten in Carol Reed's classic 1949 film *The Third Man*.

For twenty years my wives and children have had to live with my love of these three works, frequently being dragged to performances all over the place. Since 2002 I have been chief classical music critic of the *Observer*, and have thus had the best seats for numerous versions at no charge. I confess to being very picky as to whom I take with me.

It was in that role, in November 2004, that I visited Venice for the reopening of La Fenice opera house, rebuilt after its (third) destruction by fire. During that visit, thanks to Marie-José Gransard, I was taken on a vivid tour of Da Ponte's Venice by the omniscient and gifted local historian and actor Lucio Zorzi. I also visited Vittorio Veneto, where Da Ponte was born Emanuele Conegliano, and excitedly found many traces of Ceneda's most illustrious son. Since that trip, Marie-José Gransard has conducted extensive, illuminating research on my behalf in the Venetian state archive and elsewhere, including Treviso and Portogruaro, while also working through the libretti with Lucio Zorzi in search of their distinctively Venetian vernacular.

In New York, after I had returned to London, Daniel Swift followed innumerable trails for me, and came up with volumes of immensely useful material on Da Ponte's thirty-three years in that city and environs. Daniel and I are grateful for the assistance of the Da Ponte Professor of Italian at Columbia University, Olga Ragusa, who composed the inscription on his tombstone at the Catholic Cemetery, quoted in full in the Prologue.

In Vienna, via my friend Desmond Cecil, and his, the music-loving British ambassador, John Macgregor, I found a diligent researcher in Zöe Kalus, who interviewed the director of the Da Ponte institute (for Librettology), Mag. Reinhard Eisendle, and trawled through the state archives – largely, alas, in vain – for information on Da Ponte's ten years there.

I have been living in London while writing this book, so Da Ponte's decade here has been less of a problem. I am grateful, nonetheless, for suggestions and help on matters musical, textual and biographical from Hugh Canning, Andrew Clements, Amanda Holden, Robin Marris, Jonathan Miller, Anna Picard and Henry Ward. Ron Hall generously gave me a twelve-volume edition of Casanova's memoirs in Willard Trask's English translation. Logan Browning of Rice University, Houston, kindly sent me information on Da Ponte's text for Mozart's *Davidde Penitente* after a rare performance of the work there. And Jane Wellesley has been her habitually generous, supportive self.

I have been helped with translations from the Italian by Al Alvarez and Francine Brody, and from the German by Amrei Harrison and John David Morley.

On 10 March 2005 Professor Sir Frank Kermode gave the first Keith Walker memorial lecture at University College, London, under the title 'A Few Bars of Mozart, *ovvero* 35 bars in F minor'. An exploration of aspects of *Figaro*, with special reference to Da Ponte's adaptation of Beaumarchais, Barbarina's Act IV aria and the key of F minor, it has proved very useful to my discussion of the work in Chapter 6. Frank and I enjoyed many a happy evening together discussing and listening to the piece while he was working on his talk. Before this book was even commissioned, he gave me a copy of Patrick Steptoe's immensely illu-minating study of the Mozart–Da Ponte operas, prophetically inscribed 'Prep for your next book'. I am, as ever, very grateful for his friendship and encouragement.

It is with great delight that I find myself published again, after an indecently long interval, by the man who published my first few grown-up books, Lord (George) Weidenfeld. At Weidenfeld & Nicolson I am especially grateful to my editor Alan Samson. I am also, as always, deeply indebted to my agent Gill Coleridge and her colleague Lucy Luck, for their professional and personal support and friendship. The staff of the London Library have been as patient and helpful as always; and my researchers and I are also grateful for expert help in sundry archives and seminaries of Venice, Treviso, Portogruaro, Vienna and New York.

As with my life of Shakespeare, as much a labour of love as this book, this biography of Da Ponte would not have been written without the faith in my ability to do so of its dedicatee Alan Samson, polymath, fellow-Gooner and Publisher of Weidenfeld & Nicolson, whom I first got to know twenty years ago, while translating *Don Giovanni*. My debt to him ranks up there with those to my three ever supportive sons, and my pal Robert Butler for coming up with its elusive, all-important title.

Anthony Holden
London, 2004–5.

Index